JEWISH ENCOUNTERS

Jonathan Rosen, General Editor

Jewish Encounters is a collaboration between Schocken and
Nextbook, a project devoted to the promotion of Jewish literature, culture, and ideas.

>nextbook

PUBLISHED

FORTHCOMING

THE WORLDS OF SHOLOM ALEICHEM · Jeremy Dauber

ABRAHAM · Alan M. Dershowitz

MOSES · Stephen J. Dubner

BIROBIJAN · Masha Gessen

JUDAH MACCABEE · Jeffrey Goldberg

THE DAIRY RESTAURANT · Ben Katchor

JOB · Rabbi Harold S. Kushner

ABRAHAM CAHAN · Seth Lipsky

SHOW OF SHOWS · David Margolick

MRS. FREUD · Daphne Merkin

DAVID BEN-GURION · Shimon Peres and David Landau

WHEN GRANT EXPELLED THE JEWS · Jonathan Sarna

MESSIANISM · Leon Wieseltier

Sacred Trash

ADINA HOFFMAN & PETER COLE

SACRED TRASH

The Lost and Found World of
the Cairo Geniza

NEXTBOOK · SCHOCKEN · NEW YORK

Library of Congress Cataloging-in-Publication Data
Hoffman, Adina.
    Sacred trash : the lost and found world of the Cairo
Geniza / Adina Hoffman and Peter Cole.
        p. cm.
    Includes bibliographical references.
    ISBN 978-0-8052-4258-4
    1. Judaism—History—Medieval and early modern period,
425–1789—Sources. 2. Jews—History—70–1789—Sources.
3. Cairo Genizah. I. Cole, Peter. II. Schechter, S. (Solomon),
1847–1915. III. Title.
    BM180.H64 2010
    296.09182'20902—dc22   2010016751

Jacket photograph reproduced by permission of the Syndics
of Cambridge University Library
Jacket design by Barbara de Wilde

www.schocken.com
Printed in the United States of America
First Edition
2 4 6 8 9 7 5 3 1

For MMHC,
our Geniza's sphinx

Hidden wisdom and concealed treasure, what is the use of either?

—BEN SIRA

CONTENTS

Sacred Trash

1

Hidden Wisdom

Cambridge, May 1896

When the self-taught Scottish scholar of Arabic and Syriac Agnes Lewis and her no-less-learned twin sister, Margaret Gibson, hurried down a street or a hallway, they moved—as a friend later described them—"like ships in full sail." Their plump frames, thick lips, and slightly hawkish eyes made them, theoretically, identical. And both were rather vain about their dainty hands, which on special occasions they "weighed down with antique rings." In a poignant and peculiar coincidence, each of the sisters had been widowed after just a few years of happy marriage to a clergyman.

But Mrs. Lewis and Mrs. Gibson were distinct to those who knew them. Older by an entire twenty minutes, Agnes was the more ambitious, colorful, and domineering of the two; Margaret had a quieter intelligence and was, it was said, "more normal." By age fifty, Agnes had written three travel books and three novels, and had translated a tourist guide from the Greek; Margaret had contributed amply to and probably helped write her sister's nonfiction books, edited her husband's translation of Cervantes' *Journey to Parnassus*, and grown adept at watercolors. They were, meanwhile, exceptionally close—around Cambridge they came to be known as a single unit, the "Giblews"—and after the deaths of their husbands they devoted themselves and their sizable inheritance to a life of travel and study together.

This followed quite naturally from the maverick manner in which they'd been raised in a small town near Glasgow by their forward-thinking lawyer father, a widower, who subscribed to an educational philosophy that was equal parts Bohemian and Calvinist—as far-out as it was firm. Eschewing the fashion for treating girls' minds like fine china, he assumed his daughters were made of tougher stuff and schooled them as though they were sons, teaching them to think for themselves, to argue and ride horses. Perhaps most important, he had instilled in them early on a passion for philology, promising them that they could travel to any country on condition that they first learned its language. French, Spanish, German, and Italian followed, as did childhood trips around the Continent. He also encouraged the girls' nearly familial friendship with their church's progressive and intellectually daring young preacher, who had once been a protégé of the opium-eating Romantic essayist Thomas de Quincy.

After their father's sudden death when they were twenty-three, Agnes and Margaret sought consolation in strange alphabets and in travel to still more distant climes: Egypt, Palestine, Greece, and Cyprus. By middle age they had learned, between them, some nine languages—adding to their European repertoire Hebrew, Persian, and Syriac written in Estrangelo

script. Having also studied the latest photographic techniques, they journeyed extensively throughout the East, taking thousands of pictures of ancient manuscript pages and buying piles of others, the most interesting of which they then set out to transcribe and translate.

As women, and as devout (not to mention eccentric and

notoriously party-throwing) Presbyterians, they lived and worked on the margins of mostly Anglican, male-centered Cambridge society—women were not granted degrees at the town's illustrious university until 1948—and they counted as their closest friends a whole host of Quakers, freethinkers, and Jews. Yet Agnes's 1892 discovery at St. Catherine's Monastery in Sinai of one of the oldest Syriac versions of the New Testament had brought the sisters respect in learned circles: their multiple books on the subject ranged from the strictly scholarly *A Translation of the Four Gospels from the Syriac of the Sinai Palimpsest* to the more talky and popular *How the Codex Was Found.* Somehow the rumor spread that Mrs. Lewis had just happened to recognize a fragment of the ancient manuscript in the monastery dining hall, where it was being used as a butter dish. In fact, the codex was kept under tight lock and key, and its very fragile condition—to say nothing of its sacred status—certainly precluded its use by the monks as mere tableware. It took serious erudition and diplomacy for the twins to gain access to the manuscript in the monastery library; they then worked painstakingly over a period of years to decode the codex, as it were. "The leaves," wrote Agnes, "are deeply stained, and in parts ready to crumble. One and all of them were glued together, until the librarian of the Convent and I separated them with our fingers."

She and Margaret proceeded to photograph each of its 358 pages and, on their return to Cambridge, processed the film themselves and labored over the text's decipherment. Later they arranged for an expedition of several distinguished

Cambridge scholars to travel with them to Sinai, where they worked as a team, transcribing the codex as a whole.

All these far-flung intellectual adventures had been exciting but also exhausting. And although the twins had resolved to spend a quiet season in Cambridge, immersed in the proofs of the various texts they had lately copied from manuscript, they set out in the early spring of 1896 on still another Middle Eastern trip—their third in almost as many years— bound for Palestine and Egypt. The reason for the journey was reported later in what sounds like deliberately vague terms: "News we received from Cairo," Agnes wrote enigmatically, "seemed to indicate that there might be some chance of our finding something there." Weary as they were from their previous travels, they had not been eager to take this particular trip, "and yet," as she would admit in retrospect, "it had not been the least fruitful in results."

This understatement was typical of Agnes, and gives little sense of the startling events that had come to pass one historic May day in 1896, soon after the twins' return. Suffering from what her sister, Margaret, described as "a severe rheumatic illness, caused by undue exposure on the night when we had lost our tents in the valley of Elah," Agnes had decided that morning to stretch her legs. While out strolling in downtown Cambridge, she was especially glad to bump into a good friend— and, strangely, another twin who also took great pride in his beautiful hands—the Romanian-born Talmud scholar, Solomon Schechter.

Even more of an oddball in the donnish context of Cambridge than Agnes and Margaret, the very Jewish, very blustery Schechter must, too, have cut a remarkable figure as he strode down King's Parade. With his bushy, red-tinted beard, unruly hair, and tendency to gesticulate broadly as he spoke, Schechter had been known to set off in the broiling heat of midsummer wrapped up in a winter coat and several yards of scarf. An acquaintance remembered first meeting Schechter, with "his dirty black coat, smudged all over with snuff and ashes from his cigar, hands unwashed, nails as black as ink, but rather nice fingers, beard and hair unkempt, a ruddy complexion . . . One ear was stuffed full of wool, hanging out, and he was always very abrupt in his speech." Another recalled that his socks never matched. His resemblance to a bag lady apart, there was, as another colleague put it, "the magic of prophecy about the man." He also had, his wife would write years later, "a genius for friendship; he loved people and they loved him." Since his 1890 arrival in Cambridge, where he was first given the odd title Lecturer in Talmudic and later appointed Reader in Rabbinics, Schechter had gained the deep respect and affection of a range of the town's leading intellectuals, including the radical Scottish Bible scholar and

Arabist William Robertson Smith (who arranged for Schechter to join Christ's College, where special kosher meals were prepared whenever he came to dine); the Africa explorer Mary Kingsley (with whom he much enjoyed swearing); and the pioneering anthropologist and reclusive author of *The Golden Bough*, James Frazer, perhaps Schechter's best friend at the time. The two took walks together several days a week, discussing as they rambled "all things, human and divine." Frazer himself praised Schechter as "great in his intellect and learning, greater even in the warmth of his affections and his enthusiasm for every high and noble cause."

By turns fierce, warm, brusque, tender, biting in his wit, and thundering in his manner, "the king in any society in which he found himself," Schechter was often described in peculiarly zoological terms. Now he was "a demanding lamb," now an eagle or a bear. "I can see him in my mind's eye, at the height of a debate," wrote yet another friend, "rising from his chair, perhaps kicking it down, and pacing . . . the room, like a wounded lion, roaring retorts." Lamb or jungle cat, he inspired awe and devotion in most people, though one imagines that the formidable Agnes Lewis would not even have blinked as she sailed—however arthritically—toward Schechter that day in the street.

She and Mrs. Gibson had, she hastened to tell him, spent the last few weeks developing the photographs and sifting through the manuscripts they'd brought back from their most recent trip. Their purchases included what Agnes would later describe as "a bundle of documents from a dealer in the plain of Sharon . . . [and] a similar bundle bought in Cairo." Margaret, whose turn it was to do the sorting, had managed to identify most of the items that they'd carted home in a trunk—and which had almost been confiscated by overzealous customs officials in Jaffa. She had worked her way through the Hebrew fragments and set aside what she deemed parts of "the Canonical Books of the Old Testament" (the only sections of the Hebrew Bible that she, as a good Presbyterian, would know), assuming that the others were either talmudic passages or "private Jewish documents." But the twins were eager for Schechter to have a look at some of the items whose contents they did not recognize.

Schechter, of all people, might be able to identify the scraps. Remembered by Romanian relatives and acquaintances as having been the wildest boy in his hometown, one who "constantly had to be pulled down from the top of the chestnut trees," he had also been a prodigy. It was said that Shneur Zalman Schechter knew the Pentateuch by heart at five. And although he was by now almost fifty and—as the Anglicization of his first name indicated—had traveled a long way in both physical and psychic terms from his Hasidic Russian family in the small Moldavian town of Focsani (as had his twin brother, Yisrael, who had immigrated to the Jewish agricultural settlement of Zichron Yaakov in Palestine the same year that Schechter moved to England), he brought with him a prodigious Jewish learning, as well as a voracious appetite for all kinds of knowledge, classical and contemporary. Perhaps best known to twenty-first-century American Jews as the man for whom the Conservative movement's network of day schools is named, Schechter had been ordained a rabbi in Vienna and applied himself to the Palestinian Talmud at Berlin's influential new school of liberal Jewish learning, the Hochschule für die Wissenschaft des Judentums; he'd become skilled at the analysis of ancient manuscripts and absorbed a wide range of subjects at that city's university—everything from psychology and pedagogy to aesthetics, ancient history, Aristotle's ethics, and Syriac grammar. Besides a deep knowledge of biblical and rabbinic texts and a solid grounding in the "scientific" methods that had by then come to dominate in German Jewish scholarly circles, he had also developed a passion for German, French, and English literature.

When he first came to England in 1882—hired to serve as a tutor in Talmud to the aristocratic young Oxford-and-Berlin-trained theologian Claude Montefiore—he had not known a word of English. "The only phrase he had begged Montefiore to teach him," according to his wife, Mathilde, "was 'weak tea,' for he could not stand the strong tea the English used to drink." But he'd learned the language with typical rapidity, by sitting with his Hebrew Bible, the English translation, and a dictionary—then moving straight on to George Eliot. Herself an avid bookworm and elegant writer, Mathilde described her husband as a "tremendous reader" who took in "every good novel that appeared," devouring essays, philosophy, history, and theology. He'd wooed Mathilde with the satirical and none-too-romantic *Book of Snobs* by Thackeray, and it was joked that a more accurate title for Schechter than Reader in Rabbinics would have been "Reader in Fiction." He was especially fond of critical works by Charles Lamb, Leslie Stephen, and Matthew Arnold and had a particular fascination with anything written about the French Revolution and the American Civil War (Lincoln was a hero); he "loved Schiller and Heine above all." He also adored *The Vicar of Wakefield* and "boys' books like 'Treasure Island' and 'Robinson Crusoe.'"

No knowledge of Robert Louis Stevenson or Daniel Defoe, however, was necessary on this particular May day, and when—just a short time after meeting Schechter in town—Agnes arrived home at Castlebrae, the twins' stately Gothic Revival mansion, she found Schechter already huddled over the large dining-room table, intently examining the fragments that Margaret had spread across its surface.

Without much ado, he identified one vellum leaf as a rare and valuable page from the Palestinian Talmud.

"Then," according to Agnes, "he held up a dirty scrap of paper. 'This too is very interesting; may I take it away and identify it?' 'Certainly,'" she said.

In Margaret's own account, "I noticed that his eyes were glittering."

Although the scrap looked, in Margaret's words, "as if a grocer had used it for something greasy," Schechter, it seems, realized its importance almost instantly, and within an hour of his racing from Castlebrae with the two items, the twins received a telegram from the Cherry Hinton Road post office, just around the corner from the Schechters' gabled brick house on Rock Road:

FRAGMENT VERY IMPORTANT; COME TO ME THIS AFTERNOON

Probably accustomed to a certain easy agitation in their friend, the twins did not go rushing out to meet him, but sat down to lunch—at which point a letter arrived, splattered with unblotted ink and scrawled on Cambridge University Library stationery in Schechter's lurching hand. Agnes realized that it had, in fact, been sent before the telegram and that they should eat as quickly as possible and get themselves over to Rock Road. (Schechter's sense of urgency was such that he scrambled morning and night, writing p.m. for a.m.)

13/5/96
Dear Mrs Lewis
    I think we have
reason to congratulate
~~ourself~~ ourselves. For
the ~~piec~~ fragment I took
with me represents a
piece of the original
Hebrew of Ecclesiasticus.
It is the first time that
such a thing was

discovered. Please do
not speak yet about
the matter till to-morrow.
I will come to you
to-morrow about 11
p.m. and talk over
the matter with you
how to make
the matter known.
            In haste and
            great excitement
                yours sincerely,
                S. Schechter.

Schechter's plea for secrecy bubbled up from the fact that the original Hebrew of this apocryphal book—also known as Ben Sira—had been missing for nearly a millennium and survived, it was generally believed, only in its Greek and Syriac translations. The haste and great excitement with which he announced the discovery of this text would, however, soon give way to elation of a far more enduring and varied sort, as, within months, it brought Schechter to travel to Egypt and haul away one of the greatest finds unearthed in modern times: the astonishing cache of documents that has come to be known as the Cairo Geniza.

"Geniza" is a barely translatable Hebrew term that holds within it an ultimate statement about the worth of words and their place in Jewish life. It derives from the Persian *ganj* (or *kanj*), meaning "hoard" or "hidden treasure," and while the expression itself doesn't appear in the Bible, several of the later biblical books composed under Persian rule contain a handful of related inflections: Esther and Ezra, for instance, speak of *ginzei hamelekh*, or *ginzei malka*—"the King's treasuries," and the "royal archives." Rabbinic usage of the root is more common, if also more peculiar: in the Talmud it almost always suggests the notion of "concealment" or "storing away"—though just what that entailed isn't usually specified. The rabbis describe the light of Creation by which Adam could see from one end of the world to the other as being "hidden" or "stored up" (*ganuz*) for the souls of the righteous in the afterlife. Writing the sages deemed somehow heretical (including, at one point, the books of Proverbs and Ecclesiastes, "because [their] words contradicted one another") should, some believed, also be *ganuz*, that is, censored in the most physical manner—by being buried. In one instance, a threatening text was placed under a step in a staircase. Likewise, religious manuscripts that time or human error has rendered unfit for use cannot be "thrown out," but rather "require geniza"—removal, for example, to a clay jar and a safe place, "that they may continue many days" and "decay of their own accord."

Implied in this latter idea of geniza is that these works, like people, are living things, possessing an element of the sacred about them—and therefore when they "die," or become worn out, they must be honored and protected from profanation. "The contents of the book," wrote Solomon Schechter, "go up to heaven like the soul." The same Hebrew root, g-n-z, was, he noted, sometimes used on gravestones: "Here lies hidden (*nignaz*) this man."

The origins and otherworldly aspects of the institution aren't the only mysterious things about it. Both its development and its precise nature have remained curiously elusive. What we do know is that at some point the verbal noun "geniza" evolved from indicating a *process* to also connoting a *place*, either a burial plot, a storage chamber, or a cabinet where any damaged or somehow dubious holy book would be ritually entombed. In this way, the text's sanctity would be preserved, and dangerous ideas kept from circulating. Or, as one early scholar of the material neatly put it: "A genizah* serves . . . the twofold purpose of preserving good things from harm and bad things from harming."

Often this depositing of the sacred texts in a secure location was only an interim solution and suggested a kind of liminal existence preceding actual interment. In some communities texts that had been stored in a geniza would eventually be buried alongside a saint or righteous individual; more frequently the scrolls and scraps were ritually consigned to the earth alone. In still other cases it appears that removal from circulation to a geniza constituted the terminal stage of the process and brought the writings in question to their final place of rest.

With modifications, the practice of geniza has continued throughout the Jewish world into the present, ranging greatly from community to community. (A related though less well-known tradition exists in Islam, and in Arabic the word for funeral, *janaza*, derives from the same three-letter root implying "concealment.") In general and over time, it seems the talmudic notion of geniza as a form of censorship waned, and most genizot came to serve the more neutral function of holding obsolete texts. Beyond that, customs were idiosyncratic and highly vari-

---

*"Geniza" and "genizah" are two different transliterations of the same Hebrew word. In citations throughout this book, we have maintained the spelling used by the original authors. The plural of geniza is "genizot," which is also occasionally written "genizoth."

able. A nook near or under the synagogue's ark, a basement room, a cubbyhole—all could and did function as genizot. (One Iraqi community chose to honor their bags of tired texts by throwing them into the river.) The fragments that required this sort of treatment became known as *shemot*, or names: they were considered sacred because they bore the name of God. In some towns and cities, the geniza materials were taken out of their receptacles on a designated day and buried in an elaborate ritual that was part funeral, part carnival. Depending on local tradition, the papers and books—and often discarded ritual objects that included or had contact with a written text, such as mezuzot, phylactery straps, and the like—would be placed in straw baskets, leather sheets, or lengths of white cloth, like shrouds. Coffins draped with decorative fabrics were sometimes used to hold a no-longer-valid Torah scroll, and the privilege of pallbearing was bestowed upon those who had donated money to the synagogue. Songs were sung, cakes eaten, and arak was drunk as a procession set out for the cemetery. This act of inhumation served, in fact, as a kind of twin ritual to the dedication of a new Torah scroll, and after the old scroll was buried, pilgrimages to the "grave" would be performed, just as they were made to the tombs of certain holy men.

For reasons that remain obscure, in the case of the Palestinian Jews of Fustat, or Old Cairo—who worshipped in what would eventually become known as the Ben Ezra synagogue—the tradition of geniza was, it seems, extended to include the preservation of *anything written in Hebrew letters*, not only religious documents, and not just in the Hebrew language. Perhaps, as one scholar has proposed, "the very employment of the Hebrew script . . . sanctified written material." Another theory holds that the Jews of this community may simply have piled up papers in their homes and periodically delivered whole cartfuls to the Geniza without bothering to separate sacred from secular writing. Or, maybe, as another writer has suggested—in an effort to make sense of the hodge-podge of texts that have turned up in the Fustat Geniza—the impulse to

guard the written word may have gone beyond piety and evolved into a "generalized aversion toward casually discarding texts of any kind." Whatever the explanation, for most of the last millennium, hundreds of thousands of scraps were tossed into the Ben Ezra Geniza, which came to serve as a kind of holy junk heap.

More town square than sanctuary, the Fustat synagogue complex was the pivot around which its community's life in the busy city spun. In addition to serving as a house of prayer and center of study, it provided the congregation's welfare office, soup kitchen, hostel, clerical and book-keeping headquarters, and its court of law. As such, all manner of paper-work passed through it and—when discarded—slowly filled to the actual rafters a windowless box of a room on the synagogue's second floor. Thanks to the dry climate and various legends about a venomous serpent guarding the entrance and a curse that would visit anyone who dared disturb what it held, the haphazardly piled paper and parchment mostly remained hidden behind a wall in the women's section, until Schechter's arrival in late December of 1896.

What he discovered there astonished him, and in fact it seems almost impossible now to imagine how it is that so much could have emerged from so little. Barely more than eight feet long by six and a half feet wide, and extending to a height of some six yards, the Ben Ezra Geniza was the size of glorified walk-in closet. Yet here was an entire civiliza-tion. After Schechter had climbed a rickety ladder to reach that dim attic-like opening, and once his widening eyes had adjusted to the dark, he found himself staring into a space crammed to bursting with nearly ten centuries' worth of one Middle Eastern, mostly middle-class Jewish community's detritus—its letters and poems, its wills and marriage con-tracts, its bills of lading and writs of divorce, its prayers, prescriptions, trousseau lists, Bibles, money orders, amulets, court depositions, shop inventories, rabbinic responsa, contracts, leases, magic charms, and receipts. "A battlefield of books," Schechter called it, and at first glance it must have seemed an unlikely (and unsightly) mess. As another visitor described the physical state of the Geniza's contents: "For centuries, whitewash has tumbled upon them from the walls and ceiling; the sand of the desert has lodged in their folds and wrinkles; water from some unknown source has drenched them; they have squeezed and hurt each other."

It took, in other words, real imagination on Schechter's part to grasp what faced him in the unprepossessing room later referred to by one

Cambridge professor as "that pestiferous wrack." But grasp it he did: in the dank and musty chaos, Schechter soon came to understand that he had uncovered no less than a cross section of an entire society, and one that lay at the very navel of the medieval world—linking East and West, Arab and Jew, the daily imprint of the sacred and the venerable extension of the profane. Written on vellum or on rag paper, in ink of gallnut and soot and gum, these pages and scrolls were composed in Hebrew, Aramaic, and Judeo-Arabic, as well as Greek, Persian, Latin, Ladino, and even Yiddish—all written in Hebrew characters. Because those family and business papers were often tossed in unsorted, and stationery was precious and regularly "recycled," we also find Syriac, Arabic, Coptic, and—in one odd instance—Chinese. Their words were set down by young men and old, by women, children, students, and scribes, by rabbis and rebels, rich and poor, the famous and the forgotten.

Such was the miraculous nature of what Schechter found in the Cairo Geniza that some have compared its discovery to that of the Dead Sea Scrolls. The Cairo Geniza, goes this argument, is actually the more important find, since the sensational, ancient scriptures from Qumran were—as most scholars have seen them—a cultic aberration, "the work of men who gave up the world . . . to find God in a wilderness," whereas the Geniza embraces and embodies the world as it really was, warts and wonders alike, for the vast majority of medieval Jews. One of the twentieth century's greatest historians, S. D. Goitein, whose writing about the daily and most mundane Geniza documents unfurled a vibrant panorama of this Mediterranean society, clearly had such a comparison in mind when he titled a 1970 talk about the Geniza "The Living Sea Scrolls."

The materials of the so-called classical period of the Geniza alone (the later tenth through mid-thirteenth centuries) have occupied scores of scholars for more than a hundred years, transforming in the most fundamental way how we might understand Jewish history, leadership, literature, economics, marriage, charity, prayer, family, sex, and almost every other subject imaginable—from the nature of the silk trade to astrology, religious dissent, Hebrew grammar, glassmaking, and medieval attitudes toward death. There is, in point of fact, no other premodern period of the Jewish past about which we have so many and varied details. Because of the Geniza, we can nearly hear and see—and often almost smell and touch—the urbane world of the Arabized Jews who populated Fustat. If one is used to thinking of Judaism as a straight shot from the Bible to the shtetl, followed by a brief stopover on the Lower East Side, it may seem strange to realize that this socially integrated Jewish society was not just a product of some peculiar local circumstance but was, instead, emblematic of its epoch. Lest we forget, from the time of antiquity until around 1200, over 90 percent of the world's Jewish population lived in the East and, after the Muslim conquest, under the rule of Islam. Fustat was, in its medieval heyday, home to the most prosperous Jewish community on earth, and served as a commercial axis for Jews throughout North Africa and the Middle East and as far away as India. At the same time, the city contained nearly every race, class, occupation, and religious strain the region had to offer. "It was," as Goitein saw it, "a mirror of the world."

The story of the Geniza and its recovery is, by nature, a tale with numerous heroes, medieval and modern. Although Schechter deserves much of the credit for having, by force of his expansive historical vision and truly exceptional personality, rescued some 190,000 Geniza fragments from a kind of oblivion (or random dispersal), he was hardly the first to be drawn to the cache. Its presence was known—and at least partly appreciated—well before he arrived on the scene, and this book is, accordingly, also a chronicle of those who came before him, and others who would follow. "Looking over this enormous mass of fragments about me," Schechter wrote, in Moses-on-Nebo-like fashion, after several years of hard work breathing in the dust and spirit of this culture's *disjecta membra,* "I cannot overcome a sad feeling stealing over me, that I shall hardly be worthy to see all the results which the Genizah will add to our knowledge of Jews and Judaism. The work is not for one man, and not for one generation."

But this is perhaps as it should be. For the Geniza itself tells the tale of many generations, each of which preserved and transformed a part of the tradition it received. Maintaining the practice of concealment, ironically, made future revelation possible, as, over the centuries, an inadvertent archive was amassed. And so, in an almost unconscious manner, the Fustat community restored to the notion of geniza its ancient and essential dimension—that of history as hidden treasure. The protagonists of this story are the men and women who have brought its wisdom to light.

2

Serpents and Secrets

As a young Jewish boy in early-nineteenth-century Germany, Heinrich Heine spent hours exploring his family attic, which sounds oddly like a kind of domestic geniza and opens indirectly onto Cairo's: "a dusty lumber room," he would later call it, "a hospital for . . . old furniture that had reached the last degree of decrepitude." It was here that the poet-to-be discovered a faded notebook in the hand of his flamboyant great-uncle, a charismatic con man named Simon von Geldern.

Known as the "Chevalier" or the "Oriental," this uncle set out often on trips for the East and wrote about them in his journal, in Hebrew, which Heine could not read—he thought the letters "Arabic, Syriac, and Coptic"—though the idea of this yellowing travelogue ignited the child's imagination, and, from family legend and a good dose of his own fancy, he compiled a swashbuckling CV for his eccentric forebear. Von Geldern claimed, according to Heine, to have had a mystical vision at the site of the former Temple in Jerusalem and to have been the captain of a gang of robbers in Africa. He boasted deep kabbalistic knowledge, gambled heavily, escaped bands of pirates, and also made a great splash at various European courts, where he charmed the ladies in particular with his "pretended secret knowledge." Heine described his late uncle as a charlatan, though "not of a common kind. He was not one of those ordinary charlatans who pull the teeth of peasants at fairs, but he courageously entered the palaces of the great, for whom he pulled the strongest molars."

As it happened, Heine's uncle entered more than palaces. In his diary, dated 1752 or 1753, von Geldern makes a brief, cryptic notation, on the occasion of a visit to Fustat:

I was in the Elijah synagogue and searched in the Geniza. I gave 5:——

What was he searching for? Why did he pay? Did he take anything with him when he left? Apparently the first foreigner in modern times to enter the crammed room, von Geldern had been intrigued, according to one nineteenth-century commentator, by the "wealth of possibilities that lay hidden amid the rubbish of the *Genizot*" of Cairo. But how, we must wonder, did he know about the Geniza in the first place? Did he really possess some sort of privileged, arcane knowledge?

Word, it seems, had somehow begun to trickle out about a possible treasure housed in the formerly elegant, now derelict Ben Ezra synagogue. Some hundred years after von Geldern's elliptical adventure— and while the prepubescent Solomon Schechter was still busy hiking miles to his yeshiva through the bitter Romanian frosts—another foreign visitor reported on his own trip to Fustat. After an 1859 expedition to Egypt and points farther east to collect money for the poor of his city, the Lithuanian-born Jerusalemite Yaakov Safir described how he had coaxed the superstitious synagogue beadle to let him risk his life by climbing a ladder and sneaking a peek at a scroll that was alleged to have been personally copied by the biblical Ezra the Scribe. (Legend had it that anyone who dared disturb it would die within the same year.) Unconvinced that this "very old, very worn and decayed" manuscript was really of pre–Second Temple provenance, he did sense the proximity of something valuable—even as he realized that this particular scroll was likely a kind of medieval MacGuffin and not the genuine prize. By the time he returned some five years later, he had resolved to talk his way into the Geniza, which "they told me . . . is very ancient, a chamber filled with discarded books from days of old."

The usual warnings followed: the synagogue's beadle and its treasurer adamantly refused him entry, proclaiming the extreme danger of such an adventure—adding that "a serpent was coiled up there." But Safir remained determined, and he traipsed back yet again several months later to beg them to let him ascend to the roof, which then provided the only angle of access to the Geniza: "They laughed at me and said: 'Why would a man risk his life for nothing? He won't live out the year!' I pleaded with them and showed them that I had a small mezuza with me, for protection, and said that I knew how to charm snakes. And I promised the treasurer a reward if he'd bring me a ladder."

That last offer seems to have done the trick—and in a short while he found himself inside the Geniza, which was at the time heaped with broken rafters, wood panels, stones, and plaster from a recent roof collapse. It was also, he noted, spilling with scrolls. "After I had toiled for two days and was covered with dust and grime, I picked out a few pages of various old books and manuscripts, though I found nothing of value in them. But who knows what still lies beneath?"

As close as Safir had come, he hadn't yet penetrated the depths. "I was," he explains in a memoir of his travels, "tired of searching. But I did not find any fiery serpents or scorpions, and no harm came to me, thank God."

Snakes and ancient curses were the least of the dangers that lurked. "A perfect orgy of spoliation" was how one writer, the Scottish reverend James Baikie, later described what had gone on in and around the ancient tombs and temples of Egypt during the first half of the nineteenth century. "Every important or noble traveller had to add a few curios from Egypt to his miscellaneous collection gathered from half a dozen other lands, and sculptures, inscriptions, and papyri of the greatest value were thus uselessly dispersed in paltry private collections, where, when they had gratified a passing curiosity or ministered to a momentary spirit of emulation, they were allowed to gather dust through years of neglect, till at last the futile cabinet of curios was dispersed, and its items were lost sight of altogether." Another observer called it "unbridled pillage." And while this frenzy of grave-robbing and sarcophagus-snatching centered on Pharaonic relics alone, the treasures of the Cairo Geniza barely missed meeting a similar fate. Others, besides Solomon Schechter, would come within a hairsbreadth of carrying the whole stash off before he did.

There were, to be sure, certain basic differences at work in the way the world at large viewed—and coveted—the golden funerary masks and hieroglyph-rich steles of ancient Egypt and the way it saw (or in fact didn't see) the moldering and essentially unbeautiful manuscripts housed in that attic room in Fustat. Europe's fascination with everything ancient and Egyptian was tied up inextricably with imperial plotting and power plays—a trend that began with Napoleon's 1798 conquest of the country, which brought on its battleships an erudite army of archaeologists, surveyors, chemists, mineralogists, and engineers. But the men who first got wind of the Geniza and scrambled to uncover its  contents during those same early years were propelled by a much more ragtag blend of motives. And each worked, for the most part, alone. The Geniza's holdings were then just the faintest rumor among a tiny circle of scholars, travelers, and manuscript dealers, and hardly the object of the sort of popular mania directed at the mummies and scarabs of ancient Egypt.

Still, there are striking parallels between the unearthing of various Pharaonic tombs and that of the Geniza: in both cases, the glories of a past civilization might easily have faded into the sands had they not been hoisted out of oblivion by an active modern imagination, or several active modern imaginations. Both salvage operations went through a number of distinct methodological stages, with the so-called pillage of the first phase evolving later into a more systematic approach—and an emphasis on grand monuments (or, in the case of the Geniza, major works by famous men) giving way to a fascination with an accumulated wealth of minute, daily details. An early Egyptian explorer, according to the Reverend Baikie, "looked for colossi," while his "successor looks for crockery." The same would also prove true of later generations of Geniza explorers.

But first came the "plunderers."

The Russian Avraham Firkovitch has long been considered one of the Geniza's most bald-faced looters: "an assiduous and quite unscrupulous collector" he has been called, and "its first systematic" pillager. This is not, perhaps, the fairest designation, since Schechter himself might also be accused of a certain sort of plunder where the Geniza is concerned. (The line between ransack and redemption is thin with regard to the whisking away of such riches.) Firkovitch's name is now synonymous with the trove of manuscripts that he teased from *a* Cairo geniza in the mid-1860s and which has been held since in the State Public Library in St. Petersburg. After the fall of the Soviet Union, however, documents long off-limits to researchers revealed that the Egyptian geniza whose contents Firkovitch spirited back to Russia was not the Ben Ezra synagogue's, as had previously been assumed. That said,

Firkovitch did experience a very close encounter with *the* Geniza, which makes him a part of our story.

Born around 1786, Firkovitch was a Karaite—a member of the once surprisingly influential, now endangered Jewish denomination that challenged the authority of rabbinic oral tradition and evolved an alternative understanding of biblical law. Exceptionally tall, relentlessly pugnacious, and almost always mired in debt, Firkovitch was a man obsessed: he

was desperate to revivify and unite the various Karaite communities throughout Russia and the East. He was convinced that many of the Jews of Russia had once been Karaites. Moreover, he was eager to prove that the Karaites had been present in the Crimea for many millennia and so could not be responsible for the death of Christ. It has been claimed that, with this defensive though hardly watertight theory in mind, Firkovitch forged certain Karaite manuscripts as well as hundreds of ancient Crimean gravestones with Karaite inscriptions. However loony some of his ideas and dubious many of his methods, Firkovitch was clearly one of the first to have recognized the importance of genizot as a historical resource. From as early as the 1830s, when he first traveled to Jerusalem, he began to collect the manuscripts he found in these sacred crannies.

In the process, Firkovitch became something of a geniza-hound, and when he returned to southern Russia, he made it a habit to travel from village to village—upon arrival, immediately heading for the synagogue and sniffing out its geniza. Whether it was held in a special attic chamber, buried in the graveyard, or stashed inside a wall, Firkovitch would find it. And his sense of sight was as good as his nose. He had, it was said,

an especially keen eye for comparing the relative thickness of such synagogue walls and detecting a hidden stash.

So it was that as an energetic seventy-six-year-old, Firkovitch visited
the East yet again on another manuscript-finding mission. As he traveled, he foraged for papers in Jerusalem's Karaite synagogue, splurged on
others in Aleppo and Beirut, finagled a batch from the Samaritan community in Nablus, and bought several more from the aforementioned
Cairo Geniza visitor and self-proclaimed snake charmer Yaakov Safir.
Firkovitch eventually also made his way to Cairo, where he spent some
six months sorting carefully through and packing up much of the contents of what he characterized in a letter as "a very large geniza."

For almost a century now, scholars have accused Firkovitch of having
had "an interest in concealing the way in which he used to collect his
material" and being "reticent about the origin of the treasures which he
brought together in many years of daring travels." While he may indeed
have tried to maintain a certain air of mystery in public, now that his
private archive has at last been opened, this portrait of Firkovitch as
track-covering sham artist seems at best ungenerous: in a letter to a
Karaite friend back in the Crimea he states explicitly that the room
where he was working was "the geniza of the ancient synagogue that
belongs to the Disciples of Scripture," which is to say, the Karaites—and
not the "Rabbanite" (i.e., normative, Talmud-studying) Jews of the Ben
Ezra community.

Yet Firkovitch makes it explicit in his letters that he *also* visited the
Ben Ezra synagogue—and in fact intended, in his own words, "to take
the [Ben Ezra] geniza out from under the dust . . . I've already opened it
and seen that there's hope of finding valuable things there." (Upon hear-
ing about the wonders that had been discovered in the Karaite geniza—
which seems to have been more like a library than the Ben Ezra room,
containing as it did many more complete volumes—the head of the Rabbanite community in Fustat was, Firkovitch reports, "burning with
desire to open their genizot as well." He was suffering, in other words,

from a painful case of geniza envy—a syndrome that, we will see, grew increasingly common over the course of the next fifty years.) This time Firkovitch's eyes were bigger than his stomach, or his wallet, and it seems he ran out of time—he was much too busy sorting through the substantial Karaite stash—and lacked the money to carry out this grand plan. Or maybe, like Safir, all that frantic medieval paper-pushing had simply exhausted him. In a weary-sounding letter to his son-in-law he admitted that he was ready to come home and was "tired of traveling back and forth, for I have grown old." Though in another letter he refers to the "six pages that I took from the darkness of the cave that's in the graveyard of our brothers the Rabbanites in New Cairo, close to Egyptian Zoan." This was, it appears, one of the tombs in the cemetery known as the Basatin, located several miles from Fustat, which served as a sort of auxiliary geniza for the Ben Ezra synagogue. As the Geniza room filled to bursting, the community seems to have taken to burying their overflow there.

Whether he dug up additional documents in the Basatin we do not know, though the considerable number of fragments from the Firkovitch collection that match torn scraps found in other Geniza collections all over the world does make one wonder. Or perhaps he took more from Ben Ezra than he admitted in his letters. He describes very vaguely spending "three days there," during which time he says he was treated by a doctor for pains in the sinews of his hands, washed the synagogue's carved wooden wall inscriptions with a mixture of clay and lime, then copied them into a notebook. Could it be that such a serious geniza aficionado wouldn't also have plucked at least a few choice manuscripts from the bursting upstairs cache?

It does appear likely that, soon after Firkovitch's departure, papers he left behind in the Karaite synagogue were snatched up and put on the market by a gaggle of antiquities dealers who had begun to notice that something very interesting lay crumpled in the back rooms of Cairo's old synagogues. European libraries and collectors were ready to pay good money for these dusty scraps. Still, secrecy was key: this was too precious a quarry to simply open to the world.

Throughout the 1880s and into the 1890s, various Western travelers and collectors trotted in and out of Fustat and continued to miss what was literally right under their noses. The manuscript maven, lawyer, and brother of England's chief rabbi, Elkan Adler, visited the Ben Ezra synagogue in 1888 and came within inches of the Geniza when  he climbed a rotting ladder up to the purportedly precious "Scroll of Ezra" (almost, he wrote, breaking his neck in the process). But even this expert tracker of old Hebrew writings—a man who enthused in another context that "there is no sport equal to the hunt for a buried manuscript" and whose later role in the recovery of the Geniza would be quite important— accepted at face value the declarations of Cairo's Jewish leaders that they deposited all their worn-out books in the Basatin cemetery. When he returned home to England he published a lively account of his Eastern adventures, and went so far as to declare, "Nowadays there are no Hebrew manuscripts of any importance to be bought in Cairo."

Adler also reported that "it was not without a shudder that I heard that the respectable community of Cairo had resolved to have [the synagogue] whitewashed, cleaned and renovated in a few months." In fact, the Ben Ezra building was teetering near collapse, and several of the wealthy Jewish families of Cairo—who lived and prayed elsewhere but who recognized the historical importance of the site and continued to visit it as a place of pilgrimage—had decided to knock it over completely and construct a new building, according to the old model.

The work of razing the structure seems to have begun soon after Adler's visit—or, as a December 20, 1889, letter by one eyewitness, the retired British priest and die-hard Egyptophile Greville Chester, put it, "These wretches have demolished the most curious and interesting old building & are building a new one on the same site." Since the 1860s, Chester's poor health had sent him tilting toward the sun and the Nile every winter (by 1881 he claimed to have logged thirty-eight trips there) and, with the help of what sounds like a very developed knack for haggling and smuggling, he had become a steady supplier of small Egyptian objects—scarabs, seals, coins, and engraved gems—to the British Museum and the Ashmolean at Oxford, as well as papyri and other manuscripts to that university's Bodleian Library. (Among his more intriguing purchases for the British Museum was one of the first prosthetics in history, a

several-thousand-year-old mummy's false digit, which has come to be known as the Greville Chester Great Toe.) He also wrote scholarly articles about archaeology, including one on the ancient churches of Cairo. Chester maintained—incorrectly—as did others at the time, that the Ben Ezra synagogue had once been a church "which," he proclaimed, "it is much to be wished, could be rescued from its present state of profanation and restored to Christian worship." The irony, then, was that this unabashed anti-Semite—who opposed the election of Jews to the British

Parliament and had once referred to Prime Minister Benjamin Disraeli as "the Jew Earl, Philo-Turkish Jew, and Jew Premier"—was among the first Westerners to identify the Geniza as a potential gold mine, and to adopt an oddly conspiratorial, almost propriety attitude toward what would turn out to be one of the modern world's most important sources of knowledge about earlier Jewish literature and life.

In that same December 1889 letter to E. W. B. Nicholson, the librarian of the Bodleian, Chester writes breathlessly of "a quantity" of Hebrew manuscript fragments he had just discovered that morning. His conspiratorial letter in many ways anticipates Schechter's note to Mrs. Lewis:

> *The matter must not be <u>talked about</u> at present, but I tell <u>you</u> they come from the oldest synagogue at Mis'r el-Ateekeh—Old Cairo—once the Ch[urch] of S[aint] Michael, given in the early Middle Ages by an Arab Sultan to the Jews. . . .*
>
> *A room has been laid open whose floor is literally <u>covered</u> with fragments of MSS & early printed Hebr. books, & rolls of leather. From these I selected what I have got, & though I bought the best I could find there were doubtless numbers of others worth having. I only fear the lot will be destroyed or perhaps buried, & I could not get the people to say what will be done with them. One fragment of a book I got seems to me to be cabalistic. As I go on board my dahabeyeh [houseboat] tomorrow I cannot send off any more, but when I have time, I will sort the MSS., clean out the filth, try to straight[en] them out, & send them to you by Book Post from time to time. . . . I was almost suffocated with dust & devoured by fleas when making selections. . . . I suppose most of the bits are earlier than AD 1400 & some much more so?*

Chester's account is—like so much about this stage of the Geniza's history—more than slightly (perhaps willfully) obscure: he describes the demolition of the synagogue in the past tense, though he also seems to have seen the room, still standing, with his own eyes, as he inhaled its dust and was bitten by its fleas. Or perhaps the grit and bugs clung to the fragments brought to him by some nameless middleman, from whom he was buying the manuscripts? However he acquired them, the fragments he would sell to Oxford over the course of the next several years would form the basis of that university's Geniza collection—the first in Europe. Though even after he had gotten into a fairly regular routine of bundling the fragments up and shipping them to England, he also maintained that slightly paranoid pitch, chastising the Bodleian librarian in a January 1890 letter from Luxor: "I will beg you not to speak of the reception of MSS <u>openly on a post card</u>, as it might tend to their being watched for and confiscated in the Post! It would not be legal to do so probably, but that would make no difference with the powers that be." And again about a year later: "Please don't <u>on an open card</u> mention of <u>what</u> the packets rec[eive]d consist, as I believe they are apt to be stopped at the PO, if the contents were known." Chester appears to have been less concerned with foiling the manuscript-hungry competition than he was with sidestepping the strict customs laws governing the export of antiquities. (The British now controlled Egypt, but the French still dominated the Antiquities Service and watched the mail closely for illicit shipments.) But the nervous nature of his warning was typical of much of the talk surrounding the so-called Egyptian fragments at this stage.

Many of the reports about the 1889–90 "repairs" of the synagogue are tinged with the same cloak-and-dagger tone. "To quote from a reliable source whose name cannot be mentioned," wrote two otherwise forthright scholars in a hushed footnote to a 1927 museum catalog:

Before the late Dr Schechter transferred its remains to Cambridge, many dealers helped themselves to small bundles of fragments which they would obtain by bakshish [something between a tip and a bribe] from the beadle of the old Synagogue at Fustat (Old Cairo), where the Genizah had been discovered in an attic as a result of the work of repairing the Synagogue. The workmen on tearing down the roof dumped all the contents of this attic into the court-yard, and there the MSS were lying for several weeks in the open. During these weeks many dealers could obtain bundles of leaves for nominal sums. They later sold these bundles at good prices to several tourists and libraries.

It was only a matter of time before the manuscripts from these piles began to make their way from the dealers of Cairo out to all corners of the earth. In his capacity as Middle Eastern commissioner to the World's Columbian Exposition, to be held in Chicago in 1893, the Arkansas-born Semiticist and Jewish communal leader Cyrus Adler (no relation to Elkan) made an 1891 business trip to Cairo. "I happened one day to find," he recounted,

> several trays full of parchment leaves written in Hebrew, which the merchant had labeled *Anticas.* I saw at a glance that these were fairly old. As I wore a pith helmet and a khaki suit, like every other tourist, he thought I wanted one as a souvenir. But indicating an interest in the whole lot I purchased them, big and little, some of the pieces only one sheet, some of them forty or fifty pages, at the enormous price of one shilling per unit, and thus brought back to Europe what was probably the second collection from the *Genizah,* certainly the first to America.

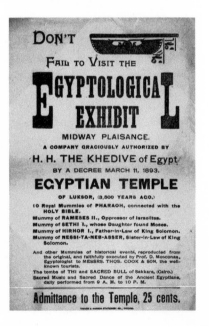

In 1892—some four years before Agnes Lewis and Margaret Gibson handed Solomon Schechter the "dirty scrap" of Ecclesiasticus they had bought from a dealer in Palestine or Cairo who may also have nabbed it off one of those same courtyard piles—Cyrus Adler showed Solomon Schechter the parchment pieces he'd bought that day. Later he wrote: "I have always flattered myself that this accidental purchase of mine was at least one of the leads that enabled Dr. Schechter to make his discovery of the Cairo *Genizah*." (Adler would, as it happened, bring more of Egypt than Geniza fragments back to the United States: the Chicago Exposition, which he helped to plan, featured not only the world's first Ferris wheel, Cracker Jacks, and Cream of Wheat, but an extremely popular attraction called "A Street in Cairo," complete with a mosque, fountains, real live "Egyptians, Arabs, Nubians, and Soudanese," and the so-called *danse du ventre*, that is, belly-dancing, advertised by the exhibit's organizers as "the wild, weird performance peculiar to the race.")

Some of the scraps dumped out in the Ben Ezra courtyard would wind up in the hands of people with a deeper and more immediate understanding than Cyrus Adler of their true origin and worth. Born in 1866 in Slovakia, the Jerusalem rabbi and independent scholar Shelomo Aharon Wertheimer, for instance, supported his large, poor family by buying and selling manuscripts. In the overgrown village that was 1890s Jerusalem, the young Wertheimer was known around town as an expert bibliophile, and so he received frequent visits from other dealers and

הרב הגאון שלמה אהרן ווערטהיימער זצ״ל
רומ״ץ בירושלים מחבר תספרים שו״ת שאלת שלמה
אור התרגום, ביאור שמות הנרדפים שבתנ״ך, בתי
מדרשות, אוצר מדרשים, גנזי ירושלם, קהלת שלמה וכו׳
נלב״ע י׳ תמוז שנת תרצ״ה בעיה״ק ירושלים ת״ו

suppliers who brought him manuscripts for inspection and possible purchase. One of these was a so-called emissary, referred to by Wertheimer's latter-day descendants simply as "the Yemenite," a man whom Wertheimer had dispatched to Egypt to buy manuscripts on his behalf. The Yemenite seems to have made several trips, returning with fragments that Wertheimer then set out to sell to the librarians at Cambridge and Oxford, to whom he announced in a series of letters and postcards—written mostly in English, but sometimes in German or (to Schechter) in Hebrew—that they came from "one of the Genizas of old Egypt."

Wertheimer's English in these missives was flawed but expressive (he addresses one note to "The Magnificent University Library"), his tone polite yet urgent—though this seems to have been more a function of financial need than any compulsion to convince his European customers of the importance of the manuscript's source. "I also come to let you know," he wrote, "that an Ancient '<u>Sefer-Tora</u>' found in one of the '<u>Geniza</u>' [*sic*] of Cairo (Egypt) written on leather of Roebuck 'צבי' should you require, let me know soon." In fact, given the monumental nature of the discovery he was more or less announcing to two of the world's great libraries, it is striking that much of the correspondence preserved in the archives consists of wrangling about postal rates: "Is it right that I should pay when your good & kind self promised me that you will send it by Registered post direct to me without my paying anything?" From 1894 to 1896 Wertheimer sold 62 Geniza manuscripts to Cambridge and some 239 items to Oxford, though just as much of the material he offered was probably sent back as was kept. One list preserved in the Cambridge files shows the piddling sums Wertheimer received for various manuscripts, of which at least some, it seems plain now, came from the Geniza; others in the same batch were marked by the librarian (whose diary indicates that he consulted with Schechter about these possible acquisitions) "not wanted," "not wanted at all," or simply "worthless."

But the contribution Wertheimer made to the gradual uncovering of the Geniza went beyond mere sales: he was the very first to knowingly transcribe and publish texts from the Geniza, and though later scholars would refer a bit dismissively to this work as "somewhat unscientific," he was, we might say, the founding father of Geniza studies. As significantly, he was also the first to make explicit mention in a publication of the existence of the trove. In an important 1893 Hebrew book of hitherto little-known rabbinical commentaries, he made conscious reference to the source of the manuscript with which he was working: it "comes from the old Geniza . . . in the land of Egypt," he announced, and he would go on to publish other volumes filled with a rich range of material from the Geniza—including more unknown midrash, rabbinic responsa, and liturgical poems. The wide scope of Geniza documents he put up for sale to Cambridge—everything from Judeo-Spanish poetry collections to marriage contracts to legal deeds to the seventh-century *Apocalypse of Zerubbabel* to medical tracts to letters to Passover hymns—also indicates a keen understanding of the vast and eclectic potential of the cache.

Yet decades later he would look back with more than a little bitterness at the fact that his own role in the recovery of the Geniza had been occluded. "It was I who made known to the world the importance of this Geniza, and other scholars and students came after me and," he complained, rather biblically, "despoiled Egypt of the Geniza manuscripts and brought to light many things from among them and earned fame throughout the world for themselves—and no one remembers the poor man who delivered the city."

Wertheimer's own close brush was, he clearly felt, with bibliographic immortality. In this sense, he was not alone. The final countdown to Schechter's "discovery" was marked by the melancholy presence of several such aggrieved and almost-famous men—now nearly forgotten.

One of the most painful of the close brushes that make up the early story of the Geniza is that of Adolf Neubauer, an extremely learned, slightly bitten Hungarian Jewish scholar and bibliographer who was Solomon Schechter's sometimes friend but more often rival, and the man who probably came nearer than anyone else to beating Schechter—and Cambridge—in the race to pack up and haul off the bulk of the Geniza documents.

Some sixteen years Schechter's senior, the multilingual Neubauer had studied in Prague and Paris and immersed himself for years in the

exacting analysis and publication of various Hebrew manuscripts. In 1868, he was hired by the Bodleian Library to catalog their extensive Hebrew holdings, and was eventually appointed sub-librarian of the entire collection. Later named that university's Reader in Rabbinics, he was Schechter's Oxford counterpart, if not in social at least in professional terms—and for several years these two erudite émigré scholars, among the only Jews in their respective Oxbridge settings, shared a wary bond, based on their common Central European background and, more important, on their passion for Hebrew manuscripts.

Their friendship was far from simple, and their personalities were quite distinct. Never one to mince words, Mathilde Schechter gently mocks in an unpublished memoir the lifelong bachelor Neubauer's severe stinginess, though she does allow that he had his winning qualities too. He had been very handsome once, "with his small features and fine blue eyes." And when she and Schechter came to know him, "in spite of [his] twenty-seven year [old] coat he always looked scrupulously clean and well-groomed, and he had a great deal of dignity. . . . [W]e really were fond of him, although it was trying sometimes."

That fondness aside, her portrait—written years later, after the friendship had completely withered—stings. ("He always had the idea that every woman he met was in love with him, and that he was irresistible," she notes, without comment.) She describes how she and Schechter found Neubauer once in his Oxford house reading manuscripts late at night beside "one little tallow candle," which was the only light in the house. Whenever Neubauer got a new manuscript he'd invite Schechter to come see it, and Mathilde would send her husband "laden with good things to eat, partly in order to observe the dietary laws and partly because I knew he would not have enough food at Neubauer's." She goes on: "Whenever I came [to Oxford] with Schechter, we stayed at lodgings, but being very polite to ladies he [Neubauer] insisted upon my coming to lunch with Schechter, where he served the cheapest fish obtainable. He was very proud of his coffee, which he made himself, and which was indeed excellent. Somebody once sent him some very good cheese, and when I asked for a second helping he put the dish far away at the other side of the table and assured me that it was not healthy for me."

Neubauer had, in certain respects, a head start where the Geniza was concerned: as early as 1876 he had been sent by the Bodleian to St. Petersburg, to report back on the Firkovitch collection. In the description he offered upon his return, he explained the idea of a geniza, and made it clear how important he thought this particular Karaite "collection of . . . manuscript *débris*," concluding his remarks with the startling (for its time) suggestion: "May I be allowed to draw the attention of the University to the treasures which Rabbanite synagogues might offer from their numerous 'Genizoth' in the East?"

While it seems Neubauer didn't immediately grasp the true worth of the Geniza manuscripts offered for sale by Reverend Chester and Rabbi Wertheimer, he did at least have the foresight to acquire some of these for the library. And it does appear that their value began gradually to dawn on him, as it was later recounted that in the early nineties a certain professor "used to see the desk of Dr Neubauer . . . covered with portions of books which Dr Neubauer told him had come from the East, his professional discretion not permitting him to disclose their exact source."

By 1894, though, Neubauer had actually announced in print the existence of a certain Egyptian geniza. Perhaps it was a way of marking Oxford's turf, but in a scholarly article from that year, he declared that "the Bodleian Library has lately acquired a considerable number of fragments of Hebrew MSS., found in a *Genizah* at Cairo, which contain a great deal of unknown matter in the branch of post-biblical literature." And in the next issue of the same journal, he again proclaimed, "The collection of Hebrew and Arabic fragments coming from a *Genizah* in Egypt, and lately acquired by the Bodleian Library, rivals that of St. Petersburg, if not in quantity, certainly in quality."

Even as Neubauer was making public the fact of a geniza, he was also plotting behind the scenes to try to get more of the stash for Oxford. Meanwhile, the situation back in Cairo had shifted. In 1892 the new synagogue building had gone up—"a hideous square abomination" in the ornery estimation of Greville Chester—and many of the manuscripts lying out in the courtyard had apparently been *returned* to the new structure's room, built, it was said, according to the original floor plan, but now made accessible by a ladder placed in the women's section. Other manuscripts from the Geniza were then buried around the synagogue grounds—a practice that, it seems, had been going on for some time before the "renovation." (So goes one plausible account. In fact, it is notable that after more than a century of research into Ben Ezra, no one has yet managed to account definitively for just what took place during the synagogue "renovations." Was the original Geniza destroyed and reconstructed completely, and then—bizarrely—refilled, or did it somehow remain standing while the rest of the building was razed and re-created? There are no clear answers.)

The idea that valuable Hebrew parchments and papers might also lie underground added a new archaeological dimension to the quest for Hebrew manuscripts. In 1889—not coincidentally, near the start of a decade in which recently excavated Greek papyri flooded the Middle Eastern market—the Egypt Exploration Fund uncovered several such fragments in the mounds around Fustat, and these Hebrew manuscripts eventually made their way to the Bodleian. Though they were donated by the Fund to the library, the man responsible for salvaging them was a

mysterious figure known as the Count Riamo d'Hulst, who claimed to have been a subject of "the Grand Duchy of Luxembourg" but who may have been a deserting German officer from the Franco-Prussian War. As an employee of the Fund, d'Hulst had been dig-ging near the synagogue when he'd come across the fragments, which he shipped back to England together with several Kufic tombstones, some pottery, coins, and glass pieces. He was later encouraged by the Bodleian to oversee a much more extensive dig at the site, and the fruits of his excavations would, in Neubauer's words, "form the nucleus of our large collection of Egyptian fragments."

D'Hulst's story is, though, yet another sad Geniza tale—as his critical contribution to the trove's retrieval was, for years, kept hidden. (He was also barely paid for his work.) According to Nicholson, the Bodleian librarian, "absolute secrecy as to the Cairo fragments was, for the time being, necessary to the interests of the Library." While this excuse might sound reasonable, it was offered grudgingly, and only *after* d'Hulst had taken to writing lengthy (sixteen-to-twenty-page) screeds in which he hounded the Oxford authorities, declaiming, for instance, "For me, it [the omission of his name in connection to the finds] is not a question of mere vanity but of justice, and having been repeatedly treated unjustly it has become a question of principle." And elsewhere, more wrenchingly: "you have not to look back as I have upon a life ruined and embittered by ingratitude & disgraceful behaviour in return for services rendered." A "pronounced Anglophile," in his own terms, he was imprisoned in Egypt during World War I as an enemy alien, and soon after died of malaria, impoverished and unknown. The full extent of his role in retrieving Geniza manuscripts was only uncovered in 2008 by a tenacious young Cambridge scholar.

It wasn't, though, just the buried fragments that were now being excavated: the entire Geniza was, in a sense, up for grabs. In an 1895 letter to Neubauer, the Assyriologist, collector, and regular traveler to Egypt A. H. Sayce (who had, through d'Hulst, been steadily supplying Oxford with Geniza manuscripts) claimed that "the Jews in charge of the place have offered to sell the whole collection for £50 with £5 bakshish [the equivalent of some $5,000 in today's currency]. But the difficulty is how to get such a large quantity of things out of the country. Could the Bodleian get the government or rather Lord Cromer [the British consul general of Egypt] to do it?" There were other obstacles too. "The three heads of the community are selling [the manuscripts]," wrote Sayce to Neubauer in a letter a few days later, "but as the one with whom the bargain was made is perpetually drunk it has been very difficult to get it completed."

For whatever reason, the plans for this sale fell through—and soon afterward, in early January of 1896, Elkan Adler returned to Cairo, where, after making a probably ample "donation," he was, as he later wrote, "conducted by [Cairo Chief] Rabbi Rafail [ben Shimon] to the extreme end of the ladies' gallery, permitted to climb to the topmost rung of a ladder, to enter the secret chamber of the Genizah through a hole in the wall, and to take away with me a sackful of paper and parchment writing—as much in fact as I could gather up in the three or four hours I was permitted to linger there."

Upon his return to England, Adler announced his discovery to Neubauer and Schechter. "The first rated me soundly for not carrying the whole lot away, the second admired my continence but was not foolish enough to follow my example."

Or, as he put it elsewhere, "Neubauer was very angry with me for not ransacking the whole Genizah. I told him that my conscience, which was tenderer then than now, reproached me for having taken away what I did, but he said that science knows no law."

Those were fighting words for such a proper gentleman. Neubauer must have felt himself a bit frenzied as he drew closer and closer to the Geniza stash: he had acquired a valuable, if small, trove of manuscripts already, and it was just a matter of time before he would somehow seize hold of the whole thing for the Bodleian. This may not have been a matter of purely "scientific" interest; he was, according to Mathilde Schechter, "of a very jealous nature" and seems not to have taken kindly to the momentous May 1896 announcement that Cambridge's own Dr. Schechter had discovered a leaf of the long-lost Hebrew Book of Ben Sira. Never mind that Neubauer had plenty of other scholarly fish to fry and that he had, until now, evinced only a passing interest in the apocryphal book: word of Schechter's find seems to have driven him around the competitive bend. Schechter, for his part, was brimming with excitement and, immediately upon identifying the ancient scrap in Agnes and Margaret's dining room that spring day, had dashed off a postcard to his difficult friend to tell him the thrilling news. After two weeks of pregnant silence, Schechter received a letter from Neubauer saying that the postcard was illegible. At the same time, Neubauer let it be known that he and his younger Oxford colleague A. E. Cowley just happened to have discovered nine leaves of Ben Sira in the Oxford collection! ("It is natural for us to think," mused Agnes Lewis, "that [the notice of Schechter's find] was of some assistance in guiding Messrs. Neubauer and Cowley to this important result.") Mathilde was more direct and declared that "for a long time he [Neubauer] could not forgive Dr. Schechter. He was very bitter about many things." That was the end of the friendship.

Now the race to get the Geniza was really on, and in October of 1896, Sayce wrote to d'Hulst: "I have persuaded the University to send Dr. Neubauer out to Cairo, since being a Jew he may be better able to get the MSS from the Jews than we are." Rumors were afoot that Elkan Adler had been in Cairo and had purchased certain manuscripts, and Sayce was eager to beat him to the rest.

But as we have heard, Neubauer already knew about Adler's Geniza finds, and though he had earlier berated the London lawyer for "not carrying the whole lot away," Neubauer now turned rather abruptly on his heel, declared Adler's fragments "a lot of worthless rubbish," and decided not to make the trip.

Was he too weary to go? Too cheap? (Adler had, it seems, committed a cardinal sin in Neubauer's eyes and "paid high prices" for his haul of useless trash.) Did he prefer to stay home and rummage for other Ben Sira fragments in the Bodleian collection? Or did he consider the ripped and dirty jumble of unsorted odds and ends that Adler had showed him— and the others that Sayce and d'Hulst had recently boxed up and shipped to the Bodleian—somehow *beneath* Oxford, which had long prided itself on obtaining valuable literary manuscripts in excellent condition, preferably more complete quires, in fine scribal hands? We may never really know—though one thing at least is sure: with that small but fateful failure of the imagination, the learned, lonely Adolf Neubauer lost all claims to the Geniza stash and, in this respect, to posterity.

3

All Sirach Now

Why Ben Sira? What drew Schechter into the spell of those fragments that May afternoon in the Giblews' dining room? What notions were kindling the glitter in his eyes that Margaret had seen when Schechter asked if he might take the leaf of Ben Sira home for inspection? His own pronouncements about the find never confront the question of motivation, at least not directly, and so in following out this psychic thread we are, to an unnerving extent, searching among shadows. Only in that half-light, however, do we stand a chance of discovering what it was about the seventeen "badly mutilated" lines of verse from the second century B.C.E. that roused the Romanian scholar and caused him to orchestrate, on the sly, his Indiana Jones–like expedition to Egypt.

In all probability, it *wasn't* the idea of the Geniza itself.

For at least a decade and a half Schechter had been working intensively with Hebrew manuscripts at the British Museum in London and in close proximity to Neubauer at Oxford's Bodleian Library—"the promised land of the Hebrew scholar," as he put it in an 1888 article. And for six of those years he had been at Cambridge, which held the "Egyptian fragments" that Shelomo Wertheimer had been selling to the university since the early nineties. By all accounts, Schechter was devoted to this work and, once he arrived at Cambridge, to the Hebraica housed in the library at what was known as the Old Schools. He was often there on the Jewish Sabbath, and the head librarian's diary entries from the pre-Geniza years register Schechter's ongoing engagement with the collection: "November 4, 1891, Schechter till too dark to write." "July 8, 1894, Schechter took me to Library to sort fragments of Hebrew MSS from Egypt . . . After tea, another hour at the Hebr. MSS." "December 31, 1894, About an hour with Schechter at Hebrew MS. fragments from R. Wertheimer." "May 4, 1896, At Library [with] Schechter, . . . Benzine failing to touch the lumps on an Egyptian Hebrew fragment on vellum. Or-

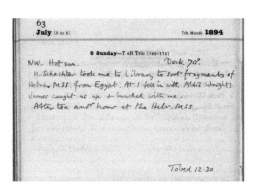

dered some chloroform." Yet none of this moved Schechter to seek out the source of these treasures.

Far from currying favor with Wertheimer, who seemed to have steady access to a heap of highbrow Hebraic trash, Schechter often made life difficult for the impecunious scholar-dealer in Jerusalem. Nor was he stirred to action by the finds of other collectors—above all the two Adlers—who had also retrieved fragments from the Egyptian capital. Moreover, many of the pieces the library had acquired while Schechter was hard at work with his manuscripts remained in boxes, unclassified in even a provisional fashion. They don't seem to have interested him at all. Finally, Schechter himself had in 1894 gone well out of his way, to Italy, in pursuit of manuscripts he required for articles he was writing. So travel itself wasn't a problem. But not until the grimy leaf of Ben Sira was in his hands did his dreams begin drifting toward Egypt. Clearly it was something about this particular work that led the burly Talmudist through that Cairene hole-in-the-wall. Again, what was the allure?

Schechter's interest in the Palestinian Talmud notwithstanding (since the 1870s he'd worked on the lesser-known, shorter, and older sibling of the Babylonian Talmud), he and the Giblews would, in their correspondence and in the public announcements of their find, focus not on that fragment of the Oral Law but on the small square of gall-eaten rag paper bearing lines of Ben Sira in a tenth-century hand. Between the blotches and the fading ink, the scrap looked like a bad photocopy of a bookkeeper's double-entry ledger, the principal information barely legible in a cloud of ambient ink. As Mathilde tells it somewhat fancifully in her memoir, Schechter returned home from the library after having confirmed his identification of the manuscript "in a very excited mood, and very pale. His first words were: 'Wife, as long as the Bible lives, my name shall not die! This small torn scrap is a page of the Hebrew original of Ben Sira. . . . I have been to the library to verify my suspicion. Now telegraph to Mrs. Lewis and Mrs. Gibson to come here immediately.' " To

stake their claim, Mrs. Lewis dashed off short pieces for two leading journals, the liberal *Academy* and *The Athenaeum*, also an independent weekly that featured a distinguished roster of contributors and a lively swirl of social chitchat and scholarly buzz, including, that particular week, notice of a revised edition of *The Anatomy of Melancholy*, a review

of a volume on *The Mogul Emperors of Hindustan*, a new poem by Algernon Swinburne (dedicated to his mother), "fine-art gossip," "science gossip," and, under the heading "literary gossip," Agnes's announcement to "All students of the Bible and of the Apocrypha" who "will be interested to learn that amongst some fragments of Hebrew MSS. which my sister

Mrs. Gibson and I have just acquired in Palestine, a leaf of the Book of Ecclesiasticus has been discovered to-day by Dr. Schechter, Lecturer in Talmudic to the University of Cambridge."

"The book interested him very much," wrote Mathilde. "Again and again Dr. Schechter would say, 'If I only had leave of absence and sufficient money, I would go in search of the rest of that lost Hebrew original.' This idea began to take so firm a hold . . . that his sleep was disturbed and his health was impaired."

Almost from the very start of his scholarly career, Schechter had been drawn to what he called "the dark ages" of Jewish history, the period extending from about 450 to 150 B.C.E.—toward the end of which Ben Sira was composed (probably in Jerusalem) and just after which it was translated into Greek by the author's grandson (in Alexandria). "No period in [our] history," wrote Schechter, "is so entirely obscure. . . . All that is left us from those ages are a few meagre notices by Josephus, which do not seem to be above doubt, and a few bare names in the Books of Chronicles of persons who hardly left any mark on the history of the times. . . . More light is wanted, . . . [and] this light promises now to come from the discovery of the original Hebrew of the apocryphal work, 'The Wisdom of Ben Sira.' "

The spectacular aspect of the discovery apart, Schechter saw in this find a redemptive sort of promise for two substantive reasons, though these dual motivating factors soon gave way to numerous and far more complicated, unconscious, and perhaps ultimately unfathomable concerns. First, and most straightforwardly, he felt that the Greek and Syriac versions—which had spawned translations into many other languages, including English—were, at times, "mere defaced caricatures of the real work of Sirach." An accurate source text would at least tell us what Ben Sira really said (if not necessarily what he meant).

Schechter's second reason for placing such hope in retrieving the original Hebrew concerns the seemingly arcane but in fact surprisingly significant matter of dating. Many of the prominent biblical scholars of the day were exponents of the interpretive approach known as "source criticism," or, sometimes, "Higher Criticism." These largely Protestant scholars used historical tools to reconstruct how and when various biblical books came to be, identifying and assigning approximate dates to distinct authorial strands, which, they believed, combined to form the texts as we know them. (Lower criticism, on the other hand, focused primarily on the words of the text—their correct reading and precise meaning.) By Schechter's time, the higher critics had concluded that a number of books in the Hebrew Bible were composed much later than previously supposed—in the latter half of the Second Temple period, that is, toward the end of the third century or the beginning or even middle of the second century B.C.E. These included the Song of Songs, the Book of Job, the Book of Ruth, and especially certain Psalms.

But this chronology, like much else about the work of the higher critics, was controversial. Noting that Ben Sira himself seems to be quoting as "classical" passages from books that some of the modern critics claimed were written at the same time as Ben Sira, or even later, Schechter remarks: "Altogether, the period looks to me rather over-populated, and I begin to get anxious about the accommodations of the Synagogue, or, rather, the 'House of Interpretation' (the *Beth haMidrash*), which was . . . a thing of moment in the religious life of those times." Schechter felt a deep-seated animus at work in this line of thought. The higher critics, he believed, were with their dating, and maybe with their very being, trying to "argue out of existence" the "humble activity [of] whole assemblies of men" enlisted in the service of religious study.

To Schechter's mind, something was wrong with this higher-critical picture, and Ben Sira might help clear things up, as it is the only quasi-biblical book for which we have a reliable date. The grandson's testimony in the prologue to his Greek version of Ben Sira indicates that he made his translation around 132 B.C.E., which would mean that Ben Sira himself wrote his work some two generations earlier—between, say, 200 and 180 B.C.E. If one had in hand a substantial sample of the original Hebrew of Ben Sira, whose date was more or less known, it could be compared with the Hebrew of these biblical books whose dates are a matter of considerable speculation, and scholars could, as Schechter put it, "test the mode of thinking as well as of the language and style of the period in question." Then readers would know just how reliable these Protestant higher critics were.

Unfortunately, the last sighting of the Hebrew original of Ben Sira had been in the tenth century, when an important Jewish scholar wrote about it. The final Christian to mention it was Saint Jerome in the fourth century. By that time Ben Sira was known as Ecclesiasticus—a Latin term meaning "Book of the Church"—as its moral thrust and presentation of ideal religious figures had earned it a place of pride among the apocryphal writings. It was seen as being "inspired by God," and many of the early Greek and Latin Church Fathers considered it authoritative. Later Catholic editions of the Bible grouped it with the standard set of Old Testament wisdom writings, and though Protestants never accepted it into the inner ring of sacred texts, the book was regularly printed as a supplement to many—though not to Presbyterian—Protestant Bibles. In short, the canonical or almost canonical Ecclesiasticus drew considerable Christian devotional and theological interest through the ages, and any major development relating to it would, the ever-canny and even competitive Schechter no doubt knew, cause a sensation. It might even pry a book like Ben Sira loose from Christian claims.

Schechter was suspicious not only of the Higher Criticism but of several other contemporary Christian approaches to theology and history as well. And for the two years prior to his identification of the Ben Sira scrap, he had been feverishly preparing a series of lectures intended to counter in respectable fashion these Christian critics and Jewish scholars of a Christianizing bent. (Speaking off the record, though, in a letter to a friend, he referred to "their" theology as an "abomination" and accused these scholars of wanting to undo history and of not being "real . . . monotheists.") It wasn't that he disagreed with the scientific impulse underlying the work in question. On the contrary, he was all in favor of serious scholarly analysis of scripture—and had gone so far as to call the fundamental effort of the Higher Criticism "one of the finest intellectual feats of this century." What he objected to was the "brutal vivisection" of Jewish history that all too often came with it.

This slashing into the living flesh of an entire people's faith was part and parcel of the distinctly anti-Jewish bias that Schechter felt lay behind the Protestant critics' line of inquiry, which perceived much of Jewish history as a continual falling off from the heights of early revelation and prophetic vision to a preoccupation with ceremony and legal sophistry. Second Temple Judaism was in this worldview reduced to a mechanical priestly cult, and post-Temple or rabbinic Judaism—which Schechter held in the highest esteem—was dismissed outright as a spiritually sterile legalism. The Law as given in the Torah, charged Julius Wellhausen, the highest of these higher critics, "thrusts itself in everywhere . . . blocks up the access to heaven, . . . and spoils morality."

Wellhausen made the case against later Judaism in disconcertingly compelling fashion. "The warm pulse of life," he wrote, "no longer throbbed in it to animate it. . . . The soul was fled; the shell remained." But it wasn't just a matter of spiritual fatigue. As this leading member of the school saw it, the problem of religious evolution also touched on fraudulence. "It is well known that there have never been more audacious inventors of history than the rabbins. But Chronicles affords evidence that this evil propensity goes back to a very early time, its root the dominating influence of the Law, being the root of Judaism itself." In Wellhausen's most important book, which was published in Germany while Schechter was taking courses at the University of Vienna in biblical grammar and other related subjects (he was just three years younger than Wellhausen), biases of this sort extended to the most fundamental level of scriptural interpretation, including philology, where, for instance, Wellhausen derived the key Hebrew word "Torah" from the root suggesting the casting of lots or the pronouncement of oracles, rather than from the three-letter radical indicating "the thing taught or reported" or "come down by tradition." "Wellhausen's hypothesis," Schechter noted, "is . . . strangely in harmony with [his] conception of the law, which thus would originate in a sort of priestly fetisch [*sic*]." For Schechter, however, the heart of Judaism was its unbroken (if often battered) line of transmission—precisely what had been reported or what had come down by tradition—without any loss of revelation's power. The teaching of Judaism embodied "the effluence of God's mercy and love," and its yoke was joyfully taken on through history by "all sorts and conditions of men, scholars, poets, mystics, lawyers, casuists, schoolmen, tradesmen, workmen, women, [and] simpletons."

Put in the plainest terms, for Schechter Higher Criticism was poorly or barely disguised "higher anti-Semitism"—"German dogs," he called the beer-loving Wellhausen and his followers—and the Hebrew Ben Sira was the newest weapon with which he could combat them.

It had already been a long fight. The very first article Schechter published under his own name was a short 1881 piece treating the essential distortion of actual Jewish practice and tradition that anti-Semitic bias in scholarship brought about. Two years later he wrote to a younger colleague studying in Germany, "It is sad to see the ways in which *Wissenschaft des Judentums* [the science of Judaism] is neglected here [in England]. As in Germany with the Bible, here the entire literature of Judaism is taken care of only by Christians. . . . There is no spiritual life and I feel like death. My only comfort is the manuscripts in the British Museum."

Over the course of the next seven or eight years, Schechter poured out a steady stream of articles on a wide range of Jewish subjects spanning the centuries, from the Hasidim to the presence of women and children in Jewish literature, from medieval figures such as Maimonides to modern historians such as Leopold Zunz—one of the founding fathers of that "scientific," which is to say also broadly humanistic, Jewish scholarship. Schechter summed up Zunz's project in an 1888 essay: "To restore the missing links between the Bible and tradition, to prove the continuity and development of Jewish thought through history, to show their religious depth and their moral and ennobling influence, to teach us how our own age with all its altered notions might nevertheless be a stage in the continuous development of Jewish ideals and might make these older thoughts a part of its own progress—this was the great task to which Zunz devoted his whole life." From that visionary if indirect statement of Schechter's own mission—he was clearly aligning himself with the great leaders of the Jewish past—it isn't far to Ben Sira's heart and substance. For an authentic Hebrew Ben Sira would confirm the existence of a moral and spiritually vital Second Temple Judaism far removed in both time and practice from the "source" revelation and yet hardly desiccated by excessive legalism or the mechanical maintenance of priestly rites.

Because of its core ethical focus and concern with transmission, Ben Sira was beloved among the rabbis of the early talmudic period. In fact, they prized the collection of hymns and homiletical verse so (one might think of it as a kind of rabbinic self-help manual—an epigrammatic miscellany of manners, morals, and the ways of wisdom and the world) that they set it almost on par in importance with the Book of Proverbs. Some scholars feel that Ben Sira was banned from the Jewish biblical canon only because of its late date or the fact that its author was known so specifically, as a particular figure from their own not-too-distant past. Though it may once have been considered a member in good standing of Israel's company of sacred writings, by the time the rabbis fixed the canon and decided what was in and what was out, Ben Sira found itself among the "outs," and along with the other "external books"—as the apocryphal writings are known in Hebrew—its study was proscribed in Judaism. Eventually the Hebrew original vanished altogether, though passages from it continued to be quoted and have left their mark on some of the prayers regularly recited by Jews today (even if most are unaware of it). Passages from the book are likewise found in the two Talmuds and other central rabbinic texts, where they are sometimes introduced with the formula "it is written"—a phrase usually reserved for quotations from scripture.

Scholarly interest apart, one is tempted to say that it was Schechter's developed literary sensibility that pulled him almost uncontrollably toward this lost valley of Hebrew letters—a path leading from the later poetry of the Bible to the next conspicuous stage in the history of Hebrew verse, the hymns and prayers of the fifth through eighth centuries. "Ben Sira," he remarked, "should rather be described as the first of the Paitanim [liturgical poets] than as one of the last of the canonical writers." It is, though, by no means clear that he intended this as a compliment, as Schechter seems to have had decidedly mixed feelings about the value of that later hymnography. In addition, like most scholars, he noted the derivative and pastiche-like quality of the Ben Sira text, which a Cambridge friend and colleague called "a tissue of old classical phrases," and which another scholar has described only a bit more generously as an attempt "to adapt the older Scriptures in order to popularize them and make them relevant to the new Hellenistic age in which [Ben Sira] lived." Still other modern writers are more blunt in their assessment of Ben Sira's limitations: "Polonius without Shakespeare," says one, suggesting that Ben Sira's wisdom is passed on without panache or anything in the way of a style that might make it memorable. Numerous commentators have found the work "tedious," and one Jewish biblical scholar has said that the Hebrew of the section identified by Schechter is "composed in an idiom which is for the most part hideous."

On the other hand, the American-Jewish classicist Moses Hadas called Ecclesiasticus "the most attractive book in the Apocrypha," adding that "it can be read almost as an essay of Montaigne is read." More than just an extender of scriptural tradition, Ben Sira's author is, says one leading Israeli Semiticist, a self-conscious, skillful, and at times even virtuoso artist whose work introduces to Hebrew notions that develop into pivotal concepts and terms in rabbinic literature (the immanence of God, for example, which later in the tradition becomes the Shekhina). The book is, he says, brimming with treasures (*genazim*).

Whatever reservations Schechter himself had about the epigonic nature of some of the writing, when Ben Sira the poet hit his stride, the results, he felt, rang a large literary gong: "The chapters containing the praise of wisdom and the praise of holy men," he wrote, "are unsurpassed in beauty of diction and grandeur of thought." He no doubt had in mind the book's opening lines—

> *All wisdom comes from the Lord*
> *and is with Him forever.*
> *Who can number the sands of the sea,*
> *and the drops of rain, and the days of eternity? . . .*
> *Who can find out the height of heaven,*
> *and the breadth of the earth, and the deep, and wisdom? . . .*

and the passage midway through the book when Wisdom speaks in praise of herself:

> *I came forth from the mouth of the most High,*
> *and covered the earth like a mist.*
> *I dwelt in high places,*
> *and my throne was in a pillar of cloud.*
> *Alone have I compassed the circuit of heaven,*
> *and walked in the bottom of the deep.*
> *In the waves of the sea, and in all the earth,*
> *and in every people and nation, I have gotten a possession.*

Schechter was almost certainly thinking, too, of Ben Sira's turn at this point from the universal toward the particular, as he asks:

> *Among all these I sought a resting place—*
> *[but] in whose inheritance might I abide?*
> *Then the Creator of all things*
> *gave me a commandment,*

and He who made me
  assigned a place for my tent,
and said: Make your dwelling in Jacob,
  and in Israel receive your inheritance . . .

And finally, if not quite consciously, Schechter may well have been alluding to the concluding verses of that same chapter when Ben Sira himself speaks out as a scholar-sage or "man of letters" and identifies in the deepest fashion with Wisdom, saying:

I came out like a brook from a river,
  like a water-channel into a garden.
I said, I will water my orchard
  and drench my garden;
and lo, my brook became a river,
  and my river became a sea.
I will make instruction shine like the dawn . . .
  and leave it to all future generations.

Wisdom in this scheme links humankind—through the Torah—to the divine and the eternal. It is a presence that survives through the ages, surfacing here through the detritus of history. Rooted in the fear of God, it involves not so much unusual insight, or cleverness, but a teachable, practical sort of knowledge that hones the ability to choose between evil and good, and helps one navigate the ethical, spiritual, and wholly ordinary challenges of living. This late expression of it—the Book of Ben Sira—culminates, some twenty chapters further on, in a great catalog of biblical heroes and the moral lessons their lives embody. The curtain call of exemplars opens with lines taken up by the American writer James Agee, who applied them to powerful effect in the title of the book he began preparing in 1936 with photographer Walker Evans about gaunt, dirt-poor tenant farmers in Alabama—radically altering the polarity of Ben Sira's verse in the process:

Let us now praise famous men
  and our fathers in their generations.

The Lord apportioned to them great glory,
His majesty from the beginning. . . .
There are some that have left a name,
so that men declare their praise.
And there are some who have no name,
who have perished as though they had not lived.

The paean goes on to celebrate the ethos and extension of Jewish teaching—from Noah and Abraham and Jacob through Ezekiel, Nehemia, and Shimon Ben Yohanan (Simon the Righteous), the high priest of Ben Sira's age, installed in the Temple and likened to the "cypress towering in the clouds" and other glories of Creation. The scholar-sage in this all-encompassing vision is an essential part of the continuum of Jewish history and of Wisdom's work in the world.

While the sensitive Schechter was, then, responding viscerally to matters of style, it stands to reason that his passion was also being stoked by a more fundamental concern: "It is one of the great tragedies," Schechter wrote in another context, "that modern Judaism knows itself so little."

So much for Schechter's nobler aspirations and his long-standing enmity toward the higher critics. What had most recently gotten his Ben Sira goat involved something much closer to home.

In 1889, David Samuel Margoliouth, the son of a missionizing Jewish convert to Anglicanism and a man of massive learning, which he would come to hide behind a stiff brush of a mustache and a cliff-like face, was appointed the Laudian chair of Arabic at Oxford. His inaugural lecture, based on a prizewinning dissertation he'd completed two years earlier, was called "The Place of Ecclesiasticus in Semitic Literature." Margoliouth had been reluctant to go public with his dissertation, he said, because he "felt that there was some secret about Ecclesiasticus which had not yet been explained." (Little did he know.) But now, he

announced, he had the key and so was ready to release his thoughts on Ben Sira to the world.

Margoliouth's lecture examined the question of textual authenticity in Ben Sira and concluded that the true nature of the lost Second Temple book is best reflected in the less-than-perfect mirror of the extant Greek and Syriac versions and, curiously, that a Hebrew *replica* could be worked up so as to provide scholars with a reliable sense of what the original Hebrew conveyed. And this he proceeded to do. He'd later claim that the original was not in fact "lost" but deliberately "destroyed," which is what he suggests is the true meaning of the g-n-z root that gives us the word *geniza*. (Margoliouth was known for having what one writer has called "the kind of beautiful mind that could see patterns where none existed" and who instead of telling his dog to " 'Sit!' . . . would order it to 'Assume the recumbent position!' ") "It is a strange feeling," he told his Oxford audience, "after reading some pages in illustration of a peculiar saying or expression to find that that saying or expression never existed."

The "key" that led Margoliouth to the convoluted argument of his lecture was his realization that the language of Ben Sira was, in all probability, not the "classical" Hebrew of the Prophets, but rather a mongrel and quantitatively metrical sort of "post-biblical language," incorporating "vulgar" Hebrew as well as elements of "Chaldean [Aramaic] and Syriac." The replicated text, Margoliouth asserted, showed that there was in fact a huge gulf between the diction and syntax (and thought) of Ben Sira and that of "the grave of the Old-Hebrew and the Old-Israel." While Margoliouth was by no means a higher—or for the most part even a Bible—critic (he argued aggressively for revelation and held wholly distinct theories of dating), he shared Higher Criticism's tendency to disparage postbiblical Judaism and to see in the history of Hebrew violent disjunction and decline rather than continuity and organic evolution. ("What a descent!" he calls it in another essay.) And in coming to his conclusions Margoliouth pointedly dismissed the many Hebrew passages of Ben Sira that appear in early midrashic literature, which he snidely referred to as "the whole rabbinic farrago." Needless to say, Hebraic hackles were raised. For Schechter in particular, Margoliouth's lecture amounted to the casting down of a gauntlet.

Margoliouth was Schechter's foil in every way. Where Schechter was educated in patchwork if serious fashion in a variety of European institutions, including the yeshiva, hadn't earned a doctorate, and was, as a non-Anglican, never granted a chair at Cambridge, Margoliouth, twelve years his junior, was an Orientalist whose prodigious learning (reflected in erudite publications examining texts in Persian, Hebrew, Sanskrit, Arabic, and Greek) earned him a prestigious professorship at Oxford and prize after prize—such that "he ceased to be quite human," as one eulogist would put it. In Cambridge the impulsive Schechter worked away with an all-consuming, Hasidic zeal; at Oxford Margoliouth was known as a cold contrarian and serial debunker—of, for example, the authenticity of pre-Islamic Arabic poetry and the Elephantine Hebrew papyri. ("Never was a learned man less apt to wax enthusiastic over the value of learning," observed Gilbert Murray, the well-known British classicist and translator.) And while Schechter sought throughout his life to demonstrate the unbroken line of Jewish vitality through the ages, Margoliouth saw Judaism through an apostate's eyes, arguing for the relevance of Ben Sira not to Jewish continuity, but to the Greek New Testament.

A year after being appointed to his Cambridge post, Schechter published a pointed response to his Oxford colleague, though he mentions Margoliouth and his lecture only in passing. This study of rabbinical quotations from Ben Sira was Schechter's first published work as a lecturer at the university. His goal with the article was to show that Ben Sira may once have been included in the biblical canon; was not composed in meter; and that "the version of Ecclesiasticus known to the Rabbis was mostly written in pure Hebrew"—that is, Hebrew as it was used by a masterful writer of scripture in the second century B.C.E., not the motley pastiche of Margoliouth's reconstructed passages, of which Schechter said: "I do not pretend to understand [them]. They are certainly not Hebrew." Finding the original version of Ben Sira would, in other words, help Schechter build a case against both the likes of Margoliouth and the more properly Protestant higher critics, who were—obviously—still very much on his mind and under his skin.

In that early study, however, Schechter was working with only a handful of quotations scattered through numerous works and handed down from rabbi to rabbi. Now, bobbing up from the depths of history was a page from what appeared to be the work itself.

The find roused him to such a degree, then, because Schechter had from the start seen Ben Sira as a critical link in the chain of Jewish bequeathal through the ages—one that connected the *Beit haMikdash* (the House of the Shrine, or the Temple) to the *Beit haMidrash* (the House of Learning, a term that first appears in Ben Sira itself, though it didn't yet denote a place of rabbinic study). That ancient house of learning was, Schechter believed, headed in spirit and possibly in fact by Ben Sira himself. Which is to say that already in Ben Sira's day—with the Temple still standing and sacrifices being offered at its altar—young men were being taught the tradition of wisdom and ethics in an early form of the *Beit haMidrash*. So in a sense, the culture that we know as Judaism today has its foundations in that fragment passed on to Schechter by Agnes and Margaret. In any event, its relevance for Judaism as he was encountering it in England seems to have virtually leapt out at the uprooted Romanian, who—noting the social circumstances and educational ideals of the book, and its author's sober assessment of mortality—characterized Jewish life in Ben Sira's time as "a world very much like ours."

For one, there was the author's grounded if not effortless attempt at absorbing elements of the surrounding Hellenistic society into his notion of Judaism. Wisdom in this Hellenized context meant "culture," and what Homer and his poems were to the Greek notion of *paideia* (or the centrality of education in the formation of character), Moses and scripture were to the Jews (at least in Ben Sira's "fantasy," which is how one scholar has described his hymn to the tradition). Moreover, the "good" for Ben Sira included not only the moral good of a purer sort, but a proper appreciation, in both ethical and aesthetic respects, of the full range of life's pleasures, subtleties, and trials: "What is life to a man without wine? / It was made to make men glad. / Drunk in season and temperately, / wine is . . . gladness of soul. . . . / A ruby seal in a setting of gold / is music at a banquet of wine." Detailed and indeed still useful instruction is given about how to behave at such a banquet, or symposium. Apart from moderation in drink, the old are cautioned not to interrupt the music with their talk and not to show off their cleverness or erudition, and the young not to be presumptuous ("among the great, do not act as their equal"). More delicate problems are also addressed. The book is hardly calling for withdrawal from the world, notes one commentator: "[Ben Sira's] godly man wears golden jewelry and bracelets on his right arm and appreciates meats and dainties. When invited as a guest, he should not greedily put his hand into the common dish. If, however, he should happen to overeat, he should leave the table, like a gentleman, and go elsewhere to vomit." (Well, some of it involves a world like ours.)

Ben Sira's consciousness of nature is also often utterly familiar and wonderfully concrete: "By His command He sends the driving snow / and speeds the lightnings of judgment. / Therefore the storehouses are opened, / and the clouds fly forth like birds. . . . The eye marvels at the snow's whiteness, and the mind is amazed at its falling." And moving into an equally physical feel for the abstract, he writes: "A mind settled on an intelligent thought is like the stucco decoration on the wall of a colonnade." At the same time the book's defense of appropriate instruction betrays an underbelly of anxiety on the part of the author, who— his grandson the translator notes—composed the book "to help the outsiders" (Jews not trained in this tradition) gain access to these vital teachings. Their reputation as People of the Book notwithstanding, ordinary Jews of the early Hellenistic period absorbed scripture only at the remove of religious practice and through oral teachings passed down through the family. Torah readings were not part of the Temple service and the study of the Torah itself was reserved for specialists like Ben Sira and his pupils. And even Jewish intellectuals educated in the traditional texts were increasingly influenced by Greek-style learning. As another of the principal twentieth-century commentators on the book puts it: "These Jews [of Ben Sira's period] had a gnawing, unexpressed fear that the religion of their ancestors was inadequate to cope with the needs of social and political structures that had changed enormously. To bolster the faith and confidence of his fellow Jews, Ben Sira published his book."

So it wasn't merely that Schechter sought to bring Judaism into the new world from the old—out of the trance of Eastern European piety and Orthodox religious observance and into the vortex of modern scholarship—but that he longed to limn a Jewish culture that reached through history with integrity and without diminishment of strength. The discovery of the original Hebrew text of Ben Sira, composed during a critically transitional phase of the Second Temple period, and essentially identical to the copy of the book possessed by the later rabbis and also by Jews in medieval Egypt, would buttress his claims for the validity of this continuous culture. "We thus see clearly," wrote Schechter, acutely conscious of his own predicament, "that what inspired Ben Sira was the present and the future of his people."

Perhaps—but for Margoliouth the newly discovered Ben Sira fragments in a tenth-century hand were "rubbish," which is to say, second- or third-rate Hebrew renderings made from a Persian translation of the original Greek and Syriac. "This . . . is the miserable trap in which all of Europe's Hebraists have been ensnared," Margoliouth sneered, noting that they were off in their dating of these fragments by no less than thirteen hundred years! If Schechter could use the discovery of the Hebrew Ben Sira to show that the Protestant critics were fundamentally mistaken in their dating of key biblical books—and better yet, if he could find the rest of the long-lost Ecclesiasticus and prove that these critics and Oxford's professor of Semitic languages were disfiguring and fundamentally misrepresenting the history of Judaism—that would help considerably to undermine their authority. The inevitable dose of Oxbridge and also personal rivalry provided by Margoliouth and Neubauer (who was, meanwhile, racing to find other Ben Sira leaves in the Bodleian collection) only added fuel to an already very serious fire.

"I am all Sirach now," Schechter would soon write to a Philadelphian confidant, noting that he was preparing "a declaration of war to [*sic*] certain results of higher criticism . . . Heaven knows that I do not want to play the savior of the orthodox party. It is for me a simple question of history. . . . We ought," he added, stating his motivation as clearly as he ever would, "to recover our Bible (Apocrypha included) from the Christians." To do so, he'd first have to make his way to Cairo.

4

Into Egypt

Schechter was now a man with a mission—a "secret mission," as Mathilde dubbed it in a letter from Cambridge to the judge and bibliophile Mayer Sulzberger, that same Philadelphian friend of her husband. True, Mathilde was writing a romance novel in her spare time and had always displayed a certain theatrical dash in her prose, though this time she wasn't dramatizing at all when she described in an epistolary whisper how Schechter had quietly slipped out of England on December 16, 1896, bound for Egypt and Palestine. He had gone, she explained, for "purposes of research (Hebrew Mss.)" though "the fact will be announced . . . only . . . about the end of January, when he will already have secured permission to work in the old Genizah, as otherwise his plans might have been defeated." He had left home for several months but— she couldn't quite contain herself

here—"glowing with love of labour and enthusiasm, to the land of bondage and land of unfulfilled promises to try his luck."

Schechter's mood was not quite so lofty. "Half-dead with fatigue and sleeplessness" on the SS *Gironde*, bound from Marseilles for Alexandria, he tried to sound circumspect as he, too, penned a note to Sulzberger and labeled his Egyptian mission simply "scientific." Schechter the former Hasid was, though, never really comfortable with such drily academic terminology and added a warmer Jewish promise to "give you details when I am in Cairo p[lease] G[od]." It was the start of the last week of an eventful year, and that same evening on the boat Schechter scribbled a letter to his "Liebe Mathilde" in the affectionate garble of English and German that would constitute his near-daily reports to her from the East. While it was his startling discovery of the long-lost Hebrew original of Ben Sira that had propelled him to set out on this covert and fairly daredevilish operation, he had more earthly things on his mind that night. Besides the usual *"Gruss und Kuss"* (greetings and kisses) that he sent his wife and *"den lieben Kinderechen"* (the dear little children—the Schechters had three), he added that the terrible heat had made him take off all his clothes. "I am pining for Cairo," he wrote, in English, "where I will put on thinner flannels."

This patchwork of high and low would mark much of Schechter's adventure in Egypt, which found him at once planting his scholarly flag at the summit of an entire society's literary, historical, religious, legal, and economic remains—and quite literally picking through some ten centuries' worth of dust, mildew, and mouse droppings in order to do the same. The Geniza spilled with riches that looked an awful lot like rubbish—and the fact that Schechter recognized the value of this putative trash, and had chosen to make his way over many miles of land and sea in order to retrieve it, is powerful testament to the force of both his imagination and his personality. An intellectual less charismatic and socially adept (a Neubauer, let us say) might have understood everything there was to know about the traditional practice of geniza and the philological and theological disputes surrounding the text of Ecclesiasticus; indeed, he might have been able to pinpoint exactly where in Fustat the stash was located and been prepared to summon an impressive list of historical sources to support that assertion. But without Schechter's dynamic presence in the here-and-now—his unvarnished ability to engage, excite, persuade, charm, and win the trust of almost all those who met him—the mission to Cairo would very likely have been an anti-climactic bust.

However vaguely, Schechter had, it's clear, known of the existence of an important geniza in Cairo for some time. Besides the hints provided by Cyrus Adler's *"anticas,"* Wertheimer's marked-down manuscripts, and Neubauer's publication of texts "found in a Genizah at Cairo," there were other clues. Margaret Gibson would later recount that after Schechter had identified the Ben Sira scrap that she and Agnes had brought back from their travels, he saw "the word 'Fostat' on several of our fragments . . . [and] suspected that [these manuscripts] had once been in the Genizah, or lumber room of the synagogue at old Cairo."

But perhaps Schechter's most important Hebraic homing device came in the person of his lawyer friend Elkan Adler: not only had Adler already ventured inside the Geniza and told Schechter in detail of his visit, showing him the sack—a worn Torah mantle—full of papers that he'd been allowed to gather up there over the course of a few hours in January of 1896, but Adler seems to have provided Schechter with the actual scent of things to come. After examining Adler's Geniza documents, Schechter had, in Adler's own words, "used his eyes and nose to very good purpose, for it was its characteristic odour and appearance that enabled him to recognise the Gibson fragment as one of the family [of Geniza documents], and so he determined to go to Cairo himself, and bring back what I had left behind."

Once having pointed his snout in the direction of Egypt, Schechter still faced the tricky task of finding money to pay for the trip and somehow keeping the expedition under wraps. Given the race then under way with Oxford to find the remainder of Ben Sira (which was, at this stage, still the ostensible reason for his journey: so far nearly a quarter of the book had been identified by the respective Cambridge and Oxford scholars), it was imperative that no one beyond the smallest circle of confidants know of Schechter's plans. He couldn't, then, ask the university for money as he had done to finance his Italian manuscript-hunting trip; the trustees of the research fund would be obliged to publicize the fact of his voyage, which would ruin the whole scheme.

Instead Schechter turned conspiratorially to several Cambridge friends for help, among them the Scottish physician Donald MacAlister, who was also close to Agnes and Margaret and was, according to Mathilde, "intensely interested" in the prospect of Schechter's search for the lost manuscript "even if there was only the slightest chance of its recovery." Understanding the urgency of the matter and the need for the utmost secrecy, MacAlister promised to approach the very next day the philosopher Henry Sidgwick, who was both a wealthy man and one of the leading liberals in Cambridge: he and his wife had been early and active advocates for the admission of women to the university. (Sidgwick cut a formidable figure in both moral and physical terms and looked, in Mathilde's estimation, "like Jupiter on the coins found in ancient Elis.") Schechter's enthusiasm seems to have been catching, as Sidgwick, for his part, was "keenly alive to the romance of [the] idea" and offered immediately to arrange a leave of absence for the Reader in Rabbinics and to pay personally for the whole trip.

In the meantime, though, yet *another* friend of Schechter's—the soft-spoken, philanthropically minded Hebraist, mathematician, Anglican priest, and Master of St. John's College, Charles Taylor—had somehow heard about the plan, and also been infected. For several years, Schechter had taught a Tuesday afternoon class that was attended by some of the most distinguished professors at the university. Taylor was nearly a decade Schechter's elder and had already published a highly regarded translation of the mishnaic *Pirkei Avot*, which he called *Sayings of the Jewish Fathers*, as well as several books with titles like *Geometrical Conics, Including Anharmonic Ratio and Projection, with Numerous Examples*. Yet for all his seniority and erudition, he was one of Schechter's most devoted students—and heir to a long and venerable tradition of Christian Hebraists at Cambridge. According to Mathilde, Taylor "insisted that he had the first right to defray expenses, being a Hebrew scholar and a pupil of Dr. Schechter's." (Here it is perhaps worth noting that Schechter's strong objections to the Protestant higher critics in no way precluded or interfered with the sympathetic feelings and respect he had for many devout Christians. Schechter held Taylor and his Hebrew

scholarship in particular in the greatest esteem, and would write after Taylor's death, "His friendship to Judaism . . . arose out of his love for Hebrew literature, to which he applied himself in his youth with a zeal and devotion hardly equalled by any contemporary Jew. To him the Rabbis were like unto [Ben] Sirah of old, 'the Fathers of the World' towards whom he never failed in the filial duty of reverence.") And so it was arranged: the honor of footing the big bill would fall to the stout Taylor, while Sidgwick would have to be content with underwriting any later expenses that might arise in conjunction with Schechter's journey. The initial outlay was £200, or some $18,000 in today's terms.

Armed with a pile of visiting cards, his good black suit, and a letter of introduction to Cairo's grand rabbi from England's chief rabbi, Hermann Adler (written, in fact, by his brother, Elkan, who vouched for the fact that Schechter was both a *"lamdan* and *tzaddik,"* a scholar and a righteous man), another to the head of the Jewish community in Cairo, and a third, from the vice-chancellor of Cambridge to the de facto ruler of Egypt, Lord Cromer, Schechter boarded the train from London to Marseilles in mid-December. Some eight days later he found himself in Cairo, which appeared, at first glance, disappointing. "Everything in it calculated to satisfy the needs of the European tourist is sadly modern, and my heart sank within me when I reflected that this was the place whence I was expected to return laden with spoils the age of which would command respect even in our ancient seats of learning." Things began to look up, though, after his meeting with the rabbi, Aharon Raphael ben Shimon, who explained that *Old* Cairo, that is, Fustat, was where Schechter should be searching—and not in the

newer city. The atmosphere there seemed more promising to Schechter, as it was "a place old enough to enjoy the respect even of a resident of Cambridge."

To Mathilde, meanwhile, referring to an earlier book he had edited, Schechter wrote that the rabbi—a bearded and bespectacled man who wore long eastern robes and a squat kind of turban—"kissed my *Avoth de Rabbi Nathan* three times. I would prefer a kiss from you. The rabbi has a younger brother who is his right hand. The way to win the heart of the rabbi is, I can see, through this brother and thus I flirted with him . . . for hours." He had decided, he told her, to take Arabic lessons three times a week. "You see how practical your old man is. If something is in the Genizah we shall, with the help of God, get it."

Schechter was eager to roll up his sleeves and start working, though he had, from the outset, to accustom himself to the meandering rhythms of the place—to the Jewish community's lengthy and involved preparations for the Sabbath (which precluded entry to the syna-

gogue on business), the regular fast days and funerals (which meant the shuttering of the whole Jewish quarter), and the leisurely courtship ritual in which he was involved with the rabbi and other officials. A few days after his first audience with Ben Shimon, Schechter offered to take him for a ride to the pyramids, which the rabbi himself had, incredibly, never seen. "It will cost me ten shillings," he told Mathilde. "But this is the only way to make myself popular." Later he would write her with an urgent request for two hundred "used English stamps" for the rabbi, a collector.

He also discovered that the hotel where he'd booked a room, the Royal, was "a true hell of immorality," and was located on a street of bordellos. "You don't need to worry about my virtue," he assured his no-doubt-alarmed wife back in England, "but I cannot let any decent person come [visit] here." Soon after his arrival, the head of the Cairo Jewish community, Moise Cattaui, found him a more suitable hotel, the Metropole, which housed many English guests, and was both cleaner and cheaper than the first. The Cattauis, as it happened, knew a thing or two about finances: they had risen from modest money-lending roots to amass a fortune in banking, real estate, and railroads, so becoming one of the wealthiest Jewish families in Egypt. As patricians who had managed to secure

the protection of the Austro-
Hungarian empire, they had
even gone so far as to refashion
themselves in the 1880s as the
"von Cattauis." They lived in a
lavish mansion in the fashionable Ismailiyya district, on a
street often referred to as rue
Cattaui. With its large private

synagogue, their house was known as a "palace" and was adjoined by a
pond and date-palm-filled garden so sprawling it looked like a park.
They welcomed Schechter in style, introducing him to the other community leaders, offering to accompany him to the Geniza, and inviting
him over for regular kosher meals. Schechter, a man of no small appe-
tites, wound up dining there several times a week for the length of his
stay in Cairo.

He may have been impatient to start work, but his wait proved worth-
while as, five days after arriving in the Egyptian capital, Schechter was
finally granted access—of the most generous and total sort—to the
Geniza: chaperoned by the rabbi, he made his way in a carriage to the
old walled area known as the Fortress of Babylon, where the Ben Ezra
synagogue was located, and the rabbi escorted him inside the compound.
"After showing me over the place and the neighbouring buildings, or
rather ruins, the Rabbi introduced me to the beadles of the synagogue,
who are at the same time the keepers of the Genizah, and authorised me
to take from it what, and as much as I liked."

"Now as a matter a fact," he would later write, "I liked it all."

Schechter's account of what he discovered when he climbed up the
ladder and peered down into the Geniza is perhaps the most famous
description ever written of that remarkable room. More than a hundred
years later, "A Hoard of Hebrew Manuscripts," published in the London
Times some six months after his return to England, also remains the

finest and most highly charged sketch of the astonishing jumble the attic chamber contained. "One can," he wrote,

> hardly realise the confusion in a genuine old Genizah until one has seen it. It is a battlefield of books, and the literary production of many centuries had their share in the battle, and their *disjecta membra* are now strewn over its area. Some of the belligerents have perished outright, and are literally ground to dust in the terrible struggle for space, whilst others, as if overtaken by a general crush, are squeezed into big, unshapely lumps, which even with the aid of chemical appliances can no longer be separated without serious damage to their constituents. In their present condition these lumps sometimes afford curiously suggestive combinations; as, for instance, when you find a piece of some rationalistic work, in which the very existence of either angels or devils is denied, clinging for its very life to an amulet in which these same beings (mostly the latter) are bound over to be on their good behaviour and not interfere with Miss Jair's love for somebody. The development of the romance is obscured by the fact that the last lines of the amulet are mounted on some I.O.U., or lease, and this in turn is squeezed between the sheets of an old moralist, who treats all attention to money affairs with scorn and indignation. Again, all these contradictory matters cleave tightly to some sheets from a very old Bible. This, indeed, ought to be the last umpire between them, but it is hardly legible without peeling off from its surface the fragments of some printed work, which clings to old nobility with all the obstinacy and obtrusiveness of the *parvenu*.

It is not clear how long it took Schechter to realize the singular nature of the cache that Rabbi Ben Shimon had put so unquestioningly at his disposal. That first night after his return from the Geniza, he could only manage an exhausted and fairly telegraphic German postscript to a letter composed and ready to send to Mathilde. He had, he reported, been working since morning in the Geniza and had emerged with two sacks of fragments, now beside him in his hotel room. Though he was (again) "half dead" with fatigue, he did have the strength to declare, "There are many valuable things there." He thought he would need "at least another week" to clear out the Geniza, because "the workers are very slow." But first things first: "I must," he announced, "take a bath immediately." He was covered in the ancient grit he called *Genizahschmutz*. As it happened, he would need to keep scrubbing off such hallowed dirt for most of the following month.

The work took a full four weeks, and throughout that time Schechter veered between states of elation and disgust. He was, on the one hand, fascinated by certain aspects of Cairo, of which "there is so much to tell . . . it is hardly possible to commence. One is drowned in embarras de richesses." And the Geniza itself certainly accounted for much of this figurative wealth. It offered far too huge and scrambled a mix to sift through in situ, so he had decided to comb out as much of the printed material as possible, then simply ship home all the manuscripts he could manage. He would worry about sorting them later. "With the help of God," he enthused to Mathilde, "quite a lot of good things will be found."

The physical labor involved in gathering and bagging the fragments was, on the other hand, punishing in the extreme. "A beastly unhealthy place," the Geniza was dark and filled with medieval dust, which "settles in one's throat and threatens suffocation," and the room was, too, "full of all possible insects." In one letter to Mathilde, he complained in his typical bilingual mishmash that he was so bitten by the mosquitoes, "ich full of spots bin."

Still worse than the bugs were the synagogue beadle and his helpers— whose assistance Schechter realized he needed in order to pack up the stash and whose incessant demands for bakshish Schechter had little choice but to meet. In public he made light of the arrangement, describing it almost as he might for the amusement of cognac-quaffing guests at a Cambridge dinner party: "Of course, they declined to be paid for their services in hard cash of so many piastres *per diem*. This was a vulgar way of doing business to which no self-respecting keeper of a real Genizah would degrade himself." Instead, they coaxed from him these endless tips, "which, besides being a more dignified kind of remuneration has the advantage of being expected also for services not rendered." It was apparently expected as well that the "Western millionaire" would provide a steady stream of handouts to everyone who came and went from the synagogue while he was toiling there—"the men as worthy colleagues employed in the same work (of selection) as myself, or, at least in watching us at our work; the women for greeting me respectfully when I entered the place, or for showing me their deep sympathy in my fits of coughing caused by the dust."

In private, meanwhile, this nonstop schnorring drove Schechter into fits of rage, and he spared no scorn when it came to the beadle Bechor in particular. "The greatest thief that ever lived," he dubbed the man in one letter and denounced the "infernal scoundrel" in another. While one can surely understand Schechter's frustration at the near-constant demands on his wallet (or Taylor's), there is, to modern ears, something unsettling about Schechter's rants on the subject of bakshish and the beadle. Consciously or not, Schechter almost seems to be echoing Baedeker's very Victorian *Egypt: Handbook for Travelers*, which he carried with him on his trip, and which warned unsuspecting European tourists that bakshish should *never* be given "except for services rendered," as "the seeds of cupidity are thereby sown." Furthermore, "most Orientals regard the European traveller as a Croesus, and sometimes too as a madman—so unintelligible to them are the objects and pleasures of traveling."

But perhaps the discomfort here springs from something more substantial than just Schechter's testy tone and his reluctance to tip. It has, too, to do with the question of his attitude toward the Geniza cache and its ownership. As the sacks of fragments piled up (at the start of what he called "the goyish new year," January 1, 1897, he had laid claim to three satchels, by the next week nine, then thirteen, seventeen, and by January 20 "about thirty bags of fragments"), Schechter had clearly come to feel the manuscripts were his own private property. "Thieves," he claimed, were trying to sell back to him "things they stole from me." The beadle himself was "stealing many good things and sell[ing] them to dealers in antiquities." One particular dealer had "some mysterious relations with the Genizah, which enabled him to offer me a fair number of fragments for sale. My complaints to the authorities of the Jewish community brought this plundering to a speedy end, but not before I had parted with certain guineas by way of payment to this worthy for a number of selected fragments, which were mine by right and on which he put exorbitant prices."

"Mine by right." That Schechter had the prescience to realize the Geniza's value rested in its integrity is not in doubt. If anything, it makes him a visionary and a hero. (The collection would be, he was wise to grasp, next to worthless were it picked apart and sold off by various profiteers; had he not arrived on the scene when he did, this would likely have happened.) Nor is there any question that the grand rabbi of Cairo himself had given Schechter carte blanche to gather up all he wanted of the Geniza. To judge from the tremendous welcome Schechter received from the city's Jewish aristocracy, his mission also enjoyed their wholehearted approval. The Cattauis, Mosseris, and other wealthy Jewish families of the place seem to have been much more interested in cultivating the goodwill of the British authorities and in establishing close relations with an elite European institution like Cambridge than in mucking around in what they must have perceived as nothing more than filthy clutter. Though the Cattauis had Egyptian roots that may have stretched back some seven or eight hundred years, many of the other leading families were relatively recent arrivals to the country, having

immigrated over the course of the last few centuries from Italy and else-where in the Levant; it seems likely that they felt no strong connection to the longer history of the local community. Neither did any of them live in Fustat, which was by this time a slum. Still, Schechter's assertion—*"mine by right"*—seems a rather presumptuous one for a Romanian-born wanderer-rabbi and naturalized citizen of England to have made after spending just a few weeks in Egypt.

To be fair, Schechter's proprietary attitude toward the Geniza frag-ments extended well beyond the borders of Egypt—and may have had as much to do with scholarly territorialism as it did with the assertion of colonial privilege. In a January 12 letter (marked "private") to the mild-mannered Cambridge librarian Francis Jenkinson, Schechter outlined his work in Cairo, describing the dust and bugs and aggravating interactions with the beadle, as well as the thirteen sacks of fragments he had col-lected to date, then moving on to a "great request" he wished to make of Jenkinson. Schechter was "anxious to send the first lot home to England" and wanted to know if Jenkinson would be willing to "give them a place in the University Library till I return." The emphatic underlinings are all Schechter's own:

> *The MSS will probably belong soon to your library. I want only to hear first whether you and the syndics will agree to certain conditions which I have to make. Money plays no important part in these conditions and I am sure you will find them very fair and just. But till then I want the MSS to be considered as my private property; so that the boxes must not be opened before I have returned. For I am very anxious to [be] the first to examine them properly. If you cannot agree to these condition [sic] will you do me the favour to send at once—when the boxes arrive for Mrs Schechter (2 Rock Road) and hand her over the boxes, who will bring them into some place of safety till I return P[lease].G[od].*

While he was waiting for Jenkinson's answer, a somewhat skittish Schechter announced to Mathilde that "I do not think it is safe to keep here all my fragments" as "there is such a thing as an evil eye of certain people." He believed it best to set about arranging for an export permit so that the manuscripts could be shipped off sooner rather than later.

Meanwhile, he found time to spend a day examining what he called "the second Genizah," which was in the "cemetery"—apparently the Basatin—and to unearth certain fragments there. (It is hard to say what, precisely, Schechter took from the graveyard or other local synagogue storerooms; he occasionally refers in his letters to the "Genizas," plural, and though he says he "found almost nothing" in "the other Geniza"—*which* geniza is not specified—his final count of manuscripts includes what he described as "one and a half sacks from the other Genizas.") He toured the Coptic churches of Old Cairo with some English friends; prayed in the Karaite synagogue; received a visit from the first secretary to Lord Cromer; took a drive with Cattaui; stopped in at the English embassy; and ate several Sabbath dinners with the rabbi who "kisses me every minute (which is not very pleasant)." He also befriended, among others, a Jewish waiter at his hotel—who supplied him daily with a little piece of grilled kosher meat—and a British businessman, Reginald Henriques, who lived in Cairo and wound up acting as a kind of private manuscript scout after Schechter left Egypt, writing in 1898 to announce that "I have been having most exciting times lately in your Geniza." He had, he reported, intercepted the excavations that Count d'Hulst and "some twenty Arabs" were carrying out in the Ben Ezra courtyard. Henriques eventually sent to Cambridge several shipments of these newly unearthed fragments, which "but for my timely intervention . . . would now have been carried off to the Bodleian Library."

On the whole, Schechter found Cairo "a glorious place, enjoying an Italian opera, French dancing masters, English administration, and Mohammetan huris. The last are very ugly, and I do not wonder they are so careful to cover their faces." Schechter had, it seems, made a splash in fashionable circles. A rich Jewish acquaintance told him that "there is much talk in the Turf (English) Club about the great Jewish Savant etc.

etc." And toward the end of his stay he finally met the consul general, Lord Cromer, "who was exceedingly kind. He expressed the wish that I should be presented to him." The fact that the most powerful man in Egypt was so intrigued by Schechter was more than flattering: it was useful. The customs officials had the right to confiscate all antiquities marked for export, but the British authorities—working, it seems, on Cromer's orders—were quick to arrange all the papers Schechter needed to make his removal of the Geniza's contents legal.

For all his hobnobbing Schechter missed his family deeply: "Could you manage," he wrote Mathilde early on, "to have yourself and the children photographed and surprise me with it[?]" Later, his pangs grew more acute: "I sympathize with Baby [possibly their younger daughter, Amy]. I also feel homesick and cry sometimes in the night. I want my wife and children." Especially his wife, it seems, to whom he proclaimed

a few weeks before he returned home, "never again on a Journey without you. I cannot stand it any longer."

They were no substitute for his Liebe Mathilde, but when Agnes and Margaret arrived in Cairo on January 20, he was

very happy to see them. The original plan had been for them to travel with him in the first place, but Agnes's severe arthritis detained them; she joked that her rheumatism had flared up when she'd inhaled "the microbe of Ecclesiasticus, a creature that may have come into existence in the ninth century, and fattened on the very dirty paper whereon [the fragment they'd shown Schechter] was written." They did eventually set out, bound again for Sinai, but eager to stop in the Egyptian capital. "Our movements were greatly stimulated," as Agnes put it, "by the news of Dr. Schechter's having obtained access to the Genizah synagogue and having dived into a hole filled with Hebrew fragments." Besides familiar faces, they came bearing gifts from home: quinine, a magnifying glass, and—best of all—a respirator, which the good doctor Donald MacAlister had thought to send along to help Schechter breathe while inside the Geniza. ("An inspiration" Schechter dubbed "this saving thing.") Agnes reported in immediately to Mathilde about "your dear Husband" and described how "Mr. Schechter is rather tired of and tired with the work he has been at. He has found a few good things amongst heaps of, well, I won't say rubbish but unimportant stuff. This is the way in all Eastern libraries. But in this case he has been choked with dust and bad air and has worked like a horse. . . . Mr. Schechter was disappointed that we had not brought 'Tommy' [the 1896 novel *Sentimental Tommy* by the Scotsman and *Peter Pan* author J. M. Barrie, about a young man with an overactive imagination; Mathilde promptly sent him a copy] but we are going to lend him Robert Louis Stevenson's last book, 'Weir of Hermiston' to make up for it. And really he has enough to see and study in Cairo without distracting his mind with novels."

The twins meant, as usual, to do more than socialize when they were in Cairo. They had come to work, and a few days after their arrival, Schechter took them to see the Geniza. Agnes's aching joints kept her from ascending that "roughest of rude ladders," which led to the room, but both Margaret and one Miss de Witt, a student from Girton (Cambridge's first college for women) who had accompanied them on their journey, climbed up and peered in. Much to Agnes's regret, they had forgotten their small Frena camera back in the hotel. Had they brought it along, we might have some visual record of the "heterogeneous mass of confusion . . . [that] filled the loft of the Genizah." As it is, only such verbal portraits remain: there is no photograph of the Geniza before its contents were carted away.

Agnes and Margaret understood that they could best help Schechter by visiting the various antiquities shops around town and buying whatever fragments they found there. (Margaret would later describe how they returned to the same neighborhood and shops where they had been regular customers for several years and had bought the original Ben Sira page. "We have no doubt whatever . . . that these . . . had come from this Genizah without the cognizance of the Grand Rabbi." It seems Mrs. Lewis's original announcement that the Ben Sira scrap had come from Palestine had been meant to throw the academic competition off the scent.) They also bought a leather portmanteau in which to pack these purchases, and, "as there is no particular satisfaction in importing dirt," set about cleaning the manuscripts in their hotel room. Agnes performed this task with what she described as "great eagerness," since "every scrap that I detached from its neighbours might possibly have been concealing another leaf of the Hebrew Ecclesiasticus, but in this I was disappointed. They were so wet that I had to spread them out on trunks and tables in the sunlight to dry, removing a quantity of sticky treacle-like stuff with bits of paper which I afterwards destroyed."

Schechter, meanwhile, was grateful for their company ("They are very friendly and in no way intrusive," he wrote Mathilde) if a bit skeptical about the results of their shopping trips. ("I think that they have bought the things which I have declined to buy from the dealers, for I have only bought what seemed to me important." That said, once back home he did arrange to buy several sacks of fragments from a dealer named Raffalovich, who shipped them to Cambridge, where—after a session of sorting with Schechter—Jenkinson declared the contents "very poor stuff.") And he continued to work—tussling with the beadle till the very end about how deep to dig in the heap of paper and vellum—and on January 28, he announced that he had "finally finished the big Geniza. I have emptied all." By the last day of the month "about a hundred thousand" fragments had been packed into "8 big wooden cases" and were ready to be shipped. (In fact more recent counts show the tally closer to 190,000 pieces.) He was, he told Mathilde, "anxious that they would go away from here for in the last days some began to grumble that I take away so much etc."

He planned to wait another week or so before setting out to visit his brother in Palestine. Even though the Geniza crates had already been sent off to England, he wanted, he wrote, to stay in town to keep an eye on "the thieves" to see whether they "will throw on the market things they stole from me." In the meantime, he invited Agnes and Margaret to tea to meet the rabbi, had another meal with the Cattauis (who packed him a kosher basket to take on his trip), and ate dinner again with the rabbi, "with the usual consequence of indigestion." But for all his sarcasm, Schechter still knew enough to be extremely grateful: "These people are so kind that they are worth some inconvenience."

5

Sorting

Clouds and sun, with a westerly wind, were recorded neatly in Francis Jenkinson's diary on May 11, 1897, as was the "squall of rain & hail" that burst out in Cambridge that evening. On this particular Tuesday, the meteorologically hypersensitive and headache-prone university librarian—a devoted amateur botanist, entomologist, bird-watcher, and chamber music enthusiast—also noted the peppermint geranium he'd given a friend, mentioned the recovery from influenza of a well-known literary critic he'd happened to meet on his way to work, and, without veering from the same even script and tone, reported: "Began unpacking the first box of Hebrew fragm[en]ts, most anxious stuff."

Most anxious indeed. Although Jenkinson remains tactfully close-mouthed in his journal about the particulars of what went on that afternoon—noting simply: "Hurried lunch & back by 2.0: Schechter, Ma[ste]r of St. John's [Charles Taylor], Mrs. Lewis and Mrs. Gibson set to work at the fragments in Centre First Floor Room"—it is not hard to imagine the tense scene that must have unfolded as, under the supervision of the gentle and fastidious librarian, the first crate of Geniza documents was pried open, and the excitable Solomon Schechter plunged his hands into the heaps of dirty fragments.

Schechter had been eagerly anticipating this moment for months now. He had returned from the Middle East at the end of March, traveling home on the boat from Port Said with none other than the leading English Egyptologist of the day, Flinders Petrie, who—while Schechter was busy emptying the Geniza—had examined the site of the Ptolemaic and Roman-era town of Oxyrynchus, 120 miles south of Cairo; that very same month enormous trash heaps had been discovered there that bore an uncanny resemblance to the Geniza and yielded a trove of Greek papyrus rolls: a thousand years' worth of tax documents, census records, letters, contracts, receipts, as well as a forgotten poem by Sappho, three unknown sayings attributed to Jesus, and a long-lost comedy by Menander. Hellenic Egypt wasn't Petrie's purview, however, so he'd left that dig in the hands of two young Oxford archaeologists (who would spend the rest of their lives unearthing and analyzing their finds—some five hundred thousand pieces in all) and set off to investigate the Old Kingdom rock tombs at Deshasheh.

He and Schechter were already friends—Mathilde mentions in her memoir that while Schechter was staying in Cairo he had visited Petrie in the desert and "found him working in his night-shirt"—and these two bearded and charismatic pioneers in their respective fields enjoyed their time together on the steamer. One wonders if they discussed the Geniza-Oxyrynchus connection and Petrie's belief in the archaeological importance of "unconsidered trifles" for the reconstruction of history: "bits of boxes, string, thread, sandals and . . . even linen." (The Geniza was spilling with its own such textual "trifles.") Then, near Marseilles, their boat hit a rock and almost sank. Petrie predicted they'd be underwater in no more than ten minutes, when a passing ship stopped and managed to take everyone on board, thereby rescuing Schechter and Petrie, and with them, in part, the very future of Egypt's past.

This near shipwreck was not, as it happens, the only threat to Schechter's health. His month of work in the Geniza had taken a real physical toll, and while still in Cairo and complaining of how the "dust of centuries [had] nearly suffocated and blinded" him, he had already undergone medical treatment. As soon as he returned home, he fell more seriously ill and his doctor ordered him to travel south for a rest cure—and to distance himself from all manuscripts and books. (Schechter being Schechter, that was a futile bit of advice; even as he was ailing, he happily reported to a friend that he'd discovered an eleventh-century Geniza letter stuffed in his very own pocket.) His good friend James Frazer offered to pay the expenses for such a therapeutic trip, but in the end Schechter chose to convalesce in Cambridge. He did gradually recover, though he would never quite return to his former strength. According to his biographer, "he passed in a year or two from robust vigor to the appearance of an old man."

Still, by the late spring afternoon when the first crate of fragments was finally opened, Schechter was well enough and ready, as he put it, to "wade . . . through these mountains of paper and parchment." At the end of May, Charles Taylor offered, in his own name and Schechter's, the "Cairo MSS brought to England by Mr. Schechter to the University, in due time, on certain conditions," chief among which was that Schechter be granted permission to borrow whatever he wanted. It took another year for the particulars of this gift to be ironed out, but eventually the library syndics agreed to the terms, which included the proviso that it be designated "a separate collection, to be called by some such name as the Taylor-Schechter Collection from the Genizah of Old Cairo." The university would, meanwhile, make arrangements for the binding or mounting of the fragments, and designate £500 "for the purpose of obtaining expert assistance in classifying and making a catalogue of the collection." The task would, it was reckoned, take ten years.

Three quarters of a century later the fragments were still being sorted.

Even-keeled university decrees were one thing. The actual process of sorting the fragments was another—and the first few days of Schechter's work were especially turbulent, with Jenkinson reporting to his diary, "When I got to the Library, I found Schechter had been making a row & declaring someone had cut one of his fragments—(it had been folded & then snipped so as to leave diamond-shaped holes). Luckily I had noticed it before, & had in fact myself put it on his table; so I was able to give him a good setting down for his impertinence and violence."

Schechter was combustible by nature. He was also, it seems, nervous about the prospect of ceding any control over "his" fragments, which explains why it was that the very same day that Jenkinson recorded Schechter's tantrum, Agnes Lewis wrote the librarian a letter in which she explained that she had "fully intended coming again this afternoon and giving what little service I could to Mr. Schechter in the way of cleaning his fragments without trying to identify any of them." But then she had happened to meet Mrs. Schechter, who explained that "her husband is quite able to clean and arrange them himself, after he has ascertained what they are. So I think I had better not trouble them again without a further invitation to do so, especially as I have more than enough at home to occupy myself with." Agnes was, on the one hand, minding her manners, and clearly sensed that Schechter viewed her presence as an annoyance. On the other hand, she of all people could understand what it meant to feel protective of one's manuscripts. Besides, all this talk of cleaning and straightening the fragments may have been missing the point. Perhaps—she seemed also to be saying—it was best to let Schechter manhandle the documents in whatever way he saw fit. As she explained to Jenkinson: "I admire and respect Mr. Schechter for things that are quite apart from neatness and tidiness."

Such tensions, together with Schechter's somewhat eccentric work habits, may have been what led to the decision to set aside a special room where he could sort the fragments in peace. (It may also have had something to do with their stench.) And so it was that Schechter would daily repair to "the Cairo apartment"—as it was sometimes called—

with a big dust-coat and nose-and-mouth protector, working steadily for many hours at a time, although the odor of the mss. which had lain buried for so many centuries was so overwhelming that visitors could hardly stand it more than a few minutes. He had around him a great many grocery-boxes, labeled "Philosophy," "Rabbinics," "Theology," "Literature," "History," "Bible," "Talmud," etc. and with his magnifying glasses he would study each little ragged piece, and then put it into its proper box with so much alertness that it was almost like a housewife counting different articles of laundry.

Or, as another Cambridge memoirist more succinctly put it: "No one who saw him in his nose-bag among the debris is likely to forget it."

Throughout that first summer in particular, Schechter toiled obsessively at sorting the fragments, and as he did, he found a sympathetic ally in Francis Jenkinson, who provided both practical help and psychological support. For all their cultural and stylistic differences, the portly rabbi and the gaunt curate's son were—yang and yin—joined by that very

alertness that Mathilde describes. After Jenkinson's death, a friend remembered his "curious bird-like movement[s]" and another recalled that he'd had a face "from which all color was absent . . . like parchment, lined and wrinkled." His late-Victorian, pressed-flower delicacy notwithstanding, Jenkinson was keenly alive to the natural world: he had, it was said, "hawk-like vision," and his diaries provide an extraordinary record of a sensibility attuned in almost microscopic fashion to the toads, verbena, phlox, caterpillars, and sycamore in his garden, as well as to the "occasional smoked glass sun," the "watery moon," and shooting stars above him. His ear, too, was finely calibrated, and he noted with a similar sharp-ness the sounds of the different birds: "<u>Swifts</u> screaming in a pack of 50 or so as late as 9 p.m." and, on another evening, "Coming home heard 'kŭ-kŭ-kŭk' over Sheep's Green or thereabouts." A friend from his days as a student offered this moving portrait of the li- 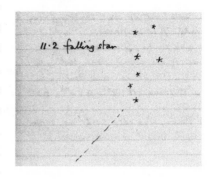 brarian as a young man: "I shall never forget how, one night in the Great Court of Trinity, he stopped our (probably flippant) conversation with his finger on his lip; some of us, I have no doubt, thought he was reproving the style of our talk and indeed, one will never forget occa-sions where some quiet reproof or look of disapproval made one deter-mine never to utter unseemly words in his presence again. This time, he was not chiding us, but trying to get us to listen to a sound he could hear though most of us could not, a flight of wild geese passing far above our heads."

It is not too much of a stretch to say that Schechter, for his part, was just as fiercely focused on the once-living world of his written scraps. And as he worked his way through those stinking heaps of *shemot*, he seems to have felt it his duty to resuscitate or even resurrect the frag-ments, so in a way bringing the process of geniza full circle. Relations between the two men were at times wobbly: Jenkinson admitted at one point to his diary that he had had "much too much" of Schechter at the library, and on another occasion reported that Schechter "has upset a large box of fragments in the darkest part of the room close to the pipes." This distressed Schechter, and he begged the librarian to gather up and protect the pieces he'd spilled: "Meanwhile," wrote Jenkinson "he tramples them like so much litter." But despite occasional friction, they seem to have shared a desire—almost a compulsive need—to pay the most careful attention to the identification of animate, or metaphorically animate, things, whether moths or manuscripts. It is no coincidence that Jenkinson was trained in what was known as "the natural history method" of bibliography, which took up a lepidopterist's approach to the classification of incunabula, and required that catalogs of these earliest printed books scientifically detail a volume's printer, typeface, and other such specifics. So it was that he would report in his diary with the same excitement that Schechter had "just found the colophon of Sirach!!" and "At night four slugs at the Linaria alpina!!" For Jenkinson, Ecclesiasticus and toadflax belonged in a single field guide.

And there was, that summer, much for the librarian to punctuate emphatically in his journal, as Schechter's sorting turned up a parade of major documents: a letter in the hand of Maimonides, fragments written in old French, Coptic, and Georgian, pages from the Palestinian Talmud, a Greek prayer book, more Ben Sira. ("Schechter found a double leaf of Ecclesiasticus and nearly went off his head," according to Jenkinson.) In June Schechter wrote his article for the *Times*, "A Hoard of Hebrew Manuscripts," which explained the cache and its history for the general reader, and Jenkinson read the proofs, then helped him compose a reply when, the day after Schechter's article appeared on August 3, an anonymous reader—"a viper," in Jenkinson's words—wrote the following letter to the editor:

> In his interesting description of the ancient "Geniza" in Cairo, Mr. Schechter omits to mention that the honour of the discovery of this treasure belongs truly to the learned librarian of the Bodleian, Dr. A. Neubauer, who was the first to light upon it and to obtain a large number of important fragments for that library. He has published, already some six years ago, a few of these documents, and has placed others at the disposal of scholars. . . . The other who

went to that "hiding place" of the ancient synagogue in Cairo was Mr. Elkan N. Adler, who not only brought last year very valuable MSS. from there, but practically gave the key to it to Mr. Schechter. In apportioning the honours of the discovery we must be just and fair.

The letter was signed "Suum Cuique," To Each His Own, and though it was a very public slap, the response that Schechter and Jenkinson composed is, given Schechter's usual quick temper, notable for the calm it exudes. Perhaps this was Jenkinson's influence: "The honour of discovering the Genizah belongs to the 'nameless' dealers in antiquities of Cairo, who for many years have continually offered its contents to the various libraries of Europe," they wrote in Schechter's name. Certain credit was indeed due to Adler, who "spent half a day in the Genizah. I learnt from him that he had been presented with some MSS. by the authorities. This is 'the key he gave me.' As to being fair and just 'in apportioning the honours of the discovery of the MSS,' " he went on, "I could tell, unfortunately, a long tale about it, as 'Suum Cuique' is perhaps aware. Priority questions, however, are tedious, and I do not intend to become a burden to your readers."

Behind the scenes, Schechter was understandably upset by this attack, though as is clear from a letter he wrote to Elkan Adler on the subject, he also had it in perspective. It seems Adler had written Schechter to assure him that *he* was not Suum Cuique, and Schechter responded with relief, "I had first some suspicion about you, thinking that it must be some distinguished person from whom the Times would receive an anonymous letter. But I saw afterwards that the English was too bad. Besides you are too openhearted for such mean tricks. . . . I do not mean to enter into a controversy. When one finds an autographed letter of Rabbenu Chushiel [an important eleventh-century biblical and talmudic commentator] one has no time for fighting with insects."

Schechter understood he had much more critical things to do than draw out this petty controversy.* Around the same time, in a letter to Mayer Sulzberger, Schechter rattled off a list of the discoveries he had made over the previous few weeks and proclaimed that "the contents of the Genizah turn out to be of much greater importance than I ever dared to hope for." He would not, he wrote, change these riches "for all Wall Street. I am finding daily valuable treasures. A whole unknown Jewish world reveals itself to us."

That revelation did not come suddenly, of course, but was the product of slow and extremely painstaking labor on the part of many people. In the now-iconic photograph taken of Schechter "at work" in the Geniza room that month, we see a man entirely alone, his brow resting on one hand—a rabbinic version of Rodin's *The Thinker*—as he contemplates a single scrap and seems to bear the entire weight of Jewish history on his sloped shoulders. He is surrounded on all sides by papery chaos: it is as though a tornado or a flood had just blasted through a huge stationery store. Yet Schechter sits still, like Prospero having tamed a phenomenal tempest.

The photograph was, as it happens, staged (there is, you will notice, no nose-bag in sight), and we know that Schechter was not often by himself in the room, which had quickly become a popular Cambridge "attraction" where visitors would often drop by to see the Romanian wonder in action: one of them described how "he may be found almost at any hour of the day deeply engaged in sorting and examining his fragments, with an expression in his face constantly changing from disappointment to rapturous delight." When a guest came to call he would

---

*The identity of "Suum Cuique" has to this day never been determined, though certain clues would seem to point in the direction of A. E. Cowley, Neubauer's younger colleague at the Bodleian. (Cowley was also coeditor, with Neubauer, of both the Oxford edition of Ecclesiasticus, published when Schechter was still in Cairo, and that library's Hebrew catalog.) Not only would he have had good reason to want to defend Neubauer's—and the Bodleian's—name, but Cowley was a fellow of Magdalene College, Oxford, which prided itself on a special toast, called "Jus Suum Cuique," which it had celebrated every October 25 since 1688.

"tak[e] them from box to box, pointing out to them the significance of this or that MS. or the peculiarity of the specimens of Hebrew writing which lie scattered about on the long tables."

But more than visitors, Schechter had partners. As he himself had grown to understand perhaps better than anyone, this was not work for one person. "The Geniza is a world," he wrote, "with all its religious and secular aspirations, longings, and disappointments, and it requires a world to interpret a world, or at least a large staff of workers." Among the most committed of Schechter's collaborators was Charles Taylor, who was responsible for sorting the postbiblical Hebrew fragments and palimpsests, and he came almost daily to the Cairo room "to revel there," as Schechter put it, "in the inspection of the faded monuments of the Jewish past. This was probably the only sightseeing in which he ever indulged." Agnes and Margaret, meanwhile, took on the task of sifting through the Syriac fragments, another Cambridge professor studied the Greek, and outside experts—one a lecturer in Arabic and Syriac from

Jews' College in London, the other a Cambridge-trained Jewish convert to Christianity (later ordained an Anglican priest)—were hired to handle, respectively, the Arabic and Judeo-Arabic fragments and the Hebrew Bible pages. At the same time, Jenkinson helped Schechter sort "select fragments" into drawers and oversaw the work of Andrew Baldrey, an employee of the library bindery, who had been assigned the task of cleaning and smoothing the fragments and placing them between glass.

And so on—and on. "The day is short and the work is great," quoted Schechter, in an 1898 sequel to his "Hoard of Hebrew Manuscripts," a wide-ranging progress report in which he surveyed more of the gems he'd plucked from the piles over the course of the previous year: leaves with gilt letters; children's primers; shorthand Bibles, which featured what is called trellis writing ("In the beginning, G. c. the h. a. the e."); pages of Mishna and other compilations of Oral Law; a papyrus hymnal; as well as copious historical material, especially from the period between the birth of the towering communal and intellectual figure Saadia Gaon in 892 and the death of Maimonides at the start of the thirteenth century. This era, wrote Schechter, "forms, as is well known, one of the most important chapters in Jewish history." But that chapter would now require serious revision, as "any number of conveyances, leases, bills, and private letters are constantly turning up, thus affording us a better insight into the social life of the Jews during those remote centuries."

He was not exactly complaining, but even as he rehearsed these discoveries, there was a new tone of melancholy fatigue creeping into Schechter's words. Since his return from Egypt, he had devoted himself

to the Geniza night and day, sun and snow—sacrificing his health and working himself past the point of exhaustion. He suffered especially in the winter, when his work was slowed to a snail's pace by the lack of artificial light at the library. He was, he wrote to Sulzberger, red-eyed after a mere hour's sorting, and forced to bathe his eyes in lotion. One "very dark" day he walked the two miles from his

house to the library and "was unable to read a single fragment on account of the fog. It was never as bad as this minute."

The irony, though, was this: as Schechter had come to grasp the truly miraculous magnitude of the Geniza, he had also begun to recognize the limits of his own strength—and to see, perhaps, the sun setting on his own role in the history of the Geniza's retrieval. "It will," he admitted, "occupy many a specialist, and much longer than a lifetime." And he had other matters to attend to besides. In a strange twist of fate, the very same day that Jenkinson supervised the opening of the first Geniza crate at the library, Schechter had been approached with a tentative offer to become chancellor of the Jewish Theological Seminary in New York. He would eventually take the job (of JTS president)—driven by a number of factors, including his sense that he was underappreciated by the powers that be at Cambridge. Upon his return from Cairo, he had been named curator of the Oriental Department at the library, given a small raise, and awarded an honorary degree, but as Mathilde wrote, "some felt it keenly that . . . if he had been a member of the Church of England he would have got a bishopric." There was, then, the related and more substantive question of his growing alienation from British Jewry and the non-Jewish milieu in which he found himself in Cambridge. ("Life among the goyim means spiritual death to me," he wrote at one low point, and at another painful moment he wondered aloud, "What shall become of my children in this wilderness?") Most pressing of all, Schechter felt honor bound to serve. "Believing as I do," he explained, "in the future of Judaism in America, I think it is my duty to be with my people where I may become some influence for good."

Perhaps he had also taken to heart the admonitions of his old friend, student, and patron Claude Montefiore, who was extremely critical of the price his work on the Geniza had exacted from Schechter's scholarly writing, and even went so far as to declare that if it had cost him his great work on theology, he wished the Geniza "had been burnt" before Schechter had ever come across it. "You think me a Philistine. Not so. But it makes me unutterably sad when I see your unique powers not turned to noble account." This was shortsighted of Montefiore: Schechter's unique powers had certainly been turned to noble account through his work on the Geniza, but—after five years of sorting manuscripts—he himself clearly sensed it was time for something else. Or something more.

Even though he was glad to be leaving England behind, Schechter's sense of debt to his friends in Cambridge was great. So many people there had helped him during what was perhaps the happiest and most fruitful period of his life. And though as the blustery Eastern European Jew surrounded by all these hushed-voiced, well-bred Englishmen he'd occasionally acted the bull in a china shop, he was one sensitive bull. In a letter to Jenkinson, composed shortly after he'd announced his resignation, which would take effect at the end of the Lent Term in March of 1902, he wrote in his emotive scrawl to thank the librarian for "the many kindnesses you have shown me during the last ten years. I only hope I have not drawn too much upon your patience and good will. But the times, especially since my return from Egypt, were not quite normal[,] my excitement finding expression in the most curious ways and counting upon your forbearance."

Among the many gifts that were showered on Schechter upon his departure were a complete set of the Babylonian Talmud, a clock that rang the Cambridge chimes, and—from Agnes and Margaret—a silver kiddush cup engraved with the words of Ben Sira that they had discovered together: "Happy is the man who meditates on wisdom and occupies himself with understanding." He was lauded in speeches and toasted at banquets—at one of which he responded by quoting his hero Abraham Lincoln's farewell address, delivered in Springfield in February of 1861, before he traveled to Washington to assume the presidency: "No one not in my situation can appreciate my feeling of sadness at the parting. . . . Here I have lived nearly twenty years, and have passed from young man to old man. Here my children have been born. I now leave not knowing when, or whether even, I may return, with a task before me greater than that which has rested on me." He went on, as Lincoln had, to wish for the assistance of "Him Who can go with me and remain with you, and be everywhere for good" as he bid them all "an affectionate farewell."

He had not, as it happens, completely left the Geniza behind, but arranged to have sent to his Manhattan address 251 pieces—41 in glass and 210 unbound. Neither had he cut off contact with his Cambridge friends and colleagues. In October of 1902, still settling into his new home and job, he wrote to Jenkinson to reassure him that the fragments he'd borrowed had a secure resting place in the "large fireproof safe" the trustees of the Seminary had installed in his house. Like Schechter, they had traveled a long way from that dusty room in Fustat to the crisp air of Morningside Heights.

And though this was a kind of ending, it was also a beginning, as several of the intellectual chain reactions that Schechter had set into motion during his Cambridge years would—long after he had left for New York and even departed from this world—continue to ripple forward, causing later scholars to look back across the centuries with a new sense of the old. There is, say the rabbis, no early or late in scripture. They seemed (before its time) to have known a thing or two about the Cairo Geniza.

6

Palimpsests

I

Well before he set sail for Manhattan, Schechter had assigned the sifting of the Greek manuscripts to Francis Burkitt, a rich, good-looking, and eschatologically inclined up-and-coming Anglican scholar of Semitic languages and biblical history. Burkitt had already worked closely, though not without rivalry, alongside the Giblews. In the early 1890s he'd helped Agnes identify the twins' first and perhaps greatest discovery—the very early Syriac version of the Gospels, which differed in several respects from the canonical text and held out the promise of bringing readers nearer to the actual words and truth of the historical Jesus. But that truth was by no means easy to grasp, since the reddish-yellow ink in which it had been cast constituted the "underwriting" of a palimpsest text—that is, a manuscript that had served double duty, as a kind of medieval Etch A Sketch pad—and had been layered over by a late-seventh- or eighth-century work treating the lives of female saints.

Because parchment was scarce in the early Middle Ages, scribes would often recycle it. Old writing no longer in demand would be scraped away with a pumice stone or the edge of a knife, and the relatively clean if not quite pristine surface that resulted would be used for a newer and presumably more important, or at least more urgent, work. (The English word encodes that process in the fossil poetry of its etymology: Greek *palin*, "again," and *psaein*, "to rub.") Normally a palimpsest contains two strata, though on at least one Geniza occasion we find three. "There is nothing that does not leave its mark, however, in this serious world of ours," noted Margaret, and parchment, like paper, has a memory—and secrets—of its own. With expertise and considerable effort, and some-times with the help of an "ill-scented" ammonium and hydrogen sulfide–based reagent (from which the common stink bomb is made), or simply with "the action of common air," scholars were able to coax these words out of hiding.

Enlisting the help of his generally skeptical mentor, the eminent sixty-two-year-old Cambridge Orientalist R. L. Bensly, Burkitt exam-ined the twins' photographic reproductions of the Sinai palimpsest and confirmed Agnes's assessment of its importance. But the grainy photo-graphs only whet their collective appetite for the thing itself, and soon Burkitt and his wife were invited to join a small group the Giblews were assembling for a return expedition to Sinai to prepare a complete tran-scription of the codex. All this was part of the twins' sense of their larger mission, which Margaret would later describe in terms that also suited, to a tee, the work that the layered world of the Cairo Geniza would require. It is, she said, "like mending broken chain . . . which is of more use than making a few feet of new chain, as it makes all the existing links more useful."

Now far more experienced, Burkitt was again drawn into the force field of palimpsestic erasure, in part by the charismatic Schechter, in part by accident. It seems that his wife, the socially adroit and cameo-pretty Amy Persis Burkitt, had attended one of Mrs. Schechter's "after-noon at Homes" and spoken there with Mr. Schechter, who had gone on and on about "the wonders of the Geniza" and urged her to come have a look at the hoard in the library. Back at her own home, she told her hus-band about Schechter's offer, and of his fervor, and said that Burkitt had "better go and see." Which he did, though he seems not to have made much of the mounds of Geniza rags until, just as he was about to leave the sorting room, Schechter casually gestured toward a certain box, saying that it contained Greek fragments. Burkitt picked up the one on top and stared at it, trying to bring what he saw into focus. Tattoo-like signs covered both sides of the parchment, with the thick Hebrew upper writing obscuring the Greek beneath it. After a few minutes Burkitt ventured an opinion: "This is very important," he said, noting that the text was an early Greek translation of the Hebrew Bible. The enthusiastic though equally overwhelmed and overworked Schechter had his doubts, but he urged Burkitt to take the whole lot away with him, give the fragments a thorough examination, and—if in fact they did contain something of substance—to edit them as soon as possible. Perhaps because he was so excited, Burkitt crashed his bicycle on his way home and, as he tells it, "while semi-conscious . . . was haunted by the fear that the precious fragments had been destroyed in the mix up."

But they had survived for more than a thousand years, and they would survive Burkitt's bike crash. And so he got down to the job of editing three tawny 12 x 9–inch leaves of vellum that were, he thought, "of substance." They made—and still make—a striking impression. Often it seems as though the surface of the parchment, like soil, had just given way under great pressure, the words forced out of their matrix by the weight (in fact the corrosive effect) of the ink's iron gall, if not by the force of the words themselves. There is, as a result, something distinctly ominous about this arena of inscription, where so many letters are pitched at the edge of these gashes in history's skin, while others are already lost forever, having slid into oblivion. The Hebrew is a sooty black—its characters tight but highly articulated, their diamond-like serifs sharp—and it arrays itself like a marching band, brass blaring and drums pounding, as it struts across this fifteen-hundred-year-old leathery field. The faint and far less legible Greek, meanwhile, floats upside

down beneath it, as though below the surface of a pond. What looks like stains from moisture on the pages makes it seem, paradoxically, as though the parchment had been burnt.

Schechter guessed that the Hebrew text was liturgical, "in a hand [from] the 11th century"—probably a hymn for the Sabbath—and all eyes turned to the Greek, which Burkitt recognized as passages from a late-fifth- or early-sixth-century copy of a second-century C.E. translation of the biblical Book of Kings. Their translator, Aquila, was a convert to Judaism who had married into the pagan emperor Hadrian's family and spent most of his adult life in Rome and Jerusalem, where he joined the Christians before converting to Judaism. In Jewish circles he was, according to the Talmud, a disciple of the great rabbi Akiva. Though Burkitt realized that it was highly likely they would find more palimpsests, "the critical interest of these few leaves is so great," he would explain, "that it seems a pity to delay their publication." By the end of that first year of feverish sorting—1897—he had seen into print an edition of the *Fragments of the Books of Kings According to the Translation of Aquila*, which included astonishingly vivid facsimiles of the palimpsests themselves.

The translation's importance was, on the whole, historical: Aquila's version of the Bible had been widely used by Greek-speaking Jews, and the Church Father Origen had placed it closest to the Hebrew in his compendium of six scriptural translations known as the Hexapla (the sixfold work) because of its extreme literalism, which lent it an air of authenticity, even as it also made for awkward reading: "It is written in a Greek more uncouth than has ever before issued from the Cambridge University Press," Burkitt noted, offering by way of example his own English rendering made from Aquila's calque-like Greek for 2 Kings 23:25: "And like him did not come to pass to his face a king who returned unto Jehovah in all his heart and in all his soul and in all his muchness according to every law of Moses, and after him arose not like him."

To be fair, Aquila's aim wasn't to produce a work of art; he wanted to make a Greek version of scripture that would be so faithful to the original register, its syntax and its every particle—all of which were of paramount importance for Jewish exegesis—that it could be read more or less as the rabbis read Hebrew. In other words, Aquila's translation was, as Burkitt put it, "a colossal crib," and he concluded that the underwriting must have been used by Greek-speaking Jews in a Fustat synagogue before it was scraped away and replaced by the Hebrew.

Burkitt's hunch that other layered manuscripts would be found was soon borne out, and three years later Charles Taylor's *Hebrew-Greek Cairo*

Genizah Palimpsests from the Taylor-Schechter Collection comprised selections from Aquila's rendering of Psalms and, among other things, almost-erased pages of the New Testament. Like Burkitt's volume, Taylor's provided first-rate facsimiles of the manuscripts. In a barely visible seventh-century scribal hand, the sloping uppercase Greek letters look like the palest traces of an ancient game of tick-tack-toe concealed in what Schechter called the vellum's "depths and under-currents." Above these quiet glyphs, again, the Hebrew regiments appear in parade formation.

And there the matter stood—with the published palimpsests now on display for the entire world to see.

Or not to see. Although the finds and publications were announced in both the London *Times* and the *New York Times*, it would be almost twenty years before anyone would bother to have a close look at the louder "upper writing," which was, after all, as Taylor made clear on the very first page of his *Genizah Palimpsests* volume, "not without interest."

If ever a scholar was destined to work with palimpsests, it was Israel Davidson. By the time he was born in 1870, in the predominantly Jewish Lithuanian town of Yanova (near Kovno), his parents had already lost twelve children. Fearing the evil eye, they refused to use their son's real name, which they planned to reveal to him only once he'd safely reached "manhood." For the time being they would simply call him "Alter" or "Hayyim," Yiddish for "old" and Hebrew for "life." The strategy worked, but only partly. While the child survived, his parents died before the boy had reached his fifth birthday, and so young Alter (the little old one) was sent to live with relatives in the much larger city of Grodno. He describes his childhood surroundings as "medieval" and life at the famous Slobodka Yeshiva in terms that also anticipate his future engagement with layered texts and their merger of generations on the page: "A hundred young men bent over a hundred old folios, declaiming words that were uttered centuries ago, . . . this is the Jewish army gathered from various parts of the Pale to defend the old faith. It is an army of Peace. . . . Their mission is not to attack but to defend. They are not bent on conquering worlds, but on conquering themselves."

When he turned seventeen, Alter was drafted by that other army in his life—the czar's—and his uncle and aunt arranged for him to be smuggled out of the country along a kind of Jewish underground railroad. Following their instructions, he headed for New York, via Hamburg, carrying a pack containing a down pillow, changes of underwear and shirts, a prayer shawl and phylacteries, and a coffeepot with a cup (lest he have to drink from a *treif* receptacle). He also had money with which to bribe the guards he'd inevitably encounter, and "a few extra rubles sewn in his coat."

Having forded a stream and lost his cup, endured two homeless weeks in Germany waiting for his ship to come in, and then undergone a thorough fleecing on board—he survived the seventeen-day passage on water, bread, herring, and whiskey (to combat the seasickness)—in mid-May of 1888, he reached New York. He had a single ruble left in his pocket, a fabricated trade (he was, he would say, a bookbinder), but nothing in the way of official papers—a passport wasn't necessary at the time—and he still did not have a legal name; at any rate, not one that he knew. The long voyage across the ocean had, however, given him time to think this through, and he'd come up with a reasonable solution. His father was David; he would be Davidson. And he was, above all, a son of Israel.

So began the making of Israel Davidson's name in America.

But not before he learned to speak English. Still Alter to his friends, the greenhorn with rabbinical ordination quickly found work doing odd jobs for lodging and board on the Lower East Side—chopping wood and working as a street vendor—and soon afterward he enrolled in school. This was hardly your standard English-as-a-foreign-language institute. At the age of eighteen, the ever-thorough scholar-to-be had decided to enroll in elementary school. He started off in one of the higher grades, but seeing how little he understood, he had himself demoted to first grade and, over the course of the year, worked his way back, mastering the skills required for each level.

At this point, in the summer of 1889, a year into his new name, he was writing letters in a bizarre English, largely derived from a cross-referencing of German, English, and Hebrew Bibles, which produced something that sounded not unlike Burkitt's rendering of Aquila's crib of the Hebrew Book of Kings: "Dear friend; In a land of strangers as here, and a condition of poverty and a heart full of sorrow as my, to such a person is the only comfort if he finds a truly friend to whom he shall impart his sorrow thoughts. . . . Your mortificatious friend, Israel Davidson."

Six years later he was a graduate of City College, and in 1902, now an American citizen, he completed his PhD at Columbia on "Parody in Jewish Literature." He worked as a chaplain at Sing Sing for a number of years, tending primarily to petty thieves—not "real criminals," as he

wrote of them. "They were just unfortunate enough to be apprehended. . . . I have met plenty on the other side of the bars for whom I had less respect." Then in 1905 the thirty-five-year-old was hired by Solomon Schechter to fill a poorly paying position teaching Talmud at the Jewish Theological Seminary, and he began his gradual climb up the slippery scholarly ladder. His dissertation was published in 1907, but the turning point in his career came about, as with Burkitt's discovery of the Aquila, almost by chance.

In 1910, while looking through some of the Geniza manuscripts that Schechter had brought with him from Cambridge, Davidson happened on a seemingly trivial item. It consisted of two 5 x 4–inch pages containing instructions in Judeo-Arabic regarding the procedure of a prayer service. Of particular interest to the no-longer-fledgling scholar was the fact that the directions cited the first words of several liturgical poems, or *piyyutim* (the Hebrew term derives from the Greek *poeites*, meaning "maker," as in the archaic English word for "poet"). The hymns had been written by a legendary if obscure Hebrew liturgical poet (*payyetan*) named Yannai, about whom almost nothing was known and whose extant work, for much of the previous millennium, had amounted to a single serial composition, part of which found its way into the Passover Haggada in some Jewish communities. The instructions also explicitly stated that the poems came from a complete liturgical collection— *Mahzor Yannai*, or Yannai's "cycle" of hymns for the liturgical year—and they implied that these hymns were extremely popular: only the first lines of the poems were listed, as the manual writer assumed that his readers had the work in hand. The manuscript also mentioned melodies and refrains.

Yannai's name barely appears in medieval Hebrew literature. In the early tenth century, Saadia Gaon counts him among the "elder poets," whose verses he says are model compositions. And the name is made nearly immortal when the German-Jewish liturgical poet and commentator Ephraim of Bonn (1133–after 1196) tells the story of how a certain hymn by Yannai is *not* recited because—in an act of what the Talmud in another context calls *kinat soferim*, or writer's envy—he murdered his student Eleazar Kallir, the most prolific and celebrated of the early Hebrew liturgical poets, by placing a scorpion in his sandal! "May God forgive all those who say this of Yannai," the only quasi-compunctious Ephraim adds, "if it did not really happen."

Nor was Yannai much of a presence in the modern scholarly literature available to Davidson. One early-nineteenth-century writer thought he lived in Italy in the tenth century; later evidence had moved his date back to the mid- or early seventh century. In 1901 the pathbreaking Shelomo Wertheimer published two short compositions by the poet from among his Geniza purchases. And that was the sum total of what was known.

So the skimpy manuscript pages that Davidson had found were quite valuable, and he published them along with his commentary in the principal professional journal of the day, the *Jewish Quarterly Review*. Beyond that, however, he could go no further, and there once again the matter stood.

We don't know precisely what happened next, but one can imagine that this find would have set the wheels whirring in the mind of the unpretentious yet ambitious Hebraicist. Davidson's wife, in her much later memoir, notes that after her husband had brought out his important edition of *The Book of Delight*, a picaresque volume by the twelfth-century Spanish Hebrew poet Yosef ibn Zabara, "the urge became ever stronger to go abroad and seek manuscripts at their source." Like Agnes Lewis and Margaret Gibson, Davidson wanted to see the real thing, not a reproduction, and he was especially interested in inspecting the enormous collection of Geniza documents that Schechter had left behind at the Cambridge University Library. And so, in June of 1914, having booked passage on a freighter with the help of a friend, Davidson, his wife, and their young daughter set out on a twelve-day voyage to reach Europe.

Davidson did make one important discovery in Cambridge, of another work by Saadia Gaon, but it was after he returned from England that "the modest man . . . [with] a veritable genius for labor," as one colleague described him, found what it seems he'd been looking for. Again, we don't know when, or even how—neither he nor his wife has left a paper trail to his epiphany, and much of his eight-thousand-volume library, which was housed at JTS, was destroyed in the 1966 fire there—

but at some point (institutional lore has it on one Sabbath afternoon, waiting for students to arrive for tea), something or someone told Davidson to take the Burkitt and Taylor palimpsest volumes down from the shelf and have another look at that Hebrew upper writing, which Schechter had identified as liturgical and which Charles Taylor had gestured at in passing as he hurried on to the more alluring, underwritten Greek.

And there it was, and had been for nearly twenty years, in at least *four places* on several pages bound between covers, printed by the Cambridge University Press and distributed to libraries around the world, where no one had noticed: Yannai's name, in that bold and easily decipherable Hebrew hand, running down the spine of a poem as an acrostic "signature." It was a find that would, in time, lead scholars to the complete works of one of the titans of Hebrew poetry and a thorough reconsideration of the evolution and nature of Hebrew literature.

Given the significance of Davidson's discovery, one can't help but note what has been called the "grotesque" nature of the fact that these hymns had been lying there, available in print for two decades. Yannai's work appeared on eight of the seventeen palimpsest pages published by Burkitt and Taylor—without anyone noticing what it actually was. The palimpsestic ironies within the grotesquery of that long delay in discovering the Yannai are compounded further when one realizes that Burkitt's terse report of his accidental Aquila discovery was printed in the *Times* of London on Tuesday, August 3, 1897, *directly under* Schechter's spectacular announcement of having found "a hoard of Hebrew manuscripts." Adding to that irony was part two of Schechter's article, which was published the following year and went on at great length about the nature of the early medieval Hebrew hymns and the pleasure their coredeemer took in them. "I am particularly fond," writes Schechter,

of looking at the remnants of a Piyyutim collection . . . with their rough edges and very ancient writing. In turning those leaves, with which time has dealt so harshly, one almost imagines one sees again the "gods ascending out of the earth," transporting us, as they do to the Kaliric period, and perhaps even earlier, when synagogues were set on fire by the angels who came to listen to the service of the holy singers, and mortals stormed Heaven with their prayers. . . . These are, however, merely my personal sentiments. The majority of students would look rather askance upon the contents of the Sabbatical hymn under which the remains of Aquila were buried for nearly nine centuries.

Already in 1897, then, Schechter realized that he had before him (and over the Aquila) a liturgical hymn for the Sabbath that was very likely from the period of Yannai's famous student and reputed victim, Kallir, and he even grew rhapsodic over the transformational quality of the presence of these poems on the ancient page. And yet, inexplicably, Schechter never seems to have directed his protégé, Israel Davidson, whose field this was, to examine these works—not even after the latter's 1910 article about Yannai, which was followed by a series of pieces published over the next three years under the same heading, "Poetic Fragments from the Cairo Geniza" (all in a journal that Schechter himself

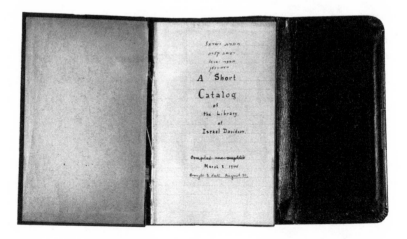

coedited). Nor did Davidson's 1914 cut-rate cruise to Cambridge produce anything in the way of a lead. Furthermore, Davidson's handwritten catalog of his private library—two highly evocative palm-sized notebooks encased in red wraparound leather, prepared in 1914 and titled *Hemdat Yisrael*, Hebrew for "Israel's Delight" (or "Desire"), shows that he owned at least one of the Cambridge palimpsest volumes, and so would have known of the other. "If the two English scholars [Burkitt and Taylor] had not published the facsimiles," Davidson noted, "the Mahzor of Yannai would very likely have remained unknown for many more years to come."

Newly oriented, Davidson went back to the palimpsests and identified forty individual units of eight long composite poems, all of which were clearly part of that Yannai "hymn book" he'd written of in 1910. Each of the elaborately orchestrated sequences was intended to accompany the portion of the Torah as it was read in Palestinian synagogues on the Sabbath during the period of late antiquity and the early Middle Ages. As such, these poems were front and center in the calendrical and spiritual consciousness of that community's Jews, who would, weekly, at the core of their sacred service, await the latest word from their poet—news that might inject life into their faith. In their serial and commissioned aspect, Yannai's composition of poems for the prayer service has been compared to Bach's production of cantatas for Sunday after Sunday while serving as musical director of the St. Thomas Church in Leipzig.

Differing from present-day Jewish practice, which is based on the Babylonian rite and completes the cycle of reading through the Torah annually, Palestinian communities in the Land of Israel and the Diaspora divided the Torah into much shorter portions and so they took three times as long to read from Genesis to the end of Deuteronomy before starting all over again. This "triennial" division of the Five Books of Moses, along with the distinctive Palestinian spelling of the poet's name (*yod, nun, yod, yod*—rather than *yod, nun, alef, yod*—though both were pronounced ya-NIGH), and the fact that there were no references in the poetry whatsoever to Islamic presence in the Holy Land, confirmed previous speculation that the poet hailed not from Italy, and certainly not from the tenth century, but from Palestine prior to the seventh-century Muslim conquest of the region.

Looking from the other end of the telescope for the work's earliest possible date, we see both that the poet makes extensive use of particular collections of midrash that were edited in the late fifth century C.E. and that his hymn book assumes the existence of a standardized, if still flexible, core liturgy, which was established shortly before that. This leads most scholars to date the poet to the mid-to-late sixth or early seventh century, which is to say, around the reign of Justinian the Great and the height of Byzantine achievement and influence, when architectural monuments such as the Ravenna mosaics were being marveled at and the rebuilt Hagia Sophia was worshipped in. It is also when the preeminent Byzantine hymnist of the jeweled style, Romanos, was writing his ornate, theatrical poems.

But just as the triennial system contributed to the development of Hebrew liturgical poetry—in that the brevity of the weekly readings left much more time for embellishment and literary commentary in the form of hymns and midrashim—it was also responsible for the tradition's demise. For one, the proliferation of liturgical poems eventually provoked widespread rabbinical opposition to the phenomenon itself, and, increasingly, pressure was put on communities to rid their worship of these overgrown baubles. More significantly, when the triennial reading fell out of practice—by the ninth or tenth century in Palestine and, it seems, early in the thirteenth century in Fustat—Yannai's hymns and others like them were rendered obsolete or fundamentally distorted in attempts to dismantle them and adapt them to the annual (Babylonian) reading. As a result, they disappeared almost entirely.

Now that work was back, at least in part—though what it was saying was by no means clear, as one example of many makes plain:

[when any man hath an issue] out of his fle[sh] and . . .

As who [. . . . .] on high . . . .
[B . . . .] turn [. . . . .]
Circumscribed by justice as well. . . . .
[D . . . . .] as an issue of . . . .
Each who [. . . . .] made him
For his desire. . . . . . . if . . . it [. . . . .]
[G] . . . of his from him, and his law and ma[. . .]
[H] . . . .
Impurity lies within him, if his ethic ends
J . . . . . . upon him his corrector
[K]ept his yeast leavened from youth
Leaving the issue to flow from his skin

And the Lord spoke to Moses and to Aaron, saying: Speak unto the children of Israel and say unto them: When any man hath an issue out of his flesh, his issue is unclean

Despite the gall-eaten gaps that Davidson found in the manuscript—chasms, really, into which the words of our palimpsest long ago tumbled—several characteristic elements of Yannai's poetry are immediately apparent, even in rough translation. Like many poems in this tradition, the hymn develops along an alphabetical acrostic. The final line of this opening section (*alef* through *lamed* in the Hebrew) leads into the first verse of the portion of the Torah read in the synagogue that week—in this case the *seder* (literally, the order) consisting of Leviticus 15:1–24, which treats the question of ritual purity, bodily discharge, and their attendant expiatory offerings—hardly the stuff of an inspiring lyricism. And yet, pus, too, was part of the early medieval Hebrew poetic process.

For it was incumbent upon the poet to make use of all the literary devices at his disposal in order to revive the experience of worship and wonder for his synagogue listeners. In this the *payyetan* was more mediating priest than scolding prophet.

However exotic or ingrown their compositions might seem by our own standards, at their best *payyetanim* produced real poetry, sometimes of a major sort. A vast allusive range; a feeling for dramatic possibility; an ability to extend scriptural narration; a varied repertoire of virtuoso musical strategies; and above all a developed sense of the tradition's homiletical potential and the congregation's hunger for the nourishment it might afford—all these were used to intensify the liturgical moment, to suck marrow from the seemingly dry bones of routinized prayer and to make it matter afresh, as the Mishna demanded: "Whosoever makes his prayer a fixed task," it cautions, "his prayer is not a true supplication." Other sources echo that call: "One's prayer should be made new each day," the Palestinian Talmud tells us, and "As new water flows from the well each hour, so Israel renews its song." Extending that notion, other writers still have likened the *piyyutim* to angels, which—according to one midrash—are created by God for specific missions and vanish after completing them. Among certain Jewish communities of the East, from roughly the fifth through the end of the ninth centuries, it seems to have been considered disgraceful for a prayer leader to recite as part of the prayer service work that wasn't his own.

Part three of Yannai's long sequence based on the Levitical discussion of impurity contains the telltale acrostic "signature" that quietly, if precariously, copyrights the poet's work. Though scholars before Davidson did not know it, and therefore did not *see* it, in Yannai's *mahzor* this section always involves a four-line (or eight-hemistich) stanza, strung along the poet's acrostic signature and concluding with an allusion to the first verse of the week's *haftara*, or supplementary reading from the prophetical books (in this case, Hosea 6:1 and its notion of returning to God—

"who has torn, that he may heal"). While here, too, the manuscript is damaged, it is clear from the opening two lines and other *piyyutim* that the poet is employing full rhyme. This turns out to be an important literary discovery in its own right, as it represents the earliest known systematic employment of end rhyme in Hebrew, and one of the earliest in Western and Near Eastern literature.

> *You, Lord, who are faithful, our God and healing's master—*
> *your healing power is readied for all you summon with desire.*
> *Now we return, [turning] to[ward] you, ...*
> *as you give strength to our weakened hand . . . in yours*
> *Into the rain of fresh blows . . . . . he . . . .*
> *and to the blow of ap . . . . [ah], blind wandering*
> *Instill our remnants with wholeness . . . [our . . . ess],*
> *Our father and healer, return to restore us.*

In short—and notwithstanding the many lacunae in the manuscript—Davidson's discovery of Yannai's work made it possible for the first time to follow the elliptical, complex, and even symphonic development of this new kind of liturgical poem, which was known in Hebrew as a *kerova*—from the Aramaic *karova*, meaning cantor or prayer leader, who would draw *near* (*karov*) to the ark in the synagogue as he led the prayers or offered a sermon. Given the emphasis in so many *piyyutim* on the priestly dimension of worship, a powerful link was established in these hymns between poetry and prayer as a substitution for sacrifice (which was no longer possible after the destruction of the Temple in 70 C.E.). The synagogue by this time had evolved from the house of study it was during the time of Ben Sira to a place of worship, a *mikdash me'at*, or little sanctuary. Like a cultic rite, and perhaps not unlike an opera, the poem's ability to move an audience was, in large part, rooted in the spectacle and splendor of its structure. For while it posed a challenge, socially and intellectually, and in many ways involved a code that had to be cracked, this product of an age obsessed with endless renewal and experience of the sublime in prayer was, apparently, sufficiently compelling to draw at least to certain synagogues large crowds—young and old—who would come, as one writer has put it, not with a prayer book they'd memorized, but anxious for a "fresh, living, and instructive word, one that would also console, as it provokes thought and serves as a spur to the imagination."

And so, Sabbath morning after Sabbath morning, Yannai's poems and others like them would be recited, or sung, ornamenting the opening benedictions of the liturgy's central prayer—the *amida*, or standing prayer. (To a certain extent the *piyyutim* were originally intended to *replace* the standard liturgy.) The variegated and sometimes powerful Hebrew of the *kerovot* (plural) gave expression to virtually every aspect of the people's life as a people (though not as individuals), and it led worshippers into the innermost layers of their faith's foundational text. For these poems were devotional devices, spiritual machines made of words that were designed with a particular function in mind. And just as Burkitt had proposed that the Aquila hovering beneath Yannai's Hebrew came from a synagogue copy of the Bible in Greek translation, so Davidson concluded that this collection of hymns, written over Aquila's Greek, was also intended for synagogue use—most likely by the Palestinian Jewish community in Fustat, where these manuscripts were found.

The slim collection of some forty poems by Yannai that Davidson managed to bring quite elegantly between navy blue covers in 1919 was just the beginning. Alert now to the presence of a singular and major body of poetry among the some quarter million or so Geniza fragments held in libraries around the world, scholars turned their attention to the obvious—the upper writing, as it were, of the Geniza collection as a whole, where Hebrew liturgy (both hymns and prose prayers) constituted some *40 percent* of the cataloged documents, and they began rummaging. Davidson himself continued to identify and publish additional Yannai fragments as well, but the next serious advance in the field came, oddly, if indirectly, from the shelves of a German department store.

II

Early in 1928, the fifty-one-year-old self-made businessman and cultural patron Salman Schocken, looking a lot like a Roman patrician, traveled to Stuttgart to attend the opening of a new store, part of a chain he'd founded and operated throughout Germany. He had come a long way from his first job as a textile salesman based in Leipzig—that city of Bach's cantatas—but he'd clearly taken a great deal with him. Schocken's department stores were designed by some of the country's finest architects, and the buildings themselves instantly became monuments of a kind. Implausible as it sounds, they were part of a broad, revolutionary vision that combined commerce and culture in an effort to bring "taste" of both a material and a spiritual sort to the hardworking members of German society at large. Just as he found new ways of making Bauhaus-inspired furniture, form-fitting cotton clothes, cologne, and the latest fashions in lingerie available to middle- and working-class people at affordable

prices, so Schocken sought to disseminate the products of the humanist tradition to the masses—serious fiction, progressive cultural criticism, and both German and Jewish classics. By the time the Stuttgart store was completed, the Schocken chain was one of the largest in Europe.

While Schocken's marketing strategies extended through all registers and regions of the country, the cultural renaissance he helped lead was initially limited to a small and radical circle of Jewish intellectuals he supported, including the Hebrew novelist and future Nobel Prize winner

S. Y. Agnon; the soon to be world-famous scholar of Jewish mysticism Gershom Scholem; and the philosopher Martin Buber. But Schocken had plans to start a major publishing house, which would make classy, compact editions of those and other writers, including Kafka and Walter Benjamin, widely available. Eventually the German and then Palestinian and Israeli firm sprouted an American branch (which published the book you're now reading), and in time, Schocken bought what would become the daily Hebrew paper of record in Palestine, *Haaretz*, which the family still runs. Apart from that—or not at all apart from that—Schocken was an avid collector of valuable German and Jewish books and manuscripts

(he had nearly thirty thousand in his personal library at the time), and it was this latter passion that led him that day from the Stuttgart train station directly to an antiquarian-book dealer, who, without delay, showed him an old and very large poetry manuscript that had recently come onto the market and might be of interest to

him. While the dealer didn't know what the manuscript contained, Schocken—whom Scholem would dub "the mystical merchant"—had, it seems, a sense that the cache was special.

Schocken had long been obsessed with finding a Jewish equivalent for the foundational works of German literature, such as the national epic *The Nibelungenlied* (The Songs of the Nibelung), a poem based on pre-Christian heroic motifs, which eighteenth-century scholars had brought to light. Discovering a work of this magnitude would, Schocken believed, contribute to the strengthening of a precariously vulnerable and insecure modern Jewish culture, and could refute the common assumption of the day that Jews had no distinctive art form of their own. And so, after looking through the stack of old scraps, which he too could not read, Schocken agreed to the steep selling price of 28,000 marks (roughly $75,000 today) for the mysterious pile of papers.

To appraise his purchase, Schocken called in his A-list of learned friends—among them the novelist Agnon and the de facto Hebrew national poet Hayyim Nahman Bialik—and was informed in short order that his hunch had been right and that he had on his hands a kind of mother lode of Hebrew literature. Prepared by a single anonymous copyist either in Egypt or Turkey in the seventeenth century, the tightly written, two-column manuscript contained some four thousand poems, including the nearly complete works of many of Muslim and Christian Spain's greatest Hebrew poets (among them Shelomo ibn Gabirol and Moshe ibn Ezra). Some of this work had been lost for centuries. This portable private library of Hebrew Andalusian poetry had passed through various hands, in Iraq, in Bombay, and again in Iraq—where it was rescued by an antiquarian-book dealer and writer from a pile of papers just before being used to heat the next day's wash water. After all this, it somehow landed in Schocken's lap in Stuttgart. Ever the practical visionary, Schocken decided to build on this spectacular find by opening a research center that would publish both scholarly studies and critical editions of this manuscript and others like it. On November 4, 1930, Das Forschungsinstitut für hebräische Dichtung—the Institute for the Study of Hebrew Poetry—opened its doors in Berlin. While Schocken 37, as the manuscript came to be known, was *not* from the Geniza, the literary enterprise it gave rise to would go on to play an axial role in the Geniza's history.

The Institute's director was Heinrich (Hayyim) Brody, a Hungarian-born former chief rabbi of Prague, who also happened to be the world's leading scholar of medieval Hebrew poetry. Within a short time Brody had hired several gifted young research assistants, including a thirty-year-old Galician Jew named Menahem Zulay—who had recently trans-posed his name from the German Billig, meaning "cheap," to its rough Hebraic equivalent. Like Davidson, Zulay had been orphaned early and raised by an aunt. Barely twenty, he left Poland for Palestine, where he worked in construction before enrolling at a teacher's seminary in Jerusalem. Not long after taking up a position in the Jezreel Valley, he was approached by Schocken, who, during a visit to Palestine, was seek-ing among other things a Hebrew tutor for his young children. Zulay, a fellow *Ostjude*, or Eastern European Jew, came highly recommended, and in 1927 Schocken brought him back to Saxony. While instructing the rich man's children and living awkwardly in his house, Zulay enrolled at the University of Leipzig. Eventually he transferred to Berlin.

When he joined the Institute, the small-framed, mild-mannered young scholar with a soft, open face and an almost secretly potent imagi-nation—along with a fierce patience beaming from within his blue-eyed gaze—had recently completed his doctorate at the University of Bonn under Paul Kahle, a Lutheran Semiticist who had spent six years as a pastor in Cairo, and would go on to become one of the pioneers of

Geniza studies. Brody and his other assistants at the Institute concen-trated on the Spanish and Ashkenazic material, which added considerably to the work done by nineteenth- and early-twentieth-century German-Jewish scholars; facing east, Kahle's modest and musically inclined protégé (Zulay's daughter recalls his delicate voice singing prayers and hymns that accompanied the family's religious rituals) took up research in "terra incognita"—the Hebrew poetry of late antiquity. This was an area that had been barely touched, apart from Davidson's groundbreaking publication, which, Zulay later said, "flashed like lightning across the skies of this scholarly field."

What that lightning briefly revealed to Zulay, as though in a dream-vision, was the possibility of *much much more:* the gaps in Davidson's time-eaten manuscript pages filled in; the discovery of Yannai's poems for the remainder of the Palestinian liturgical cycle; poems by the poets that preceded him and whom he admired, those who followed and perhaps rebelled. . . . In other words, an entire literature embodying the middle millennium of Jewish poetry's three-thousand-year history. Far too little was known about that period, said Zulay, though it had given normative Judaism its shape and character. "In my dream," he wrote, "I see some thirty volumes containing the work of the writers of sacred poetry throughout the generations, those whose hymns now languish in the Geniza."

Call it, as many did, a vision of dry bones returning to life. Or, to take up an appropriately Egyptian metaphor (courtesy of Schechter's Cambridge walking companion James Frazer and his monumental *Golden Bough*), a gathering of the limbs of Osiris—the god who had taken the Egyptians into civilization, introducing them to the cultivation of grain and a social structure that would ensure nourishment and sustenance. Osiris spread his message abroad then returned home, only to be murdered and dismembered by envious rivals and kin, who scattered the parts of his body far and wide until his sister, Isis, gathered these severed parts together and, using her sorcery, brought Osiris back to life so that "his genius would be always at work in the world."

Bones, or limbs, or both, they were lying in Geniza collections around the globe—mostly in Cambridge, but also in Oxford and London and Berlin, Frankfurt and Leningrad, Warsaw, New York, Philadelphia, and Paris—and month by month, week by week, packages containing photostats of these manuscripts were dispatched to the Institute. For five years Zulay's efforts were concentrated almost solely on this ingathering. But the pieces of the puzzle were scrambled in a heap that boggled even the very best minds. The work, it seemed, called for an almost impossible combination of vision and patience, passion and science. And perhaps for a kind of Isis-like magic—albeit one born of tremendous labor and prodigious powers of recall. ("Memory," said Zulay, "is the finest index.")

For while it was tempting to dive in and cherry-pick one's way through the chaos—looking for work by major poets in whatever form one might find it and tossing the rest to the side—Zulay realized that this wouldn't do. He would have to begin at the beginning (like the eighteen-year-old Davidson returning to first grade) and sift through the thousands of copies of fragments with loving care and steady devotion, as he himself put it, likening the work to a sacred task that has no measurable worth and would never come to an end.

"Each photostat is a prayer congealed," he wrote. "Each page a poem frozen in place. The dust of the generations has to be shaken from them; they have to be woken and revived; and the workers are busy; and a day doesn't pass without resurrection. . . . And at the center of [it all] stands Yannai."

The pressures were enormous. The economic crisis of 1929 had put new wind in the sails of the German National Socialist Workers' Party, and anti-Jewish sentiment was mounting. Department stores in particular (Schocken owned some sixteen of them by then) were singled out as representative of Jewish parasitism, with the Nazi Party platform calling for their immediate communalization and for their being "leased at low rates to small tradesmen." In 1929 Schocken's Stuttgart store was attacked by thugs with stink bombs—putting to perverse use the same chemicals the Giblews and Burkitt had employed to help bring the fading foreign past to light; now they were intended to drive it into darkness. And in 1933, Sigmund Freud—who two years earlier had been awarded Frankfurt's Goethe Prize, which he considered the culmination of his public life—saw his writing burned in the same city and elsewhere in Germany. Also that year Schocken joined a wave of Jewish intellectuals, as well as their endangered Christian supporters (including Kahle), who had begun to flee; he announced his imminent departure for Jerusalem. Zulay and the Institute followed.

In both Berlin and in Jerusalem, Zulay was painstakingly sorting the fragments that reached him and gradually beginning to see the figure in the carpet, though he was, he felt, working against the clock and being driven by another sense of time altogether. As he would later write, "It seemed as though it wasn't me working, but something working within me, some hidden power that was fed at once by hope and despair, and served as a kind of opium during these difficult times. Day after day as I entered the Institute I would forget the outside world entirely, and when I left it [at the end of my workday] I felt like someone emerging from a deep mine who had to let his eyes readjust to the light of the sun."

The world around him was, in other words, collapsing; but as it crumbled, Zulay constructed—sifting and checking, marking and imagining, and, virtually line by line, reaching back through his own catastrophic historical hour to another era and a transcendent literary force. And his labor was bearing fruit: in 1938, *Piyyutei Yannai* (The Poems of Yannai) was published by Schocken Books. Zulay's persistence had allowed him to piece together, bit by dispersed and often damaged bit, coherent fragments of some eight hundred poems—a 200 percent increase over Davidson's finds. Short on frills but long on irony, and in a handsome, dignified format, this last Hebrew volume to be published in Nazi Germany presented to the public a classical Jewish poet of mythic power and stature—precisely what Schocken had hoped for.

Obscure or bizarrely exegetical as the opening sections of the *kerovot* could often be (Yannai takes on topics like the rules of engagement in war and the multitude of cattle possessed by the tribes of Reuben and Gad), other movements of these multipart poems were more accessible.

Even the most sacerdotal of poems—Yannai's verses about pus, for example—could make way later in the same sequence for a stirring lyric that might, for readers of the day, become emblematic of twentieth-century Jewish suffering. And such was the force and range of this work that publication of these poems in popular Hebrew journals, even as Nazi power closed in, prompted one leading Jerusalem intellectual to liken the discovery of Yannai's poems to a new midrash by means of which "the Jewish tree of life, with blood spurting from its trunk, has been rejuvenated from its roots."

In their original context, many of these hymns were intended either to invite the participation of the congregation or simply to arouse its awe. The cadenza-like seventh unit of the *kerova*, for instance—known as the *rahit*, or the runner, because of the striking way in which it employs speed and density of ornament as an embodiment of virtuosity, racing from the past of scripture to the present of the listener—show-cased the poet's musical talents so tangibly that even the sleepy or merely simple members of the audience on the back benches of the synagogue couldn't help but be drawn in. One particularly stunning example involves a profound commentary on the meaning and eternal relevance of the burning bush in the Book of Exodus (which happened to give the Giblews' church its symbol and was taken up by Schechter in New York as the JTS emblem). In Yannai's vision, the heart of the unconsumed flame is understood in supercharged midrashic fashion as the embodiment of the Shekhina, the Divine Presence, or "immanence of God in the world":

> *And the angel of the Lord was revealed to him (in the heart of the flame)*
>
> > *Angel of fire devouring fire*
> > *Fire Blazing through damp and drier*
> > *Fire Candescent in smoke and snow*
> > *Fire Drawn like a crouching lion*
> > *Fire Evolving through shade after shade*
> > *Fateful fire that will not expire*

Gleaming fire that wanders far
Hissing fire that sends up sparks
Fire Infusing a swirling gale
Fire that Jolts to life without fuel
Fire that's Kindled and kindles daily
Lambent fire unfanned by fire
Miraculous fire flashing through fronds
Notions of fire like lightning on high
Omens of fire in the chariots' wind
[Pillars of fire in thunder and storm]
[Quarries of] fire wrapped in a fog
Raging fire that reaches Sheol
T[errible fire that Ushers in] cold
Fire's Vortex like a Wilderness crow
Fire eXtending and Yet like a rainbow's
Zone of color arching through sky

This sacred fire, as one commentator has noted, comes down from the heavens bearing with it the entire alphabet.

But Yannai could also be powerfully unadorned and tender. One *kerova* develops around a more human figure, the biblical Leah, whose eyes were weak and who was rejected by her husband, Jacob, in favor of her sister, Rachel. Here an analogy to the people of Israel—and in a sense to all who believe—is hauntingly constructed through a modulation of cadence and tone that reaches its lyric peak in the free-flowing form of the poem's fourth part. Once again the poet holds a literary stethoscope up to a specific narrative moment, making audible its mythic pulse:

Our eyes are weak with longing for Your love,
for we are loathed by a hateful foe:
see how afflicted we are within,
and how, without, we're abhorred—
like Leah, whose suffering you saw,
as you bore witness to her distress.
She was hated at home,
and also despised abroad.

Not each beloved, however, is loved,
and all who are hated are not hated:
some are hated below, but loved on high.
Those You despise are despised,
and those You love are beloved.
We are hated because we love
You who are holy.

In dedicating his career, in devoting his days and years to reassembling fragments of elemental poems such as this one—pieces of Judaism's cosmic puzzle—Zulay, like his colleagues, was propelled by something much deeper than a sense of professional responsibility or even the thrill of the scholarly hunt. Certainly it wasn't comfort or security, for Schocken paid the frail Zulay very little and—despite his history of heart trouble—drove him hard, demanding that he submit daily reports detailing his research. (Once when the usually reserved researcher complained to the patron about the time and energy the reports were taking, and wasting, he was duly informed: "Mr. Zulay will continue to write the reports and Mr. Schocken will continue not to read them.") Lingering tensions at the Institute aside, Zulay spoke repeatedly in public—and with particular force in the wake of the Holocaust, which took his sister and her family—of the need for both grunt work and dream work, precision *and* extension, along with the "remnant of a vital faith and naiveté into which every true scholar must tap . . . Without faith," he wrote, "there's no enthusiasm, and without enthusiasm there is no transcendence. The soul withers and one's vision narrows. Scholarship finds itself mired in trivia and the great goal is forgotten."

Like Schechter, Zulay knew that even transcendence requires traction—and that meant the continuous work of scholars across generations. Surveying the thousands of disjointed, anonymous manuscript pages—and possibly identifying with what he saw—he likened them to "mute orphans" needing a home that might let them speak. And so, hoping to make it possible for others to follow where he would one day leave off, Zulay set about the maddening task of cataloging and cross-referencing all the fragments that were arriving daily at the Institute's broad tables. Maybe he knew that his heart, which had fueled his endless and grueling labor, would soon give way. And it did. Though he worked all day and into the evenings as long and hard as he could, through a flood tide of finds in the forties and beyond, all the while suffering from a debilitating angina that forced him to stop often on his way home from the Institute to lean against walls and regain his strength, he finally succumbed, dying after a fall in his family's two-room Rehavia apartment one sunny November morning, a few months short of his fifty-fifth birthday.

But as he'd hoped, others did follow—helping to recover what he had called, in his inimitable way, this "lost page from the passport of Hebrew literature." In a moving, unpublished lecture scribbled on small notepaper and delivered at a Jerusalem rest home where he was convalescing after one of his many hospital stays, Zulay spoke on the fiftieth anniversary of the Geniza's discovery about how the essence and enduring legacy of the Jewish people cannot be apprehended by the five senses, and won't be found in conquered lands or constructed cities. Its entirety lies, he said, in what it has written, which can be grasped only by the mind and the spirit. And that literary record, he explains, "is like a tourist's passport . . . Each page bears the stamp of a different consulate. And now it happens that one of these pages becomes detached from the passport and is lost. . . . One day the lost page is found and it turns out that the owner of the passport had once, in the middle of his travels, entered his own country and stayed there for a while, then picked up and gone on his way." That lost page, Zulay explained to his audience of fellow convalescents, contains the story of the Hebrew poetry of late antiquity written in the Land of Israel.

Since the appearance of Zulay's 1938 collection of Yannai's *piyyutim*, more than half of the thirty volumes he envisioned of this verse based on

Cairo Geniza manuscripts have been published in critical editions; and month by month, as they scroll through spools of microfilm and rifle through their files and the indices of their memories, scholars continue to reunite separated pieces of poems. Almost miraculously, it seems, the literary harvest of some seven centuries has been recovered.

But *not quite* miraculously. The late Ezra Fleischer, the principal inheritor of Zulay's mantle—and someone who would also speak of the electric aspect and sorcery of the *piyyut*'s allusive, self-contained language, as well as of its distant, strange, and "uniquely Jewish beauty"—in a 1999 assessment offered a sobering reminder of just what it is that goes into the work that Zulay and his colleagues did and do. Observing that "the Geniza didn't change [this] discipline . . . it built it from the ground up," he sent forth a paean to the scholar as cultural redeemer.

"The importance of the Geniza's contribution to the study of Hebrew liturgical poetry," wrote Fleischer,

> cannot be overstated. [But] what has been garnered from this tremendous contribution . . . is not the contribution of the Geniza itself, and we err in speaking of these finds in the passive formulations [so often employed in this context]. For in this field, as in other fields of research, nothing is given and nothing is discovered. No document is deciphered and no author is identified. No item is dated, no picture reconstructed, and no theory is raised. All these acts are the achievements of a dedicated host of scholars—early and later—great and less great, who devoted their lives to the study of the Geniza and wearied in their labor, sweating blood in their efforts to sort its treasures, sometimes succeeding and sometimes failing, their eyes weakening, their hairlines receding, and their backs and limbs giving out as they grew old and frail—each in his way and at his own pace.

Looking back across the millennia of registration and effacement that the Geniza documents embody, one is tempted to say that *this*—the systole and diastole of dismissal and deliverance, of composition and copying and translation and erasure, of rejection and retrieval—is the true Isis- or maybe Ezekiel-like mystery at the heart of the enterprise. Risking desiccation for an ultimate vitality, and anonymity for the sake of another's name, the work of the Geniza's redeemers, meticulous even in their dreams, brings us back in uncanny fashion to the glory of "the famous" whom the first *payyetan*, Ben Sira, singles out for the highest praise—"those who composed musical psalms, and set forth parables in verse." In equal measure, however, the efforts of these scholars also recall the fate of the far less conspicuous, a few verses later, "who have no memorial . . . and perished as though they had not been." But like Ben Sira's craftsman, "who labors by night and by day . . . diligent in his making," and like his "smith sitting by the anvil, [as] the breath of the fire melts his flesh . . . his eyes on the pattern of the object, his heart set on finishing his work and completing its decoration," these deliverers of Hebrew's makers "maintain the fabric of the world, and the practice of their craft is their prayer." For in giving themselves day after day to poem after poem and manuscript after manuscript, they become links in the chain of transmission that Schechter himself sought to extend back to the Wisdom of Ben Sira, and from that spirit to its source. And so, in their way, they too partake of eternity.

7

That Nothing Be Lost

It wasn't always so dramatic.

Among the early toilers in what has been called the "salt-mine" of the Geniza, the young Cambridge library assistant—later curator in Oriental literature—Ernest James Worman stands out, in a way, for *not* standing out. Self-reliant, modest, and reserved to the point of opacity, he died at age thirty-eight, and his name is known only (if at all) to those involved at the fine-tooth-comb level of Geniza research. At most, a reference to one of his smattering of scholarly articles will occasionally surface in a footnote to someone else's scholarly article, though the role Worman played in the preliminary ordering and decipherment of the Geniza cache—and, indeed, in the first, tentative attempts to imagine Jewish life in medieval Fustat—was critical.

Remembered by a school friend as a loner by choice, "strong, reliable, genial and kindly: but not, I think, either enthusiastic or visionary," Worman was hardly a natural successor to the charismatic Solomon Schechter. "I felt dimly that he would do something excellently," wrote that same friend of the adolescent Worman. "What that might be I puzzled often, for it did not seem he had—at that time—any conception of it himself." Yet after Schechter's 1902 departure for New York, the Geniza collection at Cambridge was left more or less without a guardian. The English Jewish scholar Israel Abrahams had replaced his on-again, off-again friend Schechter as the university's Reader in Rabbinics, but was too busy or distracted to pay the Cairo manuscripts much attention. (His lack of interest is peculiar, to say the least, given the fact that Abrahams himself visited Cairo in March of 1898, and wrote letters to his wife declaring it "a real sell" that Schechter was "pretending he had brought away everything" from the Geniza when in fact it seemed there might be just as much remaining in Cairo as what Schechter had taken. The trail of this mysterious pronouncement gives out here—as Abrahams appears not to have brought back more than a few fragments for himself; during his time at Cambridge he basically ignored the Taylor-Schechter collection. He was, it should be said, responsible for the *Jewish Quarterly Review*, the journal he edited with Claude Montefiore, which published almost all the early articles about, and texts from, the Geniza.)

A believing Baptist and former bookshop salesman, the twenty-four-year-old Worman had been hired by the library in 1895, during Schechter's tenure, and, after being sent by his employers to study Semitic languages as a "non-collegiate" student at the university, he had been recruited to help sort the Cairo fragments. Mathilde Schechter singles him out in her memoir as having provided her husband with the most "actual help" of all those involved in this stage of the work.

Abrahams, for his part, remembered meeting Worman in 1900, when the librarian-in-training knew "little Hebrew and less Arabic." In the void created by Schechter's absence, some sense of a calling, though, seems to have stirred within Worman: he realized that the orphaned and utterly distinctive Geniza collection required care, and, finding no one else prepared to take responsibility, he rose, quietly, to the occasion. "At first," Abrahams recalled, in a memorial tribute published shortly after Worman's untimely death of an unspecified illness, "he copied mechanically, but soon revealed an unsuspected and unique power to decipher half-obliterated texts and a remarkable facility in reading doubtful passages." During this period, he was pressed into service by various far-flung scholars who lacked direct access to the collection. At times he served as a kind of belated (and anonymous) medieval scribe. Without Worman, the soon-to-be-celebrated Lithuanian-born Talmudist Louis Ginzberg, for instance, whom Schechter hired for JTS in 1903, could not possibly have written several of the books that would make him famous in Jewish circles. At one point, Worman copied out in laborious longhand for Ginzberg fifty-five fragments of the Palestinian Talmud, and in another prephotostatic instance he transcribed all the known rabbinic responsa concerning Jewish law in the Cambridge Geniza collection. And it wasn't just Semitic languages that occupied him. The librarian Francis Jenkinson reckoned that Worman could catalog books in "nearly twenty different languages" and recalled that he once helped another scholar transcribe certain Pali texts, "though he had no previous acquaintance" with that Indic alphabet.

This was drudge work, to be sure, but it seems to have served Worman as an excellent apprenticeship and compelled him to push further. According to Abrahams, "He did not long continue as a mere copyist; he resolved to understand what he transcribed." And so, "with untiring diligence and almost magical rapidity he made himself master of a difficult language and an intricate literature, his success being rare in the history of the self-taught." In 1905, after several years spent categorizing, copying, and translating hundreds of fragments onto loose scraps of paper, as he carefully assembled lists of streets, names, buildings, and the like, he published, in the *JQR*, an article that may be the first attempt to draw from the Geniza's historical materials a composite view of the Old Cairo community.

"Notes on the Jews in Fustat from Cambridge Genizah Documents" was, as its title suggests, extremely gestational, and Worman's tone was a bit cautious as he put forth the simple but—for the time—rather audacious notion that "from the business documents that come from the Genizah . . . many facts come to light which may serve to unveil something of the history of the Jewish race in a large city where they abode in great numbers, were very wealthy, and had much to endure." After tapping several classical Arabic chronicles for a précis of the history of Fustat from its founding in 640 to its conquest by the Fatimid (Shiite) caliphate in the second half of the tenth century, he proceeds to offer a rough sketch of the medieval Jewish parts of town: he accounts for the two Rabbanite synagogues located there—the synagogue of the Jerusalemites (or Palestinians, that is, Ben Ezra) and the synagogue of the Iraqians (also known as the Babylonians)—as well as the nearby Karaite synagogue. He gestures to the rabbinical courts and attempts to account for some of the officials whose names are mentioned in legal documents found in the Geniza. He lists a number of the Fustat markets (including the Big Market, the Market of the Perfumers, the Market of the Steps, and the Markets of Saffron, Wool, Linen, and Cotton). He then describes the oldest part of town, the fortress called Qasr ash-Sham' (known variously in English as the Fortress of the Romans, the Greeks, Babylon, or the Lamp), which is where the Ben Ezra synagogue is situated and which, together with an adjoining Jewish neighborhood known as Musasa, he characterizes (not entirely correctly) as "the 'ghetto' of Fustat." Musasa, he writes, was also home to "the mart of the Jews" and the chief location for the mills and millers. While the picture of Jewish Fustat that takes shape here is still very crude, and riddled with basic mistakes, the roughest outlines of the city begin in Worman's account to appear—word by word, line by line, fragment by fragment, like a blurred photograph gradually emerging in its developing fluid.

Worman went on to publish several other articles on related subjects, but he seems soon to have realized that his true gift lay not in scholarship but in bibliography. In Abrahams's words, "He determined to qualify himself for a task which he foresaw must be undertaken by himself if it were to be undertaken at all." The Geniza collection, Worman understood with uncanny prescience, would be next to worthless without a catalog.

That was easier said than done. As he set out to make sense of, and give form to, the mass of disparate paper and vellum scraps that formed the collection, the technically untrained Worman—working in almost complete isolation and with little precedent to follow—faced an enormous task that required not only advanced knowledge of several languages, expert paleographic skills, and superior eyesight, but an almost bottomless well of patience. (A devout Christian, Worman may have had the words of the Gospel of John in mind as he labored: "Gather up the

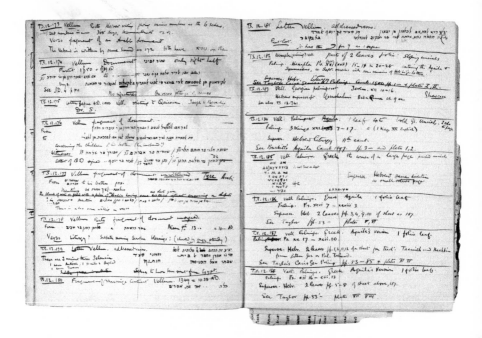

fragments that nothing be lost.") Hebrew, Judeo-Arabic, Aramaic, Arabic, and Worman's own English translations and descriptions all crowd together in the inky scrawl he left behind on hundreds of slips of paper and in six plain marble notebooks that contain his draft handlists of all the fragments preserved in glass and some of those bound in volumes— about twenty-five hundred pieces in all.

A typical page of one of Worman's handlists looks something like a working lab notebook, in which one can trace the arc of an experiment through the scientist's deliberate notations, scribbled figures, and blotchy scratch-outs. In its text-crammed and sometimes hard-to-decipher yet strangely *animate* way, it also bears a peculiar resemblance to a leaf from the Geniza:

Fustat Thursday 17 Tammuz 1383=1072 *34×22*

10 Doc. *We were with* מימון בן כלפה אלסג ... *and he was ill & we asked him*
the state of אלמערוף באבן אליחים נע
~~*About*~~ *his affairs* *He was ill in* ~~*the city*~~ בלד גרבה
confirmed
and he told us & we ~~*listened to*~~ *every word.*

Abu 'l Fadhl Sahl b. Yefeth b. Solomon "בן אלסופר" *had with him what belonged to*
him in the vessel which belonged to Abu-Surūr Perah & עטיה (סופיה טב) עטיה *this was*
a small bundle of clothes and a brass casket its lid covered & tied up ? and a
<u>*box of rolls*</u> *and a Persian flask of brass....* *a width of cloth (?)* ~~*in it inscribed*~~ *chests of*
~~*Mamainben*~~ *also things belonging to* אבו אלכיר פרג בן נחום נע /*to* אבו יחיי נוראי *3* ~~*damask*~~
<u>*robes*</u> ~~*& a fine saddle (?)*~~ *beautiful* שכארה *with rolls in it I Maimon received*
it from the house of the Abu' l-Bishr אזהר בן אברהם *on the order of Nahrai*
and ~~*In whi*~~ *his letter. And in the* שכארה *also* <u>*3 rolls of the Law & Prophets*</u>
belonging to Hasan b. כליב אלאסקלאני. *Money belonging to* ~~יאיר דן~~ *(who)*
deliver יאיר בן אברהם
owes מנשה בן מוסי: ~~pay~~ *to* מוסי בן מוסי בן מגאן *a flask or box containing 10 timmān of*
sal-ammoniac to pass on to אבו אלפרג בן אלעזר אלמגרבי
Witnesses: יוסף בן אלעזר בן השופט *(many letters above Hebrew)* משה בר שלמה נע

—

<u>*Verso*</u> *Arabic char. doc beginning (?)* هذا ما اصدق على بن طاهر البزاز

___

11 Doc. Statement: We were present at the כניסת הבבלים *25ᵗʰ Kislev 1393=1082*
Fustat & there was with us Judah b. Hayyim נע *and* ~~*related that*~~ *was talking in public to the* ממחה
that a certain ~~*someone of them present before the*~~
Joseph b. Eleazar נע ~~*one of them being*~~ זכרי *son in law of a* אבי אלכיר *had left his*
father in law. At the departure of the people from the כניסה *this* אבי אלכיר *went in from the*
street to the היכל *& took out the Law & cursed them all (?) unlawfully & went out of the synagogue*
& this Judah was talking to one אבו אלפצל בן סכר *in the street and said to this* אבו אלכיר
I have nothing to do with your cursing the Jews (!) & on the night following which was the 26 Kislev....

Compiled between 1906 and 1909, this first, fledgling handlist of Geniza manuscripts remains the only catalog of this part of the collection. And though some of the information contained there has since been superseded, corrected, or greatly expanded upon by more recent and informed readings, it offers a remarkable microcosm of the Geniza world and its riches, and shows Worman anticipating—really intuiting—a whole century of study.

Besides these chaotic drafts, Worman managed to complete two "finished" handlists, which contain brief descriptions of some of the documents, calligraphed immaculately in his fine Victorian cursive. His premature death, however, brought the process of cataloging to an abrupt halt: the bulk of the Cambridge collection would remain unclassified for another sixty years. But the descriptions that Ernest Worman left behind in that small pile of tattered notebooks would prove a great help to several others toiling in the mine.

The Polish-Jewish historian Jacob Mann, for instance, seems to have made excellent use of that handwritten legacy. Mann arrived in England from Przemysl, Galicia, in 1908—just a year before Worman's death—and while Mann had access to Worman's notebooks, it appears the two never met, a fact that somehow suits this, the loneliest period of Geniza research. If it wasn't every man *for* himself, it was certainly every man *by* himself.

That may have been the way Mann preferred it. Remembered by an acquaintance as "one of the shyest men I have ever known," he comes across in his own voluminous writings as stern, pedantic, and chronically humorless, rigid in his commitment to what he dubbed "a cautious and laborious inductive method." If that doesn't sound like a lot of fun, it must be said that the same characteristics that would have made Mann, one imagines, a singularly insufferable dinner guest may also be what rendered him precisely the (exacting, unsentimental) scholar the field *needed* at this stage. Mann's was "the genius of indefatigable and herculean industry," in the words of one admirer, who also praised his "infinite painstaking care and patience."

Raised in a household of Belz Hasidim by a ritual-slaughterer father who would offer his sons anatomy lessons based on the inner organs of a cow, Mann was considered a religious prodigy and began from an early age to study secular subjects—modern Hebrew literature, German, philosophy, and astronomy. He was by nature wary and withdrawn: it has been said that the "caution in relation to other people and the isolation" that marked him as a young man later gave way to "excessive . . . distance from his colleagues." But his aloof bearing may also have derived from an understandable instinct for self-preservation.

At age twenty, Mann convinced his father to let him travel to London to avoid the draft; they had, after all, cousins in England—and religiously observant cousins at that. In fact, Mann planned to study at both the liberal Jews' College and secular London University, and soon after his arrival, the London branch of the family picked up and moved to Antwerp, leaving him completely on his own. Impoverished, largely friendless, and new to the English language, Mann poured himself into his studies during these years, only to be pronounced an enemy alien during World War I and threatened with deportation. He had, however, already been recognized as a scholar of exceptional promise, and after the chief rabbi of England, Joseph Hertz, and the head of Jews' College, Adolph Büchler, intervened with the authorities, it was agreed that Mann could stay in London if he would report twice daily to the police.

Perhaps it was Büchler—penny-pinching Oxford librarian Adolf Neubauer's nephew and protégé—who first steered Mann toward the Geniza's untapped documentary wealth and encouraged him to take on the project that began as his dissertation and, with its 1920 publication as a book, constituted the first major historical work based on Geniza documents. *The Jews in Egypt and in Palestine under the Fatimid Caliphs* became, according to one later scholar, "a classic almost immediately after its publication." Subtitled *A Contribution to Their Political and Communal History Based Chiefly on Genizah Documents Hitherto Unpublished*, this two-volume tome charted a much more expansive realm—both physically and chronologically—than any previous modern account of medieval Middle Eastern Jewish history: Worman's inching attempts to enumerate the synagogues and markets of Fustat had given way to Mann's wide-ranging effort to chart Jewish life across the heart of an empire. By his own account, Mann had "practically gone through the whole Cambridge collection from one end to another" (wearing, it seems, a homemade gas mask, to protect himself from the fumes), and

had done much the same with the Geniza holdings at the Bodleian, the British Museum, and in the private collection—then housed in London—of that early Geniza explorer, the lawyer Elkan Adler. Yet in his typically tiptoeing way Mann insisted that "no claim is put forward of having exhausted all the available material. As with the nation of Israel, so with its literature—'scattered and separated among the peoples.' "

His book presented, according to Mann, an "attempt . . . to reconstruct the life of these Jewries [of Egypt and Palestine] from the beginning of the Fatimid reign in Egypt (969 C.E.) till about the time of Maimonides, who died at the end of the year 1204 C.E." But it was, he warned, just a start. Before all else, he needed to establish the most basic cast of characters and outline of the period. "It is my sincere hope that, as more of the Genizah fragments see the light of publication, the skeleton presented here will . . . clothe itself in flesh and blood and approach the stage of completion."

To his credit, Mann understood both the overwhelming scope of the task he had set himself and the limits of his own powers. He had made it his business to present a tremendous amount of "new" documentary material by offering in raw form the transcriptions of hundreds of mostly Hebrew fragments (communal appeals, elegies for public figures, formal "epistles," letters to and from religious leaders) plucked from the Geniza and never before published. "In Geniza research, quantity is quality," in the words of S. D. Goitein, the century's greatest explorer of the documentary Ben Ezra material. The difference between the interpretation of a single, isolated fragment and the analysis of a much larger accumulation of manuscripts relating "to the same period, the same person, the same phenomenon" was essential. Mann's triumph lay, first of all, in the sheer scale of his undertaking.

His success also derived from his ability to arrange these sources in some comprehensible order, and in doing so, to delineate a pivotal period in Jewish history, what Goitein called "the time when everything in Judaism became consolidated, crystallized, and formulated." And Mann's reading of the texts in question entailed a major historical revision: before him, the Gaonim, or presidents of the two talmudic academies of Babylonia (in the towns of Sura and Pumbedita), had been considered the leaders and sages of all the world's Jews. In Mann's version—based not on canonical religious literature or official histories but on the messier, accidental evidence found in the Geniza—the life of Jewish Palestine and the academy *there* was suddenly thrust into focus. Despite endless political and military upheavals, Jews had, it became clear, continued to live and flourish in the Holy Land, and the Gaon of Jerusalem had in fact been the leading Jewish authority in the Fatimid Empire. Mann's book was, in this sense and according to Goitein, "a revelation. It reclaimed pre-Crusader Palestine for Jewish history."

The book was also—it must be said—a serious slog to read. The result of all that maniacal document-sifting came across as what the historian Gerson Cohen has described (in relation to one of Mann's scholarly forebears) as "a staggering array of data with almost no connective thread, a vast number of trees with no forest in sight." While deeply appreciative of the "veritable gold-mine of historical information on every aspect of Jewish life in the Near East" put forth in *The Jews in Egypt and in Palestine,* Cohen respectfully wondered if Mann should in fact be classified as a historian at all. He was, rather "a master antiquarian" whose work was actually "closer to philology and textual scholarship than to historical synthesis."

Others, including Goitein, have defended Mann's claim to the historian's mantle by describing *The Jews in Egypt and in Palestine* as "not representing a consecutive narrative" but resembling, instead, "a string of pearls, held together by a chronological or associative sequence." According to Goitein, this necklace-like quality did not render the book any lesser and was, in fact, almost a given at this stage; such a piecemeal approach was attributable, he wrote, to "the very nature of Genizah research and to our knowledge of medieval history in general. Thousands of documents, often or mostly fragmentarily preserved, heaped up topsy turvy in a lumber room, and later dispersed in many different collections, have to be identified, collected, deciphered and translated, and, finally, to be understood in the context of sources, Jewish and general, otherwise known. A complete historical account will be possible only after all this work will have been done." Writing a half century after Mann, Goitein declared that "even now . . . we are far from such a final, all-comprising view of one of the greatest periods of Jewish history." Mann had, though, turned the soil and sown the seeds.

The empire that Jacob Mann worked so hard to map was a place of constant movement. The letters, edicts, and declarations he transcribed and attempted to parse had arrived in Fustat from all corners of the medieval Islamic world and Byzantium, as Jews propelled by persecution, poverty, family ties, or business opportunity took to the roads and seas.

In an odd way, the profound restlessness of this period mirrored Mann's own very mobile life and indeed his times—as, at the end of the nineteenth and start of the twentieth centuries, traditionally raised Eastern European Jews found themselves sprung from their shtetls and ghettos and bound for America, Palestine, or some other, more cosmopolitan spot than the one from which they'd come. So it was that the Przemysl-born, London-educated *Ostjude* and Austrian national Jacob Mann would pack his bags in 1920 and take up a teaching job in Baltimore, settling just a few years later in Cincinnati, at Hebrew Union College, where he would live and continue to dedicate himself tirelessly to work with the Geniza's historical materials, publishing several other major—massive—volumes of "texts and studies" before his death in 1940.

There were, of course, others on the move in these years—and as Jews wandered, so did Jewish learning. In fact Solomon Schechter's 1902 arrival in New York (by way of Romania, Berlin, Vienna, London, and Cambridge) marked more definitively than any other single event the shift of Jewish scholarship away from Europe, toward points both west and east.

Upon installing himself at JTS—and delivering an inaugural address that was criticized in the newspaper for the heavy foreign accent in which it was spoken—Schechter was quick to hire an almost exclusively European faculty, beginning with the Kovno native and great-great-nephew of the Vilna Gaon, Louis Ginzberg (whose studies in Lithuanian yeshivot were followed by years of academic work in Berlin, Strasbourg, and Heidelberg), the Polish Bible scholar Israel Friedlander (trained in Strasbourg and Berlin), the Lithuanian Israel Davidson, and the Koenigsberg-raised, Berlin-educated librarian and historian Alexander Marx. No matter how worldly this crew, there was, at first, a certain failure to communicate at the school, since several of the professors could only teach in German, and many potential students, recent immigrants themselves, were inclined to speak Yiddish. Schechter, however, was adamant that all those affiliated with the Seminary express themselves in English. (The Baltimore native Henrietta Szold, one of the first women to study at JTS and later the founder of Hadassah, the Women's Zionist Organization of America, offered the teaching staff private lessons.) Schechter also lobbied hard for JTS to emphasize rigorous European-styled textual scholarship and not what he considered the mere trade-school manufacture of congregational rabbis.

Schechter's stance was quite controversial and would remain a bone of contention for years to come. There were certain community leaders who considered his stress on the scientific study of Jewish texts "far too highbrow" for the mass of American Jews, but—at least during his own lifetime—Schechter had his linguistic and methodological way within the walls of the Seminary, where such scholarship flourished, and where Schechter also insisted that students needed to know more than just classical Jewish texts. He reportedly informed one young candidate for rabbinical school that "nobody is qualified to enter the ministry who has not read [Rousseau's] *Confessions*" and told him to apply only once he had absorbed it.

As such ideas made their way to the new world of America and, later, the old-new world of Palestine, the primary language of Jewish scholarship would shift from German to English, and, increasingly, Hebrew. The use of Hebrew for Jewish scholarly writing was, noted one German Jewish commentator in 1923, a matter of spiritual survival, as "only through its aid can a natural connection to living Judaism be found." The same year, the first lecture was delivered at the soon to be officially inaugurated Hebrew University in Jerusalem—by Albert Einstein, who uttered his opening remarks, on the theory of relativity, in the holy tongue. Another symbolically meaningful modulation occurred with the 1907 announcement by Israel Abrahams and Claude Montefiore that they were ceasing publication of the London-based *Jewish Quarterly Review;* in 1910 the journal was launched again by Philadelphia's Dropsie College for Hebrew and Cognate Learning, under the editorship of Schechter and another early collector of Geniza manuscripts, Cyrus Adler, who declared in the first issue of the resuscitated journal that "America is fast becoming the center of Jewry, and in all likelihood will become also the center of Jewish learning in the English world."

With all these scholars and scholarly notions zigzagging oceans, it is not surprising that libraries themselves—and with them, important gatherings of Geniza fragments—would also start to migrate. Since the end of the nineteenth century, various Geniza collections had made their way to all parts of the world—from Vienna to Manchester to Paris. Right around the time of Schechter's Egyptian adventure, for instance, the Moravian polymath and scholar David Kaufmann had—rather mysteriously—come into possession of a compact but valuable collection of some six hundred Geniza fragments, which were donated after his death to the Hungarian Academy of Sciences in Budapest. Although the details remain extremely sketchy, it seems Kaufmann too had been racing with Schechter and Neubauer to seize hold of the whole Geniza: Kaufmann and Schechter were regular correspondents in the 1890s, and according to one of Kaufmann's students, he had been negotiating to "purchas[e] the complete Geniza" when he learned of Schechter's Egyptian trip and "became deadly pale." Later he blamed "the careless Hungarian connection which gave it to . . . Cambridge University." The reference remains obscure—Neubauer was, it is interesting to note, Hungarian—and according to the Budapest-born Geniza scholar Alexander Scheiber, "Kaufmann never spoke of the matter."

After Schechter and his crates had departed Fustat, the aristocratic Cairene Jew Jack Mosseri had continued to gather up manuscripts left behind by those he dubbed "the wise men of the West." Poised in a privileged way between Occident and Orient, the British-educated Mosseri had a vision of local Egyptian "spiritual revival." He was also sharply, if politely, critical of what he called in 1911 "the raid on our literary treasure-house," though he admitted the Egyptian-Jewish community's role in this loss: "We did not at the time appreciate the nature of the hoard with which we so lightheartedly parted." Perhaps as a kind of compensatory gesture, from 1909 to 1912 he and a small group of French and American scholars dug for fragments in the Basatin graveyard and on the Ben Ezra grounds, unearthing Geniza manuscripts that had apparently been buried during the synagogue's 1890 renovation. The collection they rescued was substantial—some eight thousand fragments; a catalog was drawn up around the time of the excavation, some of the

collection was then photographed, and the whole lot was apparently stored in a "new Geniza" and communal library, attached to one of Cairo's more modern, Sephardic synagogues. Mosseri hoped that this would serve "not only [as] a storehouse . . . of the records of the past, but a well from which will be drawn a living stream of ideas for the present generation of Jews in and

In the Land of the Pharaohs.

INTERVIEW FOR THE *JEWISH CHRONICLE* WITH MR. JACK N. MOSSERI, OF CAIRO.

I N our last issue our Cairo correspondent gave a brief indication of the fact that the Jewish community in the Egyptian capital is "waking up" and that efforts are being made to bring its organisation into line with that of the progressive Jewries of more "modern" lands. Cairo Jewry is fortunate in having had at its head, for the past forty-three years, a wise and generous benefactor in the person of Moise Bey Cattaui, a banker of great influence and standing, who devotes a good deal of his time and a good deal more of his means to the requirements of his coreligionists, especially those of the poorer class. He has an able *aide de camp* in his communal work in the person of his nephew, Mr. Jack N. Mosseri, who, while on a recent visit to this country, gave an account of his work to a representative of the *JEWISH CHRONICLE.*

According to Mr. Mosseri's statements Cairo possesses

A Growing Jewish Community.

"Even since 1900," he said, "the number of the Jews in Cairo has been steadily growing. To-day we have a community of over 18,000 souls, or, if the Karaites are included, over 20,000."

How did the immigration commence? Was it due to persecution?

"Hardly. The idea suddenly seemed to pervade the Jewries of the East that Cairo possessed a very prosperous community, and, as if to a magnet, Jews began to flow to us from Syria, Persia, Russia, Turkey, Palestine, and Mesopotamia, especially from Bagdad. Previously we had no very serious communal problems, but naturally this large increase of the Jewish population caused us some anxiety, especially as there were a number of very poor people among the new arrivals. So we set to work, step by step, to create institutions adequate to the requirements of the large community with which we surrounded.

Mr. Jack N. Mosseri.

beyond the oldest home of the children of Israel." But Mosseri died young, in 1934, and with that his entire stash disappeared. After years of determined sleuthing by yet another Adler, the Israeli librarian and musicologist Israel Adler, the fragments eventually resurfaced—in 1970 in Paris, when the family granted Adler ten days to sort and microfilm them. Although the manuscripts were willed to the National Library in Jerusalem, they remained in a private bank vault until 2006, when they were loaned to the Cambridge library where, as of this writing, they are being preserved and cataloged. (The original handlist remains missing.)

By the second decade of the twentieth century, the United States had become home to a number of Geniza collections, including one at Dropsie College and another at the Freer Gallery in Washington, D.C. Of all the American Geniza collections, though, the largest and richest by far would make its way from Europe only after Schechter's death—to the Jewish Theological Seminary, then under the presidency of Cyrus Adler. The collection was none other than that of Schechter's old friend *Elkan* Adler, who had managed to talk his way into the Geniza a few months before Schechter had, in 1896, and to fill a Torah mantle full of fragments. As it turned out, Adler had also continued to buy up in secret large quantities of Geniza fragments for several years afterward—as the overworked and underappreciated Count Riamo d'Hulst had excavated around the Ben Ezra synagogue and supplied the Bodleian with a "great many sacks" of unearthed fragments. Since most of these were deemed by Neubauer and Cowley to contain "useless Hebrew MSS," the Oxford library chose to put them on the market, describing the transaction in their receipt book as the "sale of waste."

But the Bodleian's trash became part of Adler's cache—his extensive Judaica library, which, as early as 1916, JTS librarian Alexander Marx had been exploring the possibility of buying for the Seminary. In addition to precious incunabula, manuscripts, and rare books, the collection contained more than twenty-six thousand Geniza fragments, and the whole of it was reported to fill every room of a five-story house. "I realize it is a bold thing to ask," Marx wrote to Mayer Sulzberger, "but . . . you know what it would mean for this country to get [such a library] into the new center of Judaism." Adler may not

have been especially eager to sell, but it seems the embezzlement by a business partner of much of his firm's money made it necessary. Negotiations and fund-raising continued on and off for some seven years—with Hebrew Union College also, reportedly, "gunning for the same library" and Marx and Cyrus Adler eventually securing the support (and funds) of various influential New York Jews, including Mortimer Schiff, Felix Warburg, and Louis Marshall. Adler finally agreed to accept the sum of £25,000 (the equivalent of approximately a million dollars today) and on March 18, 1923, the *New York Times* reported the purchase of the Adler collection, the addition of which would make JTS "the greatest Jewish library in the world."

A few days later, Elkan Adler wrote to Cyrus Adler, confirming the shipping and insurance arrangements, and admitting his own sadness: "I need not tell you that it is a great wrench," he wrote, "and I feel as though I were giving away an only daughter in marriage[,] but it is a comfort to think that she will find a happy home and that she will continue to bear my name."

Cyrus Adler was quick to reply: "I fully understand that it is very hard for you to be suddenly separated from your Library to which you

have devoted so much paternal love and care and which you have brought up for more than a third of a century. But you can be sure that your 'daughter' will find a proper home. The union with her younger cousin will be very beneficial for both."

America was the setting for this bookish wedding, and, as it happens, the scene of various family feuds that had marked the Jewish community there for much of its young life—and that also had echoes in the Geniza. . . .

8

A Gallery of Heretics

"Of all the riddles the Geniza offers," Schechter wrote in 1901, as he prepared himself for the encounter with a fractured but burgeoning American Judaism and appraised a Hebrew scrap he'd come across by an upstart eighteen-year-old Persian Jewish immigrant to Babylonia, "this is one of the most puzzling." Its six pages contained parts of a loosely cadenced, rhymed expository work, and its young author's limitations as a writer "make his style," according to Schechter, "occasionally forced and even unintelligible." It was content, however, rather than eloquence, that drew Schechter into the puzzle of this not-quite-prose, and what he found there were the words of a shockingly skeptical ninth-century Jewish critic of the foundational Jewish document—the Bible. As though he'd been reading a mix of mid-twentieth-century literary New Criticism and a rationalist's guide to theology, the seemingly fearless neophyte calls into doubt the integrity of scripture on both textual and moral grounds, complaining that it lacks clarity and requires constant explanation, contains needless details and repetitions, often contradicts itself with regard to major considerations, and, worst of all, presents an implied ethics that are "inferior and in no way compatible with the moral nature of God"—whom our doubter claims is depicted in scripture as a capricious, double-dealing dispenser of punishment. Schechter also notes the "jarring" and "irreverent and irritable" tone of the questions. It is unlikely, he adds, that the writer's Jewishness was more than superficial.

This anonymous contrarian appears, however, to have had fellow believers in disbelief, and they had a teacher—who has also been delivered from the limbo of the Geniza and into a kind of tag-team denominational debate. The teacher's redeemer was the same Israel Davidson who, as a teenager, had crossed the ocean to reach New York, learned English, and entered into the Geniza's orbit when Schechter brought him to JTS.

In the summer of 1914—after he'd found the first wispy trace of the circa sixth-century liturgical poet Yannai in a Geniza fragment—Davidson, we'll recall, reversed direction and crossed the ocean once again, this time heading for Cambridge, where he was to spend a few weeks squinting his way through the University Library's Taylor-Schechter collection. We don't know for certain what he hoped to find there— though his record of publication prior to the trip, along with his wife's comments in her memoir, suggest that he was "especially anxious" to see what the collection might offer and most likely had liturgical poetry (which is to say, Yannai and company) on the brain. In a small book he published the following year, Davidson notes that he had the "privilege of examining every part of the Genizah collection," especially the "numerous fragments which had remained unclassified."

While the grail of Yannai's long-lost poetry eluded him on that round, Davidson did find something smaller and off to the side that turned out to be among his most important discoveries: a polemical work composed in response to the person scholars now believe served as the model or even mentor for Schechter's doubter. His odd name as it has reached us is Hiwi al-Balkhi—which is to say, he came from Balkh, or Old Bactria, then Persia and today northern Afghanistan. (There is considerable confusion over the name, with some scholars suggesting that Hiwi—a corruption, it seems, of the Persian "Haywayhi"—was a nickname that may have carried overtones of an Arabic word meaning "snake," or "heretic.") In the Middle Ages, Balkh was famous as the birthplace of

Zarathustra, the founder of Zoroastrianism, and the region was fertile ground for a number of religion-splintering sectarian movements, including various Shiite strains of Islam and one quasi-Jewish sect that sought to shift the Sabbath from Saturday to Wednesday(!)—the day the sun was created in the Book of Genesis. Prior to the nineteenth century, Hiwi al-Balkhi's name had been mentioned only a handful of times in the entirety of Jewish literature—always by writers who vehemently objected to his line of thought—and nothing of his work itself remained.

But here he almost was, rising revenant-like up out of the muffling mounds of Geniza documents. The fierce argument Davidson had stumbled on was with one of the most formidable Jewish minds of the age—tenth-century Jewry's greatest leader and most versatile thinker and writer, Saadia ben Yosef, who was, among many other things, the last person to have quoted from the Hebrew Ben Sira before it disappeared off the medieval radar. Born in 882, in the Egyptian district of Fayyum just south of Cairo, Saadia was appointed to the position of Gaon (Eminence), or head of the Babylonian academy of Sura, in 928. At once a conservative and profoundly revolutionary figure, it was Saadia Gaon, as he came to be known, who, more than any other individual, brought medieval Eastern Judaism into the "modern world" of Islamic civilization—"transform[ing] almost beyond recognition the intellectual and literary agendas of the cultural elite" of his day. As he did so, he fearlessly took on challenge after heretical challenge.

The scrap that Davidson had fished from the Cambridge collection was a small but tantalizing part of Saadia's polemical reply to some two hundred cutting questions that Hiwi al-Balkhi had launched at the Bible and at Judaism sometime in the ninth century, which is to say, during a period of considerable religious ferment. Saadia's thirty-one extant answers—composed before he became Gaon, and in a deft Hebrew that Davidson misidentified as rhymed prose—employed the standard prosodic components of the verse of the time, including an elaborate system of both alphabetical and signature acrostics, in addition to rhyme. It was, in other words, a kind of poetry, and it long stood as the earliest example of nonliturgical Hebrew verse, if of a merely didactic sort. In addition to being a highly influential and visionary philosopher, linguist, and commentator on scripture (which he translated into Arabic)—in many ways a much more original, critical, and attractive thinker than Maimonides—Saadia was also an innovative *payyetan*, the extent and quality of whose literary output was revealed only with the discovery of the Geniza and the work of Davidson, Menahem Zulay, and others. The tough-talking polemic Davidson had found presented him and other scholars with something like a Jewish game of *Jeopardy!* They had a set of succinct if heady answers; now they had to imagine the questions that prompted them.

As they worked out these equations, the contours of Hiwi's radical thought and doctrine began to emerge.

Judging from what we hear in the not necessarily faithful echo of Saadia's answers, Hiwi appears in his "book of questions" to have presented an eccentric, freethinking, and occasionally sneering take on the faith of his forefathers—which he may or may not have sought to leave. Deeply influenced by Zoroastrianism, certain elements of Persian philosophy, Christian and Islamic heretical doctrine, and possibly by the more controversial Jewish midrashim, he posed questions that were seen to "raise the ax over the essential principles" of Judaism as that religion emerges in the Bible and in the oral tradition: Why did God make man vulnerable to suffering? Why should the blood of animals be acceptable to Him as atonement? What would an omnipotent deity have had to fear from the builders of the Tower of Babel? Why did God choose just a single people (the Jews) and give the other nations over to the care of the angels? Why does the Bible present so many contradictory verses? Can't the biblical miracles be explained rationally? (For example, the Red Sea wasn't split supernaturally; Moses simply understood its ebb and flow, while the Egyptian troops did not. And manna wasn't sent from heaven; it's the Persian food *tarjabin*, which is found in those parts of the world. Et cetera.) In short, Hiwi seems to be saying, what kind of religion is this anyway? And what right-thinking person could believe in its scripture?

Hiwi's own theological position can be summarized along the following distinctly nonnormative Jewish lines: God, at least as He emerges in the (problematic) Bible that represents Him, is neither all powerful, all present, nor One, and—moreover—He isn't always Godlike! He engages in magic and is often neither just nor trustworthy. God did *not* create the world *in the beginning*—the world existed before Creation, and it was hardly perfect. God implanted evil in man, and He is also responsible for barbarism (sacrifice and the mutilation of circumcision). In his radical critique, and maybe also in his muttering recalcitrance, Hiwi was, as one modern scholar has put it, "a whole millennium ahead of his time."

B ut why was Saadia bothering to respond to Hiwi nearly half a century after the Bactrian Bible-basher had drawn up his questions? What troubled the Gaon so that he would risk bringing still more attention to Hiwi's heretical line of thought?

The later medieval literature reports that Hiwi composed a kind of expurgated version of scripture, shorn of "objectionable" passages, and that this was taught in schools. While modern scholarship rejects the existence of Hiwi's alternative commonsense Bible, it does leave open the possibility that he inspired just such a work by someone else, and that *this* Bible-for-doubters (perhaps by the skeptic Schechter had plucked from his crates) may have been the object of Saadia's rhymed, proto-rap-like assault. A more plausible explanation, however, lies in the evidence that derives in part from Geniza finds and indicates that Hiwi belonged to the burgeoning cluster of sectarian figures whose teachings in the second half of the eighth century had begun to creep across the periphery of the Jewish world (especially along the Persian frontier, where Hiwi was raised), and that these heretical movements had come to pose a serious challenge to rabbinic Judaism, which was gradually emerging as the mainstream expression of the faith. Saadia had spent the first thirty years of his life in Egypt and Palestine, where sects of this sort had attracted a following, and he was perhaps more alert than others to their danger.

Some seventy years after Davidson's discovery of Saadia's response, the Geniza coughed up one of the many quiet surprises that it holds in store for those who tend to its treasures like ants—patiently constructing networks of tunnels and routes along which finds and supplies might move: in 1982, a Jerusalem scholar working with microfilms of Geniza manuscripts happened on a fragment containing eleven lines of Hiwi's original composition. The page appears to come from yet another work written in response to Hiwi's dissenting position, and it quotes verbatim three of his questions (attributing one of these directly to him). The find confirms that Hiwi did indeed write in Hebrew, and for all intents and purposes employed the same style that Saadia mirrored in his reply. As with so many of the Geniza discoveries, this one too had passed through numerous hands without being recognized, despite the fact that Hiwi's name (spelled with a small difference) appeared clearly on the page, in large Hebrew characters cast into Judeo-Arabic: "And about the story of the Egyptian sorcerers, Hiwahi al-Balkhi said . . ."

In early November of 1901, the same year that Schechter published his article on the Bible doubter, he wrote to his friend Mayer Sulzberger in Philadelphia, complaining bitterly about "the dragging and haggling" of dealing with the board of directors at the Seminary as he negotiated his new position there, which he says he would gladly surrender before having even taken it up—"but for the fact that I want to live among Jews and . . . hope . . . to have, God willing, some share in shaping the future of Judaism." Then he pulls the latest rabbit out of his Geniza hat and mentions that he has just identified large fragments of a sectarian manuscript and that, again, "God willing," he "intend[s] to edit one day a volume of fragments forming *my Heretic's Gallery which will surprise the world.* [But] I am now keeping back the best things for America as I think that such publication will give the Seminary a certain prestige." A full nine years later, settled at JTS and still bickering with the board over institutional matters, he finally saw into print the manuscript he'd mentioned to Sulzberger, alongside another, older one, in a book called *Documents of Jewish Sectaries.* The contents of this volume hadn't been known before the discovery of the Geniza and were, it seemed, related to the origins of a much larger Jewish schismatic movement, the most threatening of the age. This latter group was the foe at which Saadia had aimed his rhetorical crossbow again and again in fragments found among the Fustat scraps: Karaism.

But first, Schechter's sectaries—on the face of it, a surprising shift of attention for this scholar and leader whose work and life were devoted to reinforcing the integrity and "vital" center of Jewish history and tradition. Although he was very much a man of cultural progress and in many respects a liberal, and though he believed with all his heart in the unified vision of what he called "Catholic Israel" (in which all the streams of Judaism were, in essence, one), while still in Europe Schechter had developed a pronounced aversion to the dissension of Reform Judaism, whose individualism and Protestant-style reliance on private judgment he felt merely paved the way to Christianity. As Schechter saw it, Reform Judaism in Germany and America had become a modern sect, opposed to the body of Judaism, and like the sectarian movements of the Jewish past (to which some Reformist scholars were drawn, but about which the masses of its adherents were ignorant), it would prove evanescent. Perhaps his Cairo finds would help him make his case.

A zealously particular and utterly fascinating puritanical composition, "Fragments of a Zadokite Work" (the first and principal part of the *Jewish Sectaries* volume) comprises, as Schechter diplomatically put it, "the constitution and the teachings of a Sect long ago extinct, but in which we may perhaps easily detect the parent of later schisms with which history dealt more leniently." Arguably second in importance among the Geniza revelations only to the Ben Sira fragments, the find was reported on the front page of the *New York Times* on Christmas Day 1910. A long feature story occupying the entire opening spread of the Sunday Magazine section followed on New Year's, complete with a large picture of the bespectacled Schechter and the declaration that this was a "discovery of . . . extreme importance to the history of religion." The article noted that the manuscript, which was also known as the Damascus Document, had been found "in the Genizah or Hiding Place under [*sic*] one of the most ancient synagogues in the world," and the *Times* writer plunged into the controversy that had immediately sprung up around the heretical text and which would intensify when, decades later, another copy of the work was found in the caves above the Dead Sea at Qumran: When was this work composed and who are its characters? Is it about John the Baptist, Paul, and one of the earliest Christian groups on record, or—as Schechter postulated—about a Second Temple Jewish community that in many ways anticipated the coming of Christianity and was but one of the many Jewish sects of the day?

Leading a group of Jews on the cusp, or over it, the protagonist of this cultish text—and also a central figure in the Qumran literature—is, as Schechter and most scholars translate the Hebrew, a man known as the Teacher of Righteousness. His mission is to lead Israel away from the erroneous instruction of the Man of Scoffing and back to the ways of God. Rejected by the majority of Jews and the mainstream Judaism of his time, the Teacher—who is considered "an anointed one," or Messiah from the priestly line of Aaron, not the line of Jesse and David, and was himself a priest—takes his followers to Damascus, where they form a New Covenant, or Testament. While in Damascus the Teacher dies. His disappearance—he is expected to rise again—is followed by a period of backsliding, but the sect survives as a highly organized society scattered among several cities, one of which is designated as "the City of Sanctuary," where sacrifices are offered.

The sect's congregation sees itself as the true remnant of Israel, "an Israel . . . within an Israel," and accepts the teachings, laws, and legends of the Old Testament, including the Prophets. But it also acknowledges the authority of several noncanonical or "outside" works, some of which today form part of the Pseudepigrapha—that is, falsely attributed books composed in a biblical style, usually dating from between the second century B.C.E. and the second century C.E. (for instance, the Book of Jubilees). Above all, the followers of the New Covenant distinguish themselves from the "transgressors of the Covenant" and "the builders of the fence," which is to say, the official Judaism of the Pharisees, whose motto was "Make a fence for the Torah." As Schechter bluntly puts it, this was "a Sect decidedly hostile to the bulk of the Jews as represented by the Pharisees." Schechter's translation of the document's feverish Hebrew tells how the rabbis and their followers

> searched in smooth things and chose deceits and looked forward to the breaches. And they chose the goods of the throat and justified the wicked and condemned the just and transgressed the covenant and broke the statute and gathered themselves together against the soul of the righteous man. . . . But with them that held fast to the commandments of God, who were left among them, God confirmed His covenant with Israel forever, revealing unto them the hidden things in which all Israel erred.

Among these hidden things—apart from the community's additional sacred books and highly elaborate set of laws (which called for the ritual slaughter of fish and forbade, among many other things, the employment of a "shabbos goy")—was a calendar of "new moons and seasons and Sabbaths" that differed from that of rabbinic Judaism. Likewise, the sect's interpretation of the nation of Israel's past also clashed with that of official Judaism, some of whose heroes (especially David) were singled out for abuse.

At this point a new set of questions float up before us. What was such a bizarre Second Temple sectarian text (the Dead Sea Scrolls proved Schechter right in his dating) doing in high-medieval Fustat? And why, when the manuscript was considered worn out, was it placed in the Geniza of a synagogue belonging to the Rabbanites—descendants of the Damascus Document's "Princes of Judah, [who] turned not out of the way of the traitors . . . and walk[ed] in the way of the wicked . . . and builded the wall and daubed it with untempered mortar"?

The second part of Schechter's sectarian diptych hints at a possible, though by no means definitive, answer. This Aramaic manuscript fragment by one Anan ben David, an Iraqi Jew who appeared on the Baghdadi scene some time around 770, sketches out the lines of yet another alternative Jewish system. Chafing against the ever-widening and controlling body of rabbinic law, Anan led a Muslim-influenced reform movement within Judaism proper. While he made ample use of rabbinic interpretive strategies, Anan adopted a seemingly libertarian and even postmodern line, declaring that each person was obliged to interpret the Torah for himself and that such independent interpretation of scripture took precedence over everything—tradition, community, and family— even if it led to differences in practice. But his *Book of Commandments* (*Sefer Mitzvot*), which was really a sort of maverick's Talmud ("It reads," Schechter told Sulzberger, "absolutely like Gemara"), promptly applies a corrective constrictive pressure and preaches anything but tolerance: "Father or mother, brothers or children who do not serve heaven in our fashion are persons from whom we are duty bound to separate. . . . Any Jew who does not observe the Torah is called a gentile. . . . And we must of necessity separate from them. And we are required to gather together." Of specific note in this book of precepts is Anan's forbidding not only the *kindling* of fire on the Sabbath (as the rabbis do, per Exodus 35:3), but the *burning* of fire, as the Bible states. In other words, according to Anan's literalist reading of scripture, on the day of rest *all fire had to be extinguished*, including lamps, candles, and coals for cooking that had been lit before the Sabbath had begun. (One imagines Anan and his followers sitting on the floor and eating cold leftovers in the dark.) Likewise the biblical verse that in the rabbinical tradition gives way to the prohibition against the mixing of milk and meat in a meal or a pot is understood by Anan to mean exactly what it tells us: "Thou shalt not seethe a kid in its mother's milk"—and nothing more. The consumption of milk and meat together, he ruled, was permissible, so long as the milk wasn't that of a given kid's mother. Furthermore, circumcision, Anan by way of the Geniza tells us, should be carried out with scissors, not with a scalpel; and so long as Israel was in exile, alcohol and all meat (except that of pigeons and deer) were forbidden.

These and other depressing precepts put forth in Anan's book were eventually adopted by a community of various marginal Eastern Jewish movements that were united toward the middle of the ninth century and came to be known in Hebrew initially as *bnei mikra*—disciples or champions of scripture—and in time as *kara'im*, or readers of scripture. Others believe the term Karaite (*kara'i*, in Hebrew) comes from a different derivation of the k-r-a root, meaning "to call," and reflects the influence of the sectarian Islamic Shiite movements of the time, within which the preacher was known as the *da'i*, or "caller."

Whatever the origin of the term, Karaism took hold—and the letters and documents of the Cairo Geniza shine something of a klieg light on the movement, seriously revising our view of it and showing just how critical this seemingly heretical trend was to the development of what would become normative Judaism. Evidence of the Karaites' success comes howling at us from the wrinkled pages of documents written by Rabbanite leaders on whose collective big toe they stepped. Repeatedly. The Gaon of one of the two Babylonian academies, for instance, went at them in the course of a controversy concerning alternative versions of the Passover Haggada then in circulation, and he threatened—Jews of New Jersey and the new Jerusalem take heed—excommunication for anyone who dared to shorten or in any way alter the traditional text, calling those who do so "heretics who mock the words of the sages, *and the disciples of Anan—may his name rot—*. . . who said to all those who strayed and whored after him: 'Abandon the words of the Mishna and Talmud, for I shall compose for you a Talmud of my own.' And they still persist in their error and have become a separate nation." This earliest mention of Anan's *Book of Commandments* goes on to call it a "book of abominations."

As it happens, the Geniza has also brought us more than one "shortened" version of the Haggada and, far from being an indication of heresy, the texts in question turn out simply to be Palestinian (as opposed to Babylonian) rabbinic versions of the Passover liturgy in use at the time. In some of these Geniza versions of the Haggada, the classic Four Questions (*Ma Nishtana*) that are asked at the seder table by the youngest child are reduced to two queries, or three; in one version they swell to five. In another instance the father asks them. An eleventh-century manuscript now held in a Philadelphia Geniza collection—which is among the oldest extant complete (or nearly complete) Haggadot—also presents truncated versions of both the prelude to the Passover story and the story itself.

One part of this "alternative" Philadelphia Haggada is, strangely enough, *longer* than its Babylonian and latter-day parallel: the blessing over the *karpas* (Aramaic for "celery"), which is said very early in the seder, immediately after the kiddush and the ritual washing of the hands. Instead of a single blessing recited over the typically wilted sprig-to-be-dipped-in-salt-water-reminiscent-of-our-tears, four blessings are inserted at this point in the Palestinian Geniza Haggada. This extended set of prayers makes it clear that the flimsy green thing on today's seder plate is what one distinguished scholar of classical religious thought has described as the "lonely, desiccated survivor" of a lavish and life-enhancing Greco-Roman spread of hors d'oeuvres, or the Levantine mezze of late antiquity and the High Middle Ages. Palestinian seder-goers gave thanks, in other words, not only for the fresh greens of spring, but for local fruits and diverse delicacies (most likely seasoned rice cakes), and for the different creatures that God creates—which is to say, an assortment of sweetbreads, grilled meats, and sausages that would help one through the ritual to come. As that same contemporary commentator noted, the Geniza gives us more than information—it also delivers universal wisdom: "It's all about food!"

Riding a wave of growing resentment against a ballooning Babylonian class of religious and civic administrators, Karaism spread and, toward the end of the ninth century, it reached Palestine and Egypt. This new wave of Karaite expansion was led by the Persian-born Daniel al-Kumisi, who moved to Jerusalem and helped found or at least develop what would become an aggressively missionary and relatively large, influential Karaite community there. In particular the scrupulous al-Kumisi encouraged settling the ravaged city, the destroyed Temple of which, as he saw it, should be constantly mourned: "Wake up and weep over the House of the Lord," he writes in a forceful Hebrew appeal that, like a number of his other writings, landed in Fustat: "Come to Jerusalem and stand within it at all times before Him, mourning, fasting, weeping, and wailing, wearing sackcloth and bitterness, all day and all night. . . . Hold vigils before the Lord until the day when Jerusalem shall be restored." The fragment also shows him to have differed from both Anan and previous Karaite thinkers—denying, for example, the existence of *all angels*, not merely a Logos-like being who, as one of Anan's successors had written, God appointed to create the world in His stead. In this and numerous other ways al-Kumisi embodied what became the Karaite creed, attributed to Anan, but probably coined by a later author: "Search ye well in the Torah, and do not rely on my opinion." Al-Kumisi actually upped the ante in this regard, calling Anan a "champion fool" and imploring his readers in this same appeal to rely neither on his (al-

Kumisi's) wisdom nor anyone else's, for "he who relies on any of the teachers of the dispersion and does not use his own understanding *is like him that practices heathen worship*."

Perhaps the greatest Karaite writer of this period was Ya'akov al-Kirkisani, who lived in the first half of the tenth century, probably near Baghdad. Highly educated in a broad variety of fields, al-Kirkisani read widely in contemporary Arabic linguistics as well as in its theological, philosophical, and scientific literature, and he maintained an impressive network of friendships with leading Christian and Rabbanite intellectuals. By writing in Arabic rather than in Aramaic or Hebrew, he (and many of his successors) further distanced the Karaite perspective from rabbinic thought.

Al-Kirkisani is of particular interest here because his writings contain a self-conscious history of, as he puts it, "dissension in the Jewish religion," which of course sounds like an entertaining if also vaguely tautological prospect. His long list of sectarians and heretics traces division to the heart of the notion of Israel, at least as a political entity, and it runs from the biblical Jeroboam (who led ten of the twelve tribes in revolt against Solomon's son Rehoboam, resulting in the split kingdom that lasted for more than two hundred years) to the aristocratic and priestly Second Temple Sadducees (who, in sharp distinction to the far more popular and populist Pharisees, rejected the authority of the oral tradition of the day, and differed with their rivals on numerous central points of doctrine, including belief in angels and the immortality of the soul). Post–Old Testament factions on al-Kirkisani's list of Jewish dissenters include the disciples of Yeshua (Jesus); the rival rabbinical schools of Hillel and Shammai; the Persian and then Damascene Isunians (who saw their founder, Abu Isa al-Isfahani, as the final harbinger of the Messiah); the Yudghanites (who sought to abolish the Sabbath altogether); and the followers of Anan, who was now viewed by Karaites, revisionistically, as the founder of their movement. Al-Kirkisani's schismatic survey, which concludes with Anan's successors, is our clearest if still quite distant echo of the Palestinian Talmud's noting that Second Temple Judaism consisted of no less than twenty-four different sects—the existence of which, it says, drove Israel into exile. A late-eleventh-century anti-Rabbanite tract reports that Judaism once comprised fourteen "religions" (or "paths"), but only four had survived into the writer's day: the Rabbanites, the Karaites, and two others, of which the Geniza has left us no trace.

While it's both difficult and risky to generalize about Karaite doctrine—since so much work remains in manuscript, and since the movement at root defines itself by the need for constant internal reform (al-Kirkisani wrote that "hardly two Karaites can be found who agree on everything," thereby providing historical precedent for a long line of jokes on the theme of "two Jews, three opinions")—broadly speaking, Karaism as reflected in the work of these thinkers might be summed up as follows: The Karaites saw their seemingly heretical version of the faith as the true and original Judaism, and they rejected the exclusive authority of the Talmud and its rabbis. Moreover, they refused to recognize the authority of *any* permanent religious leader (let alone a Rabbanite-appointed Gaon), and many of them embraced Jerusalem as the center of their faith's attention, mourning in sackcloth the Temple's destruction. On the intellectual plane they placed an emphasis on written rather than oral transmission, this too as a way of distinguishing themselves from the rabbinic tradition. Concomitantly, they encouraged the close study not only of scripture, but of the Hebrew language itself—taking great pains to ensure the accurate codification of the scriptural text. Ironically, in their attempt to return to a pure, unadulterated Judaism, the Karaites ended up—in ways they could not have anticipated—introducing the contemporary Arabic intellectual and religious Zeitgeist into the bloodstream of Hebraic culture, as they drew both the inspiration and technique for this linguistic inquiry from the Islamic context in which they lived.

Nowhere is that irony more pronounced than in the association between the "marginal" Karaites and the Masoretes—the eighth- and ninth-century Tiberian scholars who standardized the biblical text, and whose name (from the root "to pass on") suggests authoritative transmission of a tradition. Both groups were known as *ba'alei mikra*, masters of scripture, and speculation that their circles were related is borne out by the fact that numerous Masoretic manuscripts have been preserved by Karaite communities to whom these particular works were dedicated. In all likelihood the latter movement evolved out of the former. One curious by-product of this unlikely pairing is the Karaite practice of transliterating the Hebrew Bible *in Arabic characters* and "outfitting" them with the traditional Hebrew signs for the vowels above and below the letters. The Cairo Geniza held several mutant hybrids of this sort. We still don't know just why these Arabic-Hebrew Bibles were made. Some scholars have argued that it was out of the Karaites' desire to distinguish themselves at some point from the Masoretes (though this doesn't quite jibe with the evidence of their ongoing association); others have suggested that it was an expression of the radical and even experimental impulse at the heart of the Karaite movement. What we do know, or believe, is that it appears that these "Karabic" Bibles, as we might call them, were part of the Karaites' effort to preserve the original Tiberian reading and correct pronunciation of the text, which the living tradition of spoken Arabic may have been able to indicate more precisely.

A similar reverence and desire for the authentic lay behind the inten-

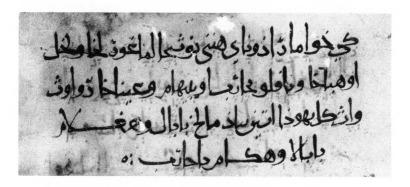

sified study of grammar among the Karaites, who believed that immersion in the intricacies and subtleties of biblical language would bring the reader closer to scripture's meaning. God in this scenario was quite literally, and absolutely, in the details, and numerous Karaite works were therefore devoted to the study of scripture's linguistic DNA—the nature and origins of language, the formation and precise definition of words, the structure of sentences, and so on. In the process, these Karaite scholars set the standard for future medieval biblical commentary—"shaming," as it were, the rabbinic leadership into matching the intensity and manner of their engagement with Hebrew and its most important literary product. In this and so many other ways, on the broader cultural level Karaism acted as what Jacob Mann called "a leavening agent" and what later scholars—having much more evidence to go on—have come to think of as a central if stealth ingredient in the renaissance and virtual re-creation of Hebrew culture that swept across the Jewish world from Baghdad to Cairo to Cordoba and Granada between the tenth and twelfth centuries.

Back in the land of practice, distinctive Karaite religious rituals included—in addition to allowing the consumption of milk with meat, and forbidding the use of any light or heat on the Sabbath (and all expressions of joy in its arrival)—the refusal to observe postbiblical Jewish holidays such as Hanukka; the eschewal of the use of phylacteries and mezuzot; the rejection of rabbinic texts of any sort for use in the prayer book (which consisted solely of biblical passages, largely Psalms); and the forbidding of sexual intercourse on the Sabbath. The Karaites understood the latter to be "labor" while for the Rabbanites it was part of the day's pleasure. In addition, the spilling of sperm was seen to cause impurity and to go against the biblical injunction of Exodus 34:21, "Six days thou shalt work, but on the seventh day thou shalt rest in plowing and in harvesting"!

One other seemingly innocuous but in fact nearly catastrophic difference between the Rabbanite and Karaite schools involved their contrasting methods of calendrical computation. While each party at times made use of the other's technique, the divergent methods resulted in the Karaites and Rabbanites employing distinct religious schedules, so that, for example, the two communities observed Yom Kippur and all the major festivals on different days. This made for serious awkwardness, especially in a place like Fustat, where the Karaite synagogue was within shouting distance of the Babylonian and Palestinian Rabbanite synagogues, and where many members of all three communities lived and worked in close proximity and sometimes owned businesses together. The Geniza makes clear that this situation and others like it led early on—especially in Iraq and Palestine—to mutual recrimination and, on occasion, to physical confrontation and attempts at excommunication. Recent scholarship, though, has demonstrated how, over time, and despite the more forceful attempts by Rabbanite leaders to draw a sharp and exclusionary line between normative Judaism and Karaism, the two communities evolved side by side, particularly in Egypt and later in Palestine, and they saw each other as part of a single religious body—the Jewish nation.

Given the "heretical" content and context of the two manuscripts that Schechter discovered, it becomes easier to see how it is that an esoteric Second Temple text and Anan's *Book of Commandments* might have wound up together in the same geniza. But their presence on the "battlefield of books" of *the* Geniza of the *Rabbanite* Ben Ezra synagogue is still something of a mystery.

Various explanations have been offered. One suggests that both these documents were considered "harmful" by Rabbanite Jews and so were taken out of circulation to prevent them from doing any more damage. Another scenario envisions these fragments coming from a different Cairo geniza—perhaps even the one attached to the Karaite synagogue, which the Russian Karaite collector Avraham Firkovitch had mined for manuscripts. A third line of reasoning proposes that the Zadokite fragment's sectarianism, along with its rejection of Pharisaic rabbinism, would have been of interest to the Egyptian-Palestinian Karaite community, but that, in the course of their normal and highly fluid social exchange with the Egyptian Rabbanites, documents moved freely and frequently between the communities and must have landed, if only by chance, in Rabbanite hands. This explanation sits well with one scholar's conclusion that, while early sectarian groups vanished from the script of history after the destruction of the Second Temple, "some of their traditions remained in circulation long enough to influence the Karaites and . . . some of the texts found at Qumran circulated in different versions among the Jews of the early middle ages." And, finally, a fourth and related possibility seems to be borne out by evidence that has emerged only in recent years and in large part from the Geniza; namely, that the Fustat Jewish community was simply far more flexible (and perhaps fickle) than we'd realized, and that there may have been serious interest in both of these "sectarian" works even within this mainstream Rabbanite context.

On a less esoteric plane, one sees that flexibility and the interaction between the different Jewish communities embodied in correspondence from the Geniza, such as when the scribe of the Palestinian yeshiva writes from Ramla to a distinguished Palestinian Rabbanite colleague in Egypt—a religious judge in Fustat—warning him about complaints that had reached the academy in Palestine that the latter's overbearing manner has been alienating his Egyptian synagogue congregation: "Because of you and your son-in-law many people have switched over to the other synagogue [the Babylonian Rabbanite synagogue in Fustat] and to the Karaite congregations." In other words, congregational affiliation was highly fluid and driven by social as much as by ideological concerns. And several *ketubot*, or marriage contracts, demonstrate the degree to which—certainly in tenth-to-twelfth-century Egypt—the two movements saw themselves as denominations of a single faith, fully aware of each other's beliefs and practices and by no means always threatened by them.

Drawn up in a Karaite court and signed in August 1117, one of these *ketubot* commemorates in Hebrew the union of a Rabbanite doctor named Yahya ben Avraham and an extremely well-off Karaite woman named Rayyisa bat Saadia. The document is decorated in unusually elaborate fashion—with biblical verses winding through the margins in a gold-and-blue-flecked lattice-like weave of miniature script—and it makes clear that, not only was this Rayyisa's third marriage, but *it was the second time she was marrying Yahya*. Their first marriage had ended in divorce and now they were trying again:

> [in the mo]nth of Elul [August], of the year one thousand four hundred and twenty eight . . . of the era of the Greeks, in Zoan [Fustat] which is on the Nile. . . . I [Yahya] declare before you an absolute, firm, and abiding declaration, being neither coerced, mistaken, in error, deceived, drunk, nor under duress, but [acting in accordance with my will and my wish and with full resolve, that I have returned to] my wife, the glorious and precious Rayyisa. . . . According to the law of Moses, the man of God, peace be upon him, and in accordance with the custom of Israel. . . . [I shall dress, clothe and] support her, and see to all her legitimate needs and desires to the best of my ability and strength, and I shall be with her in truth, justice, love, compassion, [honesty, and faithfulness. And I shall not diminish her] rights: raiment, sustenance, and sexual intercourse in the manner of the children of Israel who feed, support, and clothe their pure wives and fulfill all that is due them in faithfulness.

All this is fairly standard, including the promise of connubial satisfaction. The *ketuba* goes on to specify the particular payments exchanged and to give the shimmering details of the bride's trousseau (bracelets, rings, amber, a silver jewelry box, a deep bowl with a cover and spoon, a large and colorful wardrobe—mostly silk, wool, and linen—cushions, furniture, dishes, and utensils), then segues into the more delicate question of religious difference and tolerance:

> And our elder, dear Yahya agreed, of his own free will and resolve . . . that he shall not desecrate the festivals of the Lord as observed by his aforementioned wife according to the sighting of the moon, and that he shall not light the Sabbath candles against her [will and custom], and not coerce her in matters of food and drink. . . . And if he violates any one of these conditions he will pay one hundred dinars to the poor of the Karaites and the poor of the Rabbanites in equal shares. And this Rayyisa agreed, that while she is with her aforementioned husband she shall not desecrate the festivals of our brethren the Rabbanites.

Other Karaite Geniza documents have less sanguine things to report about mixing and matching. The prickly issue of religious conversion, for instance, is addressed in a letter that brings us the story of a leading Byzantine Karaite scholar and translator named Toviyya ben Moshe; he had married a Christian woman who'd converted to Judaism and given birth to their daughter. Its medieval locutions and concerns notwithstanding, the letter is yet another example of just how poignant and present the voices from the Geniza can be. It appears that Toviyya had moved his family to Jerusalem so that he could study with the masters at the Karaite academy there and translate key works of Karaite literature from Arabic into Hebrew, for the benefit of non-Arabic-speaking members of the community (such as those in his native Constantinople). By the time of the letter, which dates to 1040 or 1041, it's clear that Toviyya had made a name for himself in Jerusalem's Karaite intellectual circles, although that may have come at the expense of his livelihood and peace of mind. Things fell apart when his wife left him, taking their daughter with her to Egypt and returning to Christianity. Time passed and circumstances changed, and our letter, written in a plain-spoken Judeo-

Arabic, finds Toviyya now in better material circumstances but tortured by thoughts of his long-lost daughter, who has, it seems, written him with a request for money. He is trying to win her back—not only for himself, but for his faith and its followers, whom he characterizes simply as "Jews" (rather than "Karaites"):

> *I am writing you, my daughter, from Jerusalem, may God protect it. . . . Some of what I must tell you, my daughter, is what I think about your affairs, for a fire burns in my heart because of you, and God stands between me and the one who brought you harm and made you an orphan in my lifetime. . . .*
>
> *Know, my daughter, that I have sworn a solemn oath not to send you anything as long as I am uncertain about your condition and do not know what to do about your situation. God knows that I have no concern or worry other than for you. Nay, my health and my affairs are well, and my clothes cannot contain me for [my] happiness and good fortune.*
>
> *Had I been seeking nothing but worldly gain, I would regard myself today as a great success, for I have become the administrator of the government compounds in Palestine, at a handsome salary and a good [. . .] Men are under my authority. I've become powerful, and issue orders and rescind them. God has made me happier than I had been before. So good fortune has been mine and misfortune your mother's, God be praised.*
>
> *And now, my daughter, I do not know who you are with. I do not know whether you are with the Jews, who are the stock of your father, or the stock of your mother, the gentiles. But know this: if the Christians wanted to sell you to me, my own daughter, I would buy you and rescue you from their hands. What else could I do? . . .*
>
> *After [the festival of] Shavuot, I am leaving for Byzantium, for my native land and my family. Please tell me what your intentions are so that I can decide what to do about your situation, insha'allah.*

Again, we don't know how it is that this letter found its way into the Ben Ezra Geniza or what became of the broken family. Several other letters by Toviyya have also emerged from the Geniza, but scholars disagree as to what they're telling us. In one, which may have been written as many as seven or eight years later, Toviyya reports to a Fustat colleague that he has again fallen on hard times and plans to return to "my home and my patrimony," but first he would like to know with whom he can leave the money that he owes a friend. No one in the Karaite community, he says, apart from a few fellow Byzantines, cares for him at all, and then he mentions his daughter, who still "will not leave my heart."

However that sad story turned out—some say the daughter died and the wife returned to Toviyya, others say it just isn't clear—Toviyya's letters, like so many other sectarian and even heretical documents from the Cairo Geniza, throw into startling relief the question of how, through their long and sometimes lesser-known history, Jews have handled difference with regard to deepest belief and practice. More critically, these seemingly marginal contracts, tracts, letters, and appeals show us the ways in which dissension has at times come to define what Jewishness means and who, when push comes to excommunicating shove, is considered a Jew and who isn't—thus linking, after a fashion, Lower Egypt and the Upper West Side, ninth-century provincial Persia and nineteenth-century reform-minded Berlin.

9

Pieces of the Spanish Puzzle

In addition to its functioning as a de facto dead-letter office, commercial archive, and dossier of divergent religious belief, the Geniza's "mass of ragged, jumbled, dirty stuff" and its "anything but sanitary" odor hid keys to understanding the evolution of Judaism's most distinctive embodiment of elegance and order: poetry from what has come to be known as the Golden Age of Hebrew literature in Spain. Arguably the greatest poetry composed in Hebrew since the biblical period, this verse constituted such a fundamental revolution in Jewish literary culture and consciousness that its emergence far from the traditional centers of learning in the East has long been called "miraculous." And that by and large is how its story has been told—as a big Jewish literary bang, if not a full-fledged "creation out of nothing."

With good reason. For more than a thousand years after the composition of the Book of Ben Sira, the poetry that Jews produced was generated almost entirely by the engine of synagogue worship and the liturgical year. Suddenly, around the turn of the first millennium, at the northwest end of the Mediterranean and deep inside the Diaspora, Hebrew poets began writing in a radically innovative and even shocking manner, developing what amounted to a new body of literature from the unlikely alloy of Arabic literary modes and motifs on the one hand, and scriptural Hebrew and Jewish mythopoetic materials on the other. Wine, war, contemplation, wit, and erotic (as well as homoerotic) attraction—all now swam into the Hebrew poets' ken. Within a short time Andalusia's classicizing Hebrew new wave produced its first great, and some would say its greatest poet, Shmuel HaNagid, whose worldly, intimate, and supremely wise verse was followed by the work of four other major figures: the metaphysically inclined and misanthropic Shelomo ibn Gabirol; the most Arabized of the Hebrew masters, Moshe ibn Ezra, whose consummate craft acted as ballast and keel to an abiding melancholy; Avraham ibn Ezra, who was raised in Muslim Spain but whose refreshingly grounded work was written in the Christian north, as well as in Provence and Italy; and perhaps the most famous of them all, and certainly the sweetest singer of the age, Yehuda HaLevi.

The early years of the twentieth century saw quantum leaps in the study of this Golden Age poetry (as it has come to be known): scholars prepared the first serious critical editions and new manuscripts were discovered far and wide. In addition to Schocken's Stuttgart windfall, the nearly complete works of HaNagid surfaced in Aleppo, Syria, causing the preeminent Hebrew poet of the day, Hayyim Nahman Bialik, to sputter: "A kind of light shines on the marvelous prince—upon him and his period and the poets of his day. . . . The man is unrivalled in our history." Interested readers now had a reasonably clear view of the principal poetry of the period, though when it came to tracing the steps that led to the various stages of its development, there was little in the way of actual tracks. Hence the ex nihilo narrative. The Cairo Geniza, however, has changed all that—or, one should say, *is changing* all that—and as with so many dimensions of our repository's tale, demystification has not led to deflation.

On the contrary, a concatenation of discoveries stretching into the twenty-first century has only enhanced the aura of wonder surrounding the poetry's origins. Against staggering odds, patient and tenacious scholars have reunited torn pages or separated leaves or even just stray lines of manuscript fragments that had made their way from the Fustat

Geniza to libraries across Europe and North America. As "matches" large and small have been found for stranded pieces of the Spanish-Hebrew puzzle, not only new poems and new collections of poems, but new poets, new kinds of poems and poets, and the often extraordinary life stories of some of Hebrew literature's finest writers have been introduced into the modern literary mix.

In 1936 a young but already experienced assistant at the Schocken Institute for the Research of Hebrew Poetry, Jefim Hayyim Schirmann, published several important articles treating historical and literary dimensions of work by poets of the Muslim period in Spain. The most substantial of these publications—really a ninety-five-page monograph on, and provisional edition of, the period's minor poets—mentioned in passing a small fragment that Schirmann had found, like the other material he was treating, among the Geniza manuscripts. It consisted only of a short prose heading to a certain poem and that poem's first three words. The Judeo-Arabic caption attributed the poem "to Ben Labrat, of blessed memory" and described the circumstances of its composition.

Ben Labrat, Schirmann knew, had to be the unusually named Dunash ben Labrat, who was by all accounts the founder of the new Andalusian Hebrew poetry. In an imaginative shift of a high order, sometime toward the middle of the tenth century the Moroccan-born Dunash had reconceived the very nature of Hebrew verse. While studying in Babylonia under Saadia Gaon, it seems that the aspiring poet had taken seriously, possibly too seriously, his influential mentor's notion that the chosen people had more than a little to learn from the thriving Islamic society around them, including, for starters, science, philosophy, linguistics, and new modes of written discourse (much of this activity having been spurred, it seems, by the Karaite irritation and that movement's own engagement with Arabic modes of writing). For one reason or another Dunash decided to apply Saadia's line of thought to poetry as well, and he came up with a way of adapting Arabic poetry's standard of musical measurement—quantitative meter—to Hebrew. The ambitious disciple showed the results to his illustrious teacher, who offered up the decidedly ambiguous judgment: "Nothing like it has ever been seen in Israel." Dunash soon headed west, and he reached Spain by his early thirties, having brought with him the new poetics and all they implied. "Let Scripture be your Eden," he wrote in a motto-like fragment, "and the Arabs' books your paradise grove." The extant historical evidence indicates that Dunash's liturgical verse was soon sung "in every town and city, in every village and country." His secular poems also gained many admirers, despite his scorn for what he considered the provincial ways of the backward Spanish Jewish literati he encountered in Andalusia—and he eventually unseated the only rival for literary supremacy on the Hebrew cultural scene—the far more parochial, if by no means ungifted, Menahem ben Saruk (whose scant surviving work the Geniza preserves and who, in a most unfortunate case of fallout from court intrigue, had his Cordoban house quite literally razed around him, on the Sabbath no less, before he was tossed into jail by the leading Jewish patron of the day). With Dunash's success, however, came some hard-core resistance, and the disturber of the literary peace with the alien (Berber) name was accused not only of "destroying the holy tongue . . . by casting it into foreign meters," but, in doing so, of bringing nothing less than "calamity upon his people."

Although documentary material relating to Dunash's poetic revolution had been available since the mid-nineteenth century—including some of his prose (and that of his attackers and defenders in Spain who were hashing out what they clearly thought to be the major controversy of the day)—very little was known about his poetry. At the height of the modern fascination with the Hebrew Andalusian literature, when Schirmann was working at the Institute, the situation wasn't much better than the one described in 1873 by a German scholar who had written:

"[Dunash's] poems have been lost, and only a few lines remain." This, too, the Geniza would change.

Schirmann, who would go on to become a towering figure in this field, had been intensively engaged with medieval Hebrew poetry since the age of twelve or thirteen. Born to a wealthy family in Kiev in 1904, he was given an excellent general education and, thanks to his religiously observant father, was also fed the best of what Hebrew literature had to offer. But the nineteenth-century masters Mendele Mocher Seforim, Shalom Aleichem, and their like were not, as Schirmann tells it, to his taste. One of his teachers decided to return to older material he knew would interest the gifted if obviously somewhat odd Jefim, and he brought him medieval dirges for the Ninth of Av, the holiday commemorating the destruction of the First and Second Temples. Among these poems was Yehuda HaLevi's long, plaintive, and iconic ode, *"Tzion halo tishali,"* which, while not written specifically for that day of mourning, had long been incorporated into its literature:

> *Won't you ask, Zion,*
> *how your captives are faring—*
> *this last remnant of your flock who seek*
> *your peace with all their being?*
> *From west and east, from north and south—*
> *from those near and far,*
> *from all corners—accept these greetings,*
> *and from desire's prisoner, this blessing . . .*

The poem made such an impression on the budding bibliophile that he sat down and translated it into Russian. He was hooked, and from then on the teenager tried to get his hands on anything relating to medieval Hebrew poetry, scouring libraries in Rome when the family passed through that city after the revolution forced them to flee Russia in 1919, and later devouring books in his new home, Berlin, where material on the subject was easier to find. Some adolescent boys run track or join the astronomy club; by age fifteen, with German under his belt, Schirmann had begun compiling a detailed bibliography of medieval Hebrew literature, drawing up his lists along geo-cultural lines: Spain, France, Ashkenaz, Africa, and so on.

Schirmann's first contact with the Geniza came in 1930, when he joined the Schocken Institute just a few months after it opened in Berlin. Twenty-six and, it was felt, the most mobile (i.e., only unmarried) member of the research staff, he was promptly sent to Cambridge to photograph manuscripts. He would later remember the tremendous

excitement and tension of going daily to the small, richly appointed and carpeted rooms of the old university library—not the new "enormous and enormously ugly building that looks from the out- side like a factory with a large tower" (which opened in 1935)— and sitting there to work with Geniza manuscripts from the moment the doors opened until they closed. Some fragments had been sorted and placed in large cardboard boxes or in bound albums; others rested between glass; still others had barely been looked at and required basic cata- loging. "Day after day," he later recounted, "I came across heaps of important manuscripts—some containing unknown poems by well- known writers, or work by their contemporaries to whom fortune had been less than kind and [whose compositions] had fallen into the abyss. Every evening, as I looked back over the day's work, I'd dream of the dis- coveries that awaited me the following day."

In 1934 the Institute relocated to a grandly austere combination of two intersecting limestone cubes set like a toppled sans-serif capital T in Jerusalem's placid Rehavia neighborhood, just across the street from Schocken's new villa. Both buildings had been designed by the already renowned and ever-inventive "Oriental from East Prussia," architect Erich Mendelsohn, who'd planned several of Schocken's streamlined German department stores and who saw in Palestine "a union between the most modern civilization and a most antique culture . . . [a] place where intellect and vision—matter and spirit—meet." The Institute's quasi-Bauhaus style inflected for the Levantine light was in many ways the ideal place for this cultural confluence. Schirmann set himself up in the reading room beside Brody and the two Galicians who were working on Eastern and Ashkenazic *piyyut*—Zulay and Abraham Meir Habermann—downstairs from the lemon-wood walls, pale horsehair chairs, and Rembrandtlicht of Schocken's private library. There Schirmann began poring over photostat copies of "new" medieval and  Renaissance-era Hebrew poems. By the time he'd come across the Dunash (of blessed memory) heading, the now thirty-two-year-old had already produced a groundbreaking anthology of Hebrew poetry from Italy and published studies that had made a powerful impression on Bialik, who was deeply committed to the "ingathering" of great works of the literary past in an effort to catalyze contemporary Jewish culture.

All of which is to say that the single line of quantitatively metered verse at the end of the heading mentioning Dunash pricked up the ears of the poetry-saturated scholar. None of the extant verses attributed to Dunash matched it; but the fine index of Schirmann's memory at once led him back to a poem that began with the same words but which had been attributed to Shelomo Ibn Gabirol since 1879, when it was found in the Firkovitch collection.

That poem, it was now clear, had another and very different author and, with the shift of perspective brought about by Schirmann's seemingly minor "match," a somewhat plodding though conceptually effective fifty-two-line poem that existed in a single complete copy became one of the most important pieces in the entire Andalusian Hebrew canon—at the head of which it suddenly stood. For, apart from its quality, the poem emerges from what is perhaps *the* central question of the literary tradition that would take shape in Spain for the next five hundred years—namely, could Arabic forms of expression articulate the deepest Jewish concerns? Or were Dunash's opponents right and would a Hebrew poetry that evolved through and from these "alien" forms inevitably foster the erosion of those very values? "And this," says the heading,

> is another poem by Ben Labrat, of blessed memory, about the ways of drinking in the evening and in the morning . . . accompanied by musical instruments and the sound of water courses and the plucking of strings, and the chirping of birds from the branches, with the scent of all sorts of incense and herbs—all this he described at a gathering convened by Hasdai the Sefardi, may he rest in peace. And he said, "Drink, he says, don't drowse / drink wine aged well in barrels."

The poem, in other words, begins with an invitation to just such a wine party. Hasdai ibn Shaprut ("the Sefardi," who had, one assumes, by this time brought the roof down on Menaham) was the greatest Jewish patron and political leader of the day. A highly regarded court physician and bureaucrat in Caliph Abd al-Rahman III's administration, he'd developed a Jewish cultural scene in emulation of what he witnessed at the Cordoban Muslim court. As promised in the heading, the poem tells of his party in a tended grove or garden along a river, where gentle music is played, pigeons coo, and fine wines and food are served. The detailed call to drink (and, by extension, to enjoy the occasion in the spirit of the place and times) is violently interrupted by someone who objects to what he considers the courtiers' indulgence and scandalous behavior. "How could we drink wine," he scolds, "or even raise our eyes— / while we, now, are nothing, / detested and despised?" That is, how can we allow ourselves these refined pleasures while the holy city of Jerusalem is in "foreign" hands and the Jewish people can't determine its own fate? Implicit in the interlocutor's retort (is he Dunash? or a foil?) is a challenge to the entire aesthetic—and with it the worldview—of the new poetry that Dunash pioneered. And so the marvelously ambiguous literary situation both frames and perfectly embodies the tensions between the secular and sacred, radical and classical, Hebraic and Arabic dimensions of experience that would run through so much of this literature for several hundred years to come. Thanks to "this peculiar archive," as Schirmann once referred to the Geniza, we can see that cultural agon being played out at the very beginning of the period.

More than perhaps any other individual working with medieval Hebrew poetry, Schirmann was possessed of a kind of visionary precision, within which he commanded a broad view of the age and its poetry even as he labored like an archaeologist among the detritus of the Old Cairo cache. His spadework with these cultural castoffs has shown us pivotal moments in the history of the literature, including (apart from Dunash's classic and theatrical presentation of its challenge) the entrance into Hebrew of the homoerotic and widespread use of the "gazelle"—the classic image of the beloved, which the Jewish poets took over from Arabic. It also produced numerous smaller if no less startling discoveries. Among the many other pearls that Schirmann plucked out of the Geniza, in an effort to present the work of poets who were well known in their day but eventually forgotten, for instance, we find a fabulous poem about fleas, along with a satirical take on an old man who was caught "over his boy . . . / sucking on his mouth. / With his beak against that face he looked," says the twelfth-century speaker, "like a crow devouring a mouse."

But Schirmann's detailed investigations came to their most profound fruition in his landmark anthologies and prose accounts of the period, which injected Andalusian poetry into the bloodstream of modern Hebrew cultural life. Among these monuments of, and to, bygone eras of literary creation are his magisterial 1956 anthology *Hebrew Poetry from Spain and Provence;* his 1965 collection of some 250 previously unpublished Geniza poems; and his astonishingly fluid two-volume history of all five hundred years of this verse, the immaculate manuscript of which was, after Schirmann's 1981 death, found in a corner of the lifelong bachelor's small, Spartan, and essentially library-less rented Jerusalem apartment. It was still in its author's loopy, childlike handwriting, lacked annotation, and had not been revised. There were no instructions or indications of any sort as to what was to be done with the manuscript, which had most likely been composed between 1968 and 1974 and then set aside until the author's death.

The scale of his project notwithstanding, this was hardly surprising. Friends and colleagues remember Schirmann as "a riddle to all those around him"—someone who combined qualities that, curiously, one sees in the Hebrew poems of Spain, but rarely in a single person or scholar. He was, at one and the same time, remarkably disciplined, absorptive, discreet, expressive, lucid, alert to refinement and the aesthetic sublime, and both closed to people and open to the world. Almost frighteningly au courant in a tremendous range of fields, he was somehow able in his work to integrate the scholarly, literary, and musical gifts that he tended to keep apart in his life. A serious violinist, he had studied for five years at a Berlin college of music while getting his academic degrees; he'd considered a career as a soloist, and continued to play throughout his life.

As war raged in Palestine, February of 1948 provided an image that in many ways sums up the contradictory forces at work in and around the man. Following a devastating terror attack on the downtown Jerusalem street where Schirmann lived—a thunderous bombing by Arab irregulars and British deserters in which some fifty-two people were killed and well over a hundred injured—then Hebrew University professor S. D. Goitein's wife, Theresa, wrote to her oldest daughter (who was working on a kibbutz) to tell her of the blast and its aftermath. She describes seeing wounded people in their pajamas wandering around the street in a daze among the debris and recounts some of the other horrors. There were, though, also "many miracles," according to Mrs. Goitein: "For example, Dr. Schirmann, who lived on the roof—his building was entirely destroyed, but he was saved and lowered by a rope while holding his violin. I met him and he's in fine spirits."

Midair or on the street, Schirmann, observers recalled, cut a distinctly strange and disembodied figure. He had a large balding head and a face which, in pictures, suggested a mother hen's. He was tall and walked with a stoop; addressed his interlocutors in the third person; and often improvised his sometimes tedious Hebrew lectures from German notes that he held inside the daily Hebrew paper—the talk punctuated by a nervous tic, which would have the lecturer look at disconcerting intervals suddenly up to his right. Though he did as much as any other person in the twentieth century for Hebrew literature and scholarship in the state of Israel, he remained—colleagues noted—European to the end, and  after he retired from teaching in 1968 he spent much of his time with his sister in Paris, where he died and was buried.

With his work as a whole, and almost single-handedly, said one of Schirmann's most distinguished students, the Romanian-born former prisoner of Zion Ezra Fleischer—who would eventually oversee the publication of Schirmann's grand history of the entire period—"he shifted attention from the interesting or unusual to the beautiful." Schirmann was, Fleischer added, "the type of character about which novels might be written."

Over the decades following Schirmann's encounter with the Dunash heading, a few more of Dunash's poems were discovered (some from the Geniza), though his long wine poem remained among his most important works. More spectacular than the identification of its author, however, is the story of another misattribution that involves the poet.

In 1944, working from a photostat, a Jerusalem scholar named Nehemia Allony published a fragment of a Hebrew poem that had been torn vertically down the middle. The surviving left flank of the page contained a little more than half of the lyric, which had probably been raised from the Old Cairene graves that furnished much of the material for the Mosseri collection. The fragment had a Judeo-Arabic heading, which read: "Dunash ben Labrat to him." Allony extrapolated from the extant part of the poem that the lines in question were in all likelihood part of a wedding song composed by Dunash in honor of a local groom and his non-Iberian bride.

Some forty-one years and several wars later, Ezra Fleischer came across a complete version of the same lyric as he sat wading through the then seventy thousand microfilmed copies of poems housed at the Israel National Academy's Geniza Research Institute for Hebrew Poetry, which Schirmann had established in 1967 and which Fleischer himself would go on to direct for four decades. (The Institute's extensive index of meters, refrains, genres, opening lines, rhyme schemes, stanzaic structures, and scriptural citations—all of which are cross-referenced in an effort to map a fragment's "genetic" identity—today lists some ninety thousand titles.) The lines revealed by the reproduction of this tiny (5 x 3½–

inch) scrap of rag paper from the Taylor-Schechter collection also bore a heading, but it was indecipherable, at least on film. The poem, however, was as clear as could be and, moreover, it was extremely moving in that clarity, which told not of a wedding but of a couple's painful separation:

> *Will her love remember his graceful doe,*
> *her only son in her arms as he parted?*
> *On her left hand he placed a ring from his right,*
> *on his wrist she placed her bracelet.*
> *As a keepsake she took his mantle from him,*
> *and he in turn took hers from her.*
> *Would he settle, now, in the land of Spain,*
> *if its prince gave him half his kingdom?*

As Fleischer describes it, the poem's pacing and development, its transitions and rhetorical ornaments of intensification, along with its central silence and choreography framed by opening and closing questions, all combine to powerful effect and make for a small tableau of striking beauty. The find was all the more intriguing because none of the extant work by Dunash had given any indication that he was capable of writing poems as poised as this one.

Spurred by his discovery, Fleischer went back to the Mosseri collection and, working from new microfilm, within a short time he was able to find the second half of the vertically torn page Allony had published. As if in a made-for-TV *National Geographic* special, the two fragments came together before Fleischer's eyes like pieces of a map pointing to a long-

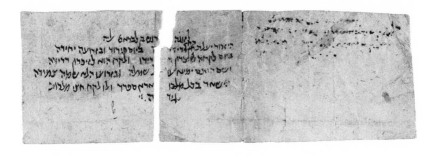

lost treasure—though what they yielded was itself the treasure, and, in its way, priceless. It seems that the 1944 fragment had been missing only a single Judeo-Arabic word in the heading, but that word was critical: *lizawjat*, meaning, "By the wife of." The full poem with its restored heading was, in other words, described as being *"By the wife of Dunash ben Labrat to him"*—making it almost certain that *she*, not her husband, was the author of this lyric. Cambridge's University Library then supplied Fleischer with an enhanced reproduction of the Taylor-Schechter manuscript containing the lines in question, and he was able to decipher the caption to the complete copy of the poem. It read: "A letter from the wife of Dunash," confirming the identity both of the poem's author and its protagonists. Furthermore, the Taylor-Schechter manuscript contained *another* poem halfway down the page—this one with a heading that read: *"His [her husband's] reply to her,"* indicating plainly that an exchange of his-and-her (or even he said, she said) poems was involved.

With this find, scholars suddenly had in hand not just a poem by the wife of Dunash ben Labrat—the sole example of her work that has come down to us—but the only poem by a woman in the entire five-hundred-year-old medieval Hebrew canon. Composed, it seems, on the occasion of her husband's forced departure from Spain (the reasons for his leaving remain obscure, but the last line of the poem suggests that he had fallen out of favor with the leader of Spanish Jewry at the time, the aforementioned Hasdai ibn Shaprut), the poem is simple but highly refined. Its restraint and quiet dignity, along with its pulsing tenderness and subtle complication of tone—melding affection, resentment, and above all a sense of acceptance of what seems to be a tragic fate—speak for this poet who has no name, but who, thanks to the Geniza and Ezra Fleischer, now has a place of pride at the very start of the canon alongside her husband and his wine poem. And not just as a curiosity. The poem by Dunash's wife, observed Fleischer, is no less than "the first fully realized personal poem in the new Andalusian style," and it far surpasses the work of her husband in quality. That it emerged at such an early stage of the poetry's evolution, he says, and from the pen of a woman, makes the find all the more remarkable.

As it turns out, there were more Dunash-related surprises still to come. In 1985, five years after the discovery of the poetic exchange between the Ben Labrats, the notion of their forced separation was corroborated by yet another Geniza find. In the upper left corner of a previously examined letter from Hasdai ibn Shaprut to the Empress Helena of Byzantium—Hasdai was corresponding with her about the plight of the Jews in her kingdom, and the letter was, scholars believe, part of his archive, which somehow landed in Cairo—Fleischer identified what appears to be a somewhat slack poem of complaint by Dunash addressed to Hasdai and composed in the local and unmetered style of Menahem. (It seems that Dunash had taken up this mode as well, though he showed little affinity for it.) Broadly translated, the new fragment picks up in medias res (the opening two lines were illegible): " . . . I served you in sorrow, for all your wares are loathsome. / I will glean no grapes, nor will I gather corn. / I betrayed a young wife and sent her a writ of divorce. / I left my home, and abandoned the son that she bore." Dunash is, in other words, bemoaning the conditions of his service under Hasdai, the pressures he faced on that job, and the heavy price he had to pay for it in the end—the destruction of his family.

The Geniza's contribution to the field of Spanish Hebrew poetry was, however, by no means restricted to the recovery of precursor, minor, or merely piquant poems of the day, meaningful as those discoveries have been. As the work of scholars from the early thirties and on has repeatedly demonstrated, and sometimes in breathtaking fashion, understanding the connections between the less heralded or seemingly tangential writers of the period has helped us see the shapes made by the lives and lines of the major poets as well.

Yehuda HaLevi is a case in point. In 1938, Schirmann prepared the first-ever biographical study of HaLevi based on a relatively complete and reliable edition of his poems. Some four decades later, in the wake of his friend S. D. Goitein's pioneering explorations of previously ignored Judeo-Arabic documents relating to Mediterranean commerce, Schirmann had to thoroughly revise his earlier work in order to take into account information contained in the fifty-five letters pertaining to HaLevi that Goitein found in the Geniza. Among this correspondence were several stylistically impressive pages in the poet's own feathery hand, several of which were scrawled while the doctor-poet was surrounded by people—probably his patients—and as a courier was waiting to get on his way.

Goitein had published only a handful of these letters, and nearly a quarter century would pass before younger scholars would look into this material again. But look they did, and once more the baton was passed—as the Giblews' motto had it, *lampada tradam* (let me hand on the torch)—from field to field (between literary scholarship in Hebrew and

documentary research in Judeo-Arabic), and then vertically, from one generation to another, as Schirmann's student Ezra Fleischer teamed up in the late 1990s with one of Goitein's prominent disciples, historian Moshe Gil, to bring out a collection of all the Judeo-Arabic and Hebrew documentary material relating to HaLevi's biography.

Dedicated to their two teachers—who worked, as Fleischer put it, in a period "when Nephilim [the legendary semidivine biblical giants] were still in the land"—*Yehuda HaLevi and His Circle* presents something akin to a wide-angle view of

HaLevi's world and takes us, as few medieval Jewish documents of this or any other era have, into the tangible scene of a major writer's day. In signed and dated formal letters sent by official post between Egypt and other parts of the Jewish world, and in more casual "notes" passed between colleagues and friends, we find the poet and his peers—businessmen and scholars, physicians and cantors, writers and hangers-on—going about their lives. They buy, sell, love, annoy, hate, and suffer illness (often elaborately described); they announce births, mourn deaths, report on travels, request books of poems, and tell of family friction, communal tension, and the pathetic competition that literary celebrity sometimes breeds.

At the same time the documents lead us back to the circumstances surrounding the composition of HaLevi's poems, multiple copies of which also emerge from the Geniza. A letter Fleischer believes to be from the summer of 1129 by the poet to his wealthy Egyptian merchant friend Halfon ben Netanel mentions HaLevi's desire to go east, thus giving us the first documentary evidence of a principal theme in his best-known work: his longing to turn his back on Spain and all it had come to stand for—poetically, intellectually, and spiritually—and journey to the Land of Israel, where he could spend his remaining days. And in fact the beating heart of this cache lies in the letters that allow us to travel with the elder HaLevi when he eventually embarks on that trip. Other letters seem to solve, or come close to solving, the centuries-old mystery of whether or not—and how—HaLevi realized his dream to set foot in Jerusalem and see, as he put it in perhaps his most famous poem, "the dust of the desolate shrine."

But the value of these letters goes well beyond the stuff of a single man's biography. Rather, they demonstrate, as Fleischer provocatively states, that the trip was not simply a personal pilgrimage so much as a full-fledged emigration, and that the rejection of the syncretic culture of Andalusia by the most prominent Jewish personality of the day was intended to serve as an educational and political model for others. (After all, HaLevi was, as one Granadan writer put it in an 1130 letter that wound up in the Geniza, "the quintessence and embodiment of our country.") The irony of this most intimate portrait of the poet, then, is that—in combination with his poems and prose writings—it reveals the embrace of HaLevi by subsequent generations to be, by and large, a celebration not of Andalusian-Jewish literary accomplishment, but of the *abandonment* of that accomplishment. In numerous places the poet characterizes the Hebrew poetry of his time as "froth on the waves of wisdom's sea" and describes the entire complex of secular Greco-Arabic learning as "all flowers and no fruit."

And so it is that we can look over Halfon ben Netanel's shoulder as, in September of 1140, in Fustat, he receives a letter from a relative in Alexandria announcing the imminent arrival from Spain of "the Sultan's new ship," which was carrying HaLevi and had dropped anchor in Alexandria's harbor on Sunday the eighth. A short while later HaLevi himself writes Halfon and tells him of the warm embrace he'd received in Alexandria, a reception that was to his mind *too* enthusiastic; it embarrassed him. The ever-gracious HaLevi played along, as he did for so much of his time in that city, but his mind was elsewhere:

> *Outwardly I participated [in the festivities], but inwardly it all weighed on me heavily. This is not what I've come for, and in fact I desired the opposite— solitude and retreat—as I am close to being like one who waits for death at any moment. However, as you know, my natural disposition will not allow me anything but to accept the kindness of those who mean well, and to greet them in friendship.*

Within a few weeks, however, things in Alexandria grow sticky for the superstar poet, as jealousy festers all around him and gives rise to misunderstanding and considerable grumbling. By September 23 an Alexandrian Jewish colleague of Halfon (who is still at home for the holiday season) writes with a report of HaLevi's time and trials in the city, saying plainly that he's amazed Halfon has allowed things to get so out of hand in his absence; one frustrated would-be host had gone so far as to involve the local police in applying pressure to lure the celebrated guest to his home. The colleague asks Halfon to make his way to Alexandria at once "to put an end to this headache."

The trail resumes several months later, after Halfon has heeded his colleague's call, plucked HaLevi out of the Alexandrian spider's web, and taken him personally to Fustat.

In early 1141, a new and apparently overeager and possessive Alexandrian friend of the poet, Abu Ala, writes HaLevi directly to say that his visit to the city has left behind a noxious cloud. It seems that some of the poems HaLevi had written in honor of his Alexandrian host were being circulated in the city by that host, as a kind of self-aggrandizing commemorative collection, and members of the community were muttering about the great poet's hypocrisy. How could a devout man on a religious pilgrimage be writing frivolous verse about fountains and chickens, and paeans to patrons (which HaLevi had been improvising, no doubt as gestures of gratitude)? Abu Ala goes on to ask if HaLevi is aware that he had, however unintentionally, offended people by turning down invitations from some and accepting them from others. All this, Abu Ala hastens to make clear, he is reporting out of "affection . . . and concern for your dignity (may it ever be great)." Above the Judeo-Arabic letter Abu Ala writes in Arabic characters, *"Burn after reading!"*

On May 11 of the same year, 1141, we hear that HaLevi—having barely survived a close scrape with the local Muslim religious authorities—is aboard an "oversized nutshell" of a boat, waiting to complete his journey to Palestine. "The ships bound for al-Andalus, Tripoli, Sicily and Byzantium, and other points East," writes one of his friends, "have found a good wind and departed." HaLevi, however, has been waiting on deck for four full days. Finally, on Monday, May 19, a partially torn fragment reports that "Our Master Yehuda HaLevi sailed on Wednesday." The wind had shifted.

That laconic word turns out to be the last sighting of the poet. Three months later a Hebrew letter is dispatched from Fustat to Damascus containing several hard-to-decipher lines that mention "our Master, Yehuda HaLevi, the pious and righteous man"; using a locution employed for the dead, it adds: "the memory of a saint is a blessing." At this point the manuscript is corrupt, though a glancing reference to the "gates of Jerusalem" follows. In any event, a legend arose according to which HaLevi was killed there by a Saracen on horseback—unlikely as that might have been, given that the holy city was under Crusader rule at the time and off-limits to both Muslims and Jews. (Testimony from this period does indicate, however, that modest pilgrimages to Jerusalem were made by Jews, who would pray on the Mount of Olives, outside the city, overlooking the site of the Temple Mount.)

HaLevi's celebrity notwithstanding, we know nothing for certain about his life after he left the harbor at Alexandria. There is reasonably convincing evidence that he survived the ten-day journey to (most likely) the Crusader port of Acre, at some point set out for Jerusalem, and that he died between June 8 and August 5, 1141, some two months after arriving in Palestine. Perhaps further particulars of this final chapter of HaLevi's life will someday surface. For now, we're fortunate to have between covers this almost implausibly tactile account of the penultimate chapter in HaLevi's life, narrated—or one should say, woven and reimagined—with characteristic artistry, and sometimes hyperbole, by Ezra Fleischer, whose own story is no less (and in some ways even more) remarkable than those of the other scholar-heroes who have brought us into the kaleidoscopic world of the Geniza.

Born in 1928 in Timisoara, Transylvania (Romania's second-largest city, near the Hungarian border), Fleischer came from a devout, cosmopolitan family steeped in Hebrew learning. His great-grandfather was a charismatic and prominent rabbi, and his Hebrew-teacher father founded a religious school that he directed from 1918 to 1948, when it was shut down by the authorities after the Communist takeover of the country. Yehuda Loeb Fleischer was also a serious scholar whose work was devoted above all to the important biblical commentator and fifth major poet of the Spanish-Hebrew period—the marvelously realistic and liturgically fecund Avraham ibn Ezra, after whom Avraham Ezra Fleischer was named.

The young Ezra, as he came to be called, received a superb if entirely informal Jewish education in a home that was, as he conjures it, "filled with Hebrew books, and suffused with scholarship and the love of medieval Hebrew literature." At the municipal secondary school he worked his way through a classical secular curriculum—including several European languages and Latin poetry. Meanwhile, the family (along with its library, the largest Hebrew collection in Transylvania) survived the war years, though they lived in constant fear of deportation or even extermination. An aspiring poet, Fleischer ended up studying law, since that was the only field for which entrance exams weren't held on the Jewish Sabbath; he took his degree but never practiced—as he was arrested in 1952 for "Zionist propaganda," coded reference to the fact that he was actively involved with a religious youth group that encouraged immigration to Israel. Held in isolation without trial for some thirty months, during which time he was repeatedly and brutally interrogated, he was eventually given the "light" sentence of six years, though he was released in 1955, after the thaw that followed Stalin's death. All told, he'd spent nearly four years behind bars, much of it in solitary confinement, where he fell ill and nearly died.

Nonetheless, Fleischer describes that period of internment not as traumatic, but as something that he would come to "wear like a crown." Imprisonment, he said, taught him an entirely new "rhythm of thought, maybe also of feeling," and out of that recalibrated cadence of being, while still incarcerated, he composed "hundreds of poems in Hebrew," though he wasn't allowed to write them down. Possessed of a phenomenal memory, however, he managed to put the poems to paper soon after his release. Three years later he wrote "The Burden of Gog," a long, vatic, defiantly ironic, and pathos-driven cry that confronted in camouflaged if dated fashion the cruelty and essential deadness at the heart of Communist rule. That poem was smuggled at great risk out of the country through diplomatic channels in Bucharest and on to Israel, where it was published in a prominent literary magazine, under a pen name supplied by the editor. By all accounts it "caused a sensation," and for this work, the thirty-one-year-old Romanian was awarded, in absentia and pseudonymously, the still-new state's highest honor, the Israel Prize. It is also a kind of "match" that, while listening one night to the radio, which Fleischer tuned regularly to the short-wave station "Kol Tzion laGola" (the Voice of Zion to the Exile, or Diaspora), he first heard that "The Burden of Gog," by someone named Y. Goleh—Goleh means "a person in exile" in Hebrew and the pseudonym had been invented without his knowledge, to protect him—would be awarded the prize the following evening, on Israel's Independence Day. The announcement, he said, left him trembling—not with joy, or pride, but in mortal fear—for discovery of the poem's author at the time would have been tantamount to a death sentence.

Less than two years later the former prisoner–poet and his wife were in Zion, where the author of "The Burden of Gog" was, at last, given his prize personally by Prime Minister David Ben-Gurion. Fleischer settled in Jerusalem and took up the study of medieval Hebrew poetry under Hayyim Schirmann.

In a certain sense the two men could not have been more different: Schirmann was a consummate European secular Jew, the product of the finest prerevolutionary Russian and Weimar training; Fleischer emerged from the heart of traditional Judaism and the prisons of the Soviet bloc and remained religiously observant all his life. The former was as famous for his cautious and meticulously mapped studies as for his seamless, spellbinding written narratives that presented psychologically pitch-perfect takes on the literature and its poets; the latter tended toward dramatic conceptual and aesthetic formulations, precisely calibrated close readings, and pioneering, if sometimes ferociously elaborated, structural analyses. The bulkier mentor was almost banker-like in his shapeless suits and black ties, and, as many have noted, something of an awkward, distant cipher; the disciple with the chiseled chin was dapper, courtly, and very much present as a legendary and inspiring teacher, and as an ethical if sometimes severe upholder of professional standards. Though he lived through critical periods of his people's history, and contributed to them in a vital fashion, Schirmann avoided political and social commentary in his work and in public; Fleischer, on the other hand, for all the nationalism evident in his scholarship—a defiant pride in the worth of Hebrew culture through the ages and a deep-seated suspicion of what he called the "mirage" of the cultural symbiosis that produced the Hebrew poetry of Spain—spoke out on the most sensitive of subjects, on several occasions offering up a devastating critique of religious and political complacency in Israeli society and, after the 1994 Ramadan and Purim massacre of Muslim worshippers by an extremist right-wing religious Jewish doctor in Hebron, delivering an astounding denunciation in a prophetic vein of this "spiller of blood" and his pious backers, "rabbis of wickedness . . . and sages of darkness," whose actions "refute our entire history . . . and pervert [Judaism's] sacred teachings."

And yet, for all their differences, Fleischer's achievement both complements and extends that of his teacher. First and foremost, the writing of both was grounded in utter and almost mind-boggling immersion in

a field that evolved radically as they wrote—which is another way of saying that the Geniza figured profoundly in their work. Second, while Schirmann concentrated on the secular poetry of Spain and viewed it, in a sense, against the backdrop of later developments in European literature, Fleischer focused, for the most part, on liturgical poetry and looked to the East (Palestine and Iraq) for keys to the Spanish accomplishment. (That said, he also made major discoveries of critical early secular and sacred

Andalusian poetry, rescuing from oblivion—in addition to Dunash's wife—the still too little known work of Yosef ibn Avitor and several key poems by Menahem ben Saruk, the poet Dunash displaced at Hasdai's court.) With this bi- or even trifocal concentration on the intricate connections between the liturgy of late antiquity, the *piyyut* of the early Middle Ages, and the Hebrew poetry of Spain, Fleischer in particular lived the Geniza as few people have and with it helped change the face of Jewish literature. Its revelations seep through all he wrote, and his accounts of what has been found there are among the most inspired since Schechter's.

Fleischer's fulcral understanding, together with his finely honed rhetorical skills, allowed him to articulate the wonder of the Geniza maybe better than any who came before him. In singularly acute fashion, for instance, he describes the discovery of the Geniza as a fourfold miracle: How else, he asks, can one explain the fact that so many thousands of documents were discovered after nearly nine hundred years of utter neglect? And, at the same time, how is it possible that so many thousands of documents were *not* discovered over the course of nearly nine hundred years? Third, that the documents *were* discovered, *when* they were discovered, *by someone who could recognize their worth and knew what to do with them* (that is, Schechter—after others such as Adler and Neubauer had come so close), is itself nothing short of miraculous. And finally, it is a miracle of at least a minor sort that the contents of the Geniza were *only gradually* revealed to scholars, who otherwise might have been paralyzed by the overwhelming size of the find.

In the final lecture he ever gave, just a year before he passed away, at age seventy-eight after a difficult illness, Fleischer stepped back and surveyed a century of, in its way, death-defying cultural accomplishment. "The study of the Geniza," he declared,

> has given us not so much a quantitative increase in knowledge (although that has been immense); and not just a qualitative advance that surpasses expectation (although this has been astonishing); and not merely an influx (dizzying as that has been) of dates and names, of hues and lights and voices. The recovery of the Geniza has meant, rather, the spectacular completion of a breathtaking landscape, the perfect, harmonious, and inevitable unity of which all of a sudden seems revealed.

Nearly five decades of devotion to that culture and its multiple miracles left Fleischer marveling at "the tens of thousands of hitherto unknown poems . . . by hundreds of unknown poets [that] were," as he saw it, "suddenly, with the Geniza's discovery, released like spirits or ghosts through the square opening of that sealed room at the end of the women's gallery of the Ben Ezra synagogue." As he sought to retrieve at least some of their lines, in painstaking and piecemeal fashion, he could sense, he said on more than one occasion, the poets themselves present beside him, guiding him through the labyrinth of redemption.

10

A Mediterranean Society

"SECRET," announced the pale blue aerogramme, handwritten in quick, clear Hebrew strokes, in Cambridge, on Saturday night, October 8, 1955. Inside the round "ס," or *samech*, of the first letter of the word *sodi*, the correspondent—the German-born Arabist, philologist, and ethnographer S. D. Goitein—had inscribed sideways and in tiny letters *"today it's very hot!"* But the unseasonably warm English weather was hardly what prompted Goitein to write in such a thrilled flush to his

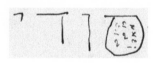 wife, Theresa ("my beloved *Ima*," as he called her, using the Hebrew for "mother"), who had stayed home in Jerusalem while he spent the summer and early fall as he'd done for the previous several years, shuttling between the Geniza collections of various British libraries in search of historical documents for a volume he'd planned about the medieval India trade.

Replete with a footnote and several professorial asides, the letter described what had taken place the day before, on the Jewish holiday of Hoshana Rabba, which is traditionally considered to be the date when final judgment—begun on Rosh HaShana, the new year—is sealed.

I never imagined that I'd have news and discoveries this time. But yesterday the head of the library, Creswick (pronounced Cresick), together with the

head of the Oriental department, Miss Skilliter, took me to the seventh floor,
under the roof—I was amazed to find that the attic of this magnificent build-
ing is just like ours: pipes and water tanks (. . . and the tanks were exposed!)
and what do I see? Actual crates, as they were sent from Egypt in
1897 . . . Schechter deposited here what he thought no longer of any value,
but not a quarter hour had passed before I pulled out a piece of a large letter
(60 lines) that's among the very best I have about travel to India—along
with another 3 documents. The librarian . . . was clearly excited and ordered
the crate to be taken down to a special room so that we could examine it (I
mean me with the help of Miss Skilliter). And so this morning, even though
it was Saturday and a holiday [Simhat Torah], I decided to celebrate the Sab-
bath by rummaging around in a virgin geniza, really like Schechter in his
day, and I stood there all morning long,* taking things out and sorting
them. . . .

*wearing a brown overall

More than their biblical first names, Cambridge setting, loving wives, erudition, and overalls joined Solomon Schechter and Shelomo Dov Goitein, who might, in a very loose sense, be dubbed respectively the *discoverer* and *rediscoverer* of the Cairo Geniza. In 1896, Schechter had rushed "in haste and great excitement" to tell Agnes Lewis about his identification of the Ben Sira fragment, asking that she "not speak yet about the matter," and now, almost sixty years later, Goitein dashed off in his enthused yet precise way this report to Theresa, also emphatically insisting on silence about his new find: "It's absolutely forbidden for anyone besides [David] Baneth [Goitein's cousin, close friend, and fellow Jerusalem scholar] to know about this. The 'librarian' asked me not even to tell the Cambridge people themselves."

In a more substantive sense, both Schechter and Goitein understood almost intuitively the promise locked in those cluttered upstairs rooms—one in the Ben Ezra synagogue, the second under the eaves of the Cambridge library. His first encounter with the material that would soon come to be known as the New Series and more than double the size of the Taylor-Schechter collection—as it also produced some of the most important fragments in the entire Geniza stash—Goitein later described in a published account: he was, he wrote, led by Creswick and Skilliter from the manuscript reading room to "the uppermost floor, just under the roof," where he beheld a crate "of dimensions I have never seen in my life. In huge letters the address Alexandria-Liverpool was written on it, but also, in another script . . . the word: Rubbish."

There it was, yet again: the wholesale dismissal of the Geniza manuscripts as nothing more than a rag-paper and parchment scrap heap was, as we have seen, a very old story. Another Shelomo, the desperate nineteenth-century Jerusalem bookseller Shelomo Aharon Wertheimer, could attest to this, having been informed repeatedly by the Cambridge library that so many of the Cairene items he'd offered for sale were "not wanted" or "worthless." Schechter himself had, after his own sometimes single-minded fashion, been blind to the value of those "Egyptian fragments" before he'd recognized the leaf of Ben Sira and caught the Geniza bug. And even after he'd realized the worth of the cache and worked so hard to rescue it, others had been decidedly unimpressed: "About a score of years ago," wrote Schechter's nutty if forbiddingly learned nemesis in the Ben Sira controversy, D. S. Margoliouth, in 1913, "the University of Cambridge was presented with the contents of a huge waste paper basket, imported from Egypt, where such stores abound. The material contained in these repositories is almost always valueless, like the gods of the Gentiles unable to do good or harm, and so neither worth preserving nor worth destroying." While certain Geniza finds were widely celebrated, a dump-like aura stuck to those fragments left behind after Schechter's departure for New York and the subsequent deaths of Charles Taylor (in 1908), Ernest Worman (in 1909), and the conscientious, bird- and bug-obsessed Cambridge librarian Francis Jenkinson (in 1923). Just four years after Jenkinson passed away in a Hampstead nursing home, one library assistant described what remained in the Taylor-Schechter boxes as "nothing of any interest or value. The late librarian would not allow anything to be destroyed which is the only reason why they were not burned years ago." Writing a report in the 1940s, Jenkinson's successor was only a bit more circumspect about his experience with one particular Geniza crate. "I have," he admitted, "once or twice rummaged in the box (a large 'tea chest') and imagine that they are the leavings after Dr. Schechter had picked over the whole collection. They might from their size and condition be fairly described as a dust-heap . . . [and] seem (to an ignorant person) to be a hopeless case."

Goitein, though, knew otherwise, and, like Schechter before him, had an uncanny gift for recognizing treasure where others saw trash. And as Schechter's "chance" encounter with Agnes Lewis in downtown Cambridge and subsequent identification of the Ben Sira fragment had in fact been the product of years of inadvertent preparation, so Goitein's unexpected "rediscovery" of the Geniza didn't just happen with a random tap on the shoulder from Creswick. ("I see you here every year working assiduously on our Geniza collections. I should like to show you something," was how Creswick put it in the too-stiff-to-be-true account that Goitein offered in print. In his diary that evening, he noted simply "2:30 with Creswick and Skilliter to the seventh floor, under the roof.") Whatever the librarian's actual words were, by the time Creswick invited the small-boned, balding, bespectacled, and vaguely Mr. Magoo–like professor to ascend to the attic and have a look, S. D. Goitein had, unknowingly but rigorously, readied himself to fathom the significance of those crates.

B efore Goitein—or B.G., as it might be called, given the eventual scale of his accomplishment—scholars of the Geniza materials had almost always focused their energies on major trends, shall we say, in Jewish pietism. What mattered were liturgical fragments, pages of Talmud and midrash, rabbinical rulings, and documents relating to important political and religious developments, or to the lives and leanings of medieval Jewish communal leaders. The dramatic discoveries like the Ben Sira fragments, the *piyyutim* of Yannai, and the Damascus Document commanded the lion's share of academic and popular attention during the first half of the twentieth century. While the materials were rich, the linguistic range of the texts in question remained, at this stage, narrow: fragments written in Hebrew and Aramaic lent themselves most readily to translation and commentary by scripturally savvy scholars of Judaica.

Several others had, it's true, ventured beyond the traditional languages of sacred Jewish writing and into the scrappier realm of Judeo-Arabic, which amounted to the Hebrew transliteration of an unadorned middle register of Arabic. This Judeo-Arabic was once the fluid language of most nonliterary written communication and instruction for the Jews of North Africa, Spain, and the Muslim East. (Classical Arabic— written in Arabic characters and considered by believing Muslims to be the holy language of Koranic revelation—was more formal, uniform, and elaborate.) At the start of the century, Ernest Worman had made a very preliminary attempt to detail some of the documents written in this language, and the historian Jacob Mann had taken a stab at Judeo-Arabic in some of his later work. In pre-state Palestine, scholars like David Baneth, whom his confidant Goitein regarded as "the father of the Geniza project," had deepened these Arabic explorations.

Language apart, however, the scholarship of this period still adhered by and large to the same high-minded conception of the Jewish past that had prevailed during Schechter's day. This approach was Victorian and set in a major key, for full orchestra: "The History of the World . . . ," wrote Thomas Carlyle in 1888, "was the Biography of Great Men." Eminent medievals like Maimonides, Yehuda HaLevi, Saadia, and the other Gaonim of Babylonia and Palestine played the prominent roles. Living proof of this all-star approach remains visible in twenty-first-century Jerusalem's leafy Rehavia neighborhood, where the Hebrew University was housed in the early years of the state (as was the Schocken Institute), and where so many of the Geniza scholars—including Goitein, Baneth, Zulay, and Schirmann—lived, alongside Gershom Scholem and much of the rest of the university faculty. (Indeed, had a large, well-placed bomb hit Rehavia in the early 1950s, it would have dealt a near-fatal blow to modern Jewish thought.) As a member of the Neighborhood Committee in the mid-1920s, yet another Geniza scholar, Simha Assaf, was charged with the task of naming the local streets, and for this purpose drew from "the period of Spanish splendor, which is close to the heart of every Jew." So it is that one can to this day stroll down Ramban (Nahmanides) Avenue, take a right on Ibn Gabirol, head left at Abarbanel, right on Avraham ibn Ezra, right again on Alharizi, and end up in a park that was once known as Yehuda HaLevi Boulevard and later as the Garden of the Kuzari—a jungle-gym-filled playground named for the poet's most important philosophical work.

While Goitein, too, was steeped in the work of the members of this Golden Age pantheon, had *he* named Rehavia's streets, the map might have looked different. The historical figures who interested him most—shopkeepers and scribes, beggars and brides—were those whose lives emerged from the fragments that earlier scholars had brushed aside as (once again that scowling estimation) without worth. "Business letter, and therefore valueless" was, Goitein noted wryly, the telling description of one such Geniza item in the catalog of a "most distinguished library." But Goitein's approach was intensely democratic and, as he understood from the very start of his work with the documents, it was precisely those fragments of a more humdrum-seeming daily nature—court depositions, merchants' accounts, bills of divorce, and the like—that would allow him to bring the Mediterranean world of the High Middle Ages alive on the page, in all its quotidian glory.

That start, however, was a long time coming. Surrounded by Geniza scholars and Geniza studies from his earliest days in Jerusalem,

Goitein had, he said, "studiously avoided" the field for years. He "read the relevant publications, though not regularly," and had the sense that "Geniza research was sufficiently taken care of by others." Besides, his hands and head were plenty full without it.

When he'd first come to Palestine in 1923, at age twenty-three, on a boat with his friend Gershom Scholem, Goitein, the Frankfurt- and Berlin-trained scholar of Islam, idealistic Zionist educator, and aspiring playwright, taught Bible and Hebrew at Haifa's prestigious Reali High School. In the wake of the lukewarm public reaction to a turgid five-act costume drama he'd published, about a Jewish woman burned at the stake in twelfth-century France (particularly devastating was a serialized, three-part pan of the play in one of the leading Hebrew newspapers of the day by Shalom Spiegel, Goitein's colleague at the Reali school, brother of Hollywood producer Sam Spiegel, and himself a future Geniza scholar), Goitein seems to have realized his severe limitations as a literary writer and been forced to consider how he might put his lively imagination to better use.

So it was that in 1927 he accepted an invitation to move from Haifa to Jerusalem and take the job of the first-ever lecturer in the History of Islam and the Muslim Peoples at the Hebrew University's newly founded School of Oriental Studies. "The whole student body turned up" for his

initial lecture, he would later remember, because "everyone was curious to learn something about the Arabs." Soon after, he married the aristocratic and strong-willed Theresa Gottlieb, a Latvian eurhythmics teacher and children's book writer who had, as a younger woman, flirted seriously with political anarchism and appeared as a butterfly in one of Berlin director Max Reinhardt's elaborate theatrical productions. By the late 1930s, with three children and a live-at-home mother (Theresa's) to support, they were both working hard to make ends meet: in addition to his full-time job as chief inspector of Jewish and Arab schools in Palestine, or—as he preferred to introduce himself—"His Majesty's senior education officer in Palestine," Goitein was teaching almost daily at the university.

He was absorbed, as well, in his own scholarship, which included intensive "ethnolinguistic" research on Yemenite Jews—the "most Jewish and most Arab of all Jews" he called them—and he found time to translate several volumes from Judeo-Arabic to Hebrew, to edit a lengthy work of classical Arabic history, and to write a number of "popular" books (on education, on the Yemenites) as well as dozens of academic articles, poems, letters, and reviews, even as he rose early every morning to put on his phylacteries and study a page of Gemara before doing his calisthenics. A grueling schedule of professional and social meetings filled his week, and even the Sabbath day was rigidly regimented: Torah study with his children in the morning, followed by a brisk and botanically instructive hike through the meadows and hills. Inquisitive and businesslike, he would also pause along the route to talk with—really *interview*—the Palestinian peasants working in their fields, or to discuss a new publication with some learned acquaintance. Later, he might set scraps of these conversations down in his journal, which reads at times like an anthropologist's telegraphic field notes. (Written mostly in Hebrew, this diary also contains occasional, particularly private notations in the obscure and extinct South Arabian alphabet.) Aside from the strictly enforced two hours of naptime silence that reigned in the

Goiteins' Abarbanel Street apartment every afternoon, S. D. Goitein rarely stopped moving.

To an onlooker it might have seemed, in other words, as though the spry and rather officious little man was suffering from a highly refined, intellectual case of A.D.D. One nonagenarian former student (now an eminent professor emeritus) recalls that Goitein was, during these years, "like a bumblebee, tasting all the flowers" and, according to Goitein's own diary, Theresa described him as the human equivalent of Grand Central Station, with trains constantly coming and going in different directions.

But then, for a critical month and a half in 1948, all those trains screeched to a standstill—and S. D. Goitein's life was altered unexpectedly and forever.

The circumstances surrounding this pivotal point in his own—and the Geniza's—history are oddly opaque, though we do know this much: with war still wracking the two-month-old state of Israel and Goitein's political mood darker than ever (he had never been sanguine about the prospects for peace, but the recent violence on all sides had compelled him to write even grimmer-than-usual letters to friends abroad, proclaiming, for instance, "I fear that our entire existence—our lives and our property—will be destroyed in a very short time if a miracle doesn't occur"), he had set off for Europe, charged with what he vaguely called "a special mission." Though the echo is inadvertent, his terminology was, bizarrely, almost identical to that Mathilde Schechter had used in a letter, some fifty-two years before, to describe Solomon's top-secret trip to Cairo.

To this day, no one knows for certain what Goitein's mission was—not his children, not his students. His diaries from the period are frustratingly blank, and his correspondence reveals few clues. There are theories (he was sent on a diplomatic errand by the Israeli government, he was dispatched to retrieve a manuscript or book collection for the National Library), but little to go on in terms of hard facts. And while he would later describe at least part of his trip as "a most innocent undertaking," it stands to reason that something urgent must have caused him to board a Piper plane in recently besieged and still tense Jerusalem and bid good-bye to his wife and children for a full three months. His sense of civic and domestic responsibility was, after all, unflagging, and the situation at home was dire: there were battles and bombings everywhere, and Theresa was serving as a volunteer nurse and witnessing all kinds of atrocities up close. Although it isn't clear that he knew how long he would be gone or that he planned from the outset for his trip to take him beyond France, he left in July for the International Congress of Orientalists in Paris and returned only in October, from Hungary—on, it seems, a plane filled with frozen chickens, shipped for the Israeli army at the cost of forty grush [at the time, the Israeli equivalent of cents] a kilogram. "It's good," he quipped in a letter to his wife, "that I've lost weight." In his later writing about this period he dispensed with the joking and took pains to mince around the specifics of what or who compelled him to embark on the Hungarian stage of this journey. (He also never explained what he was doing in Paris for more than a month.) He had, he says, planned to spend just two weeks in Budapest, recently occupied by the Soviets. But the new Communist bureaucracy was not nearly as efficient as the middle-aged Germanic scholar, and Goitein was forced to wait. And wait. And as he was waiting (for a full six weeks), he bided his time at the Academy of Sciences— again, we don't really know why—where he had a chance to examine a small bundle of Geniza fragments from the David Kaufmann collection, that important gathering of manuscripts that had been housed in Hungary since Schechter's day and which had narrowly escaped destruction after the Nazi invasion in 1944.

The thin file that Goitein encountered that fateful autumn was apparently all that remained, after the war, of the documents that had been set aside much earlier in the century by the great Hungarian Orientalist Ignaz Goldziher, widely regarded as the founder of Islamology. A religious Jew and scholarly prodigy (he published his debut book—on the history and nature of Jewish prayer—at age twelve), Goldziher was the first European to study at the all-Muslim al-Azhar University in Cairo and was also the first to examine the Judeo-Arabic materials in the Kaufmann collection. "I can say," wrote the notoriously irascible genius in 1906, "that I found the contents of the [Kaufmann] documents of extraordinary interest. To say nothing of . . . the letters and inventories which bear direct witness to every aspect of life."

It may just have been a coincidence that in the year leading up to Goitein's trip to Hungary, he had published a spate of articles (several in Hebrew and one in Arabic, for a popular Egyptian journal) about Goldziher's life and work, and the relationship between the late master's decidedly uneasy Judaism and his fascination with Islam. As rendered by Goitein—who was himself, it's worth noting, not just a student of any and all aspects of Islamic civilization but descended from a long line of Hungarian and Moravian rabbis—Goldziher comes across as (like Goitein) unquenchably curious. Goldziher, Goitein writes, was someone who knew "how to create an enormous mosaic from the tiniest of tiny details, scattered in the most out-of-the-way places."

It may also have been mere chance that the Orientalist Congress where Goitein started his European trip that summer featured a presentation by the two Hungarian bibliophiles responsible for maintaining the Kaufmann collection. This was the first meeting of the learned society since World War II, and the director of the Budapest Rabbinical Seminary, Samuel Löwinger, and the school's then librarian (later director and himself an important Geniza researcher), Alexander Scheiber, used the occasion to announce that "the scholars surviving from the annihilated Jewry of a little European country take the liberty of reporting . . . on what has remained . . . from the Hebrew and Hebrew-Arabic MSS in Hungary." The black shadow of the Holocaust, one imagines, must have trailed every step of Goitein's trip, his first to Europe in years.

The mysteries of his "innocent undertaking" notwithstanding (in the

end he declared it a failure), there is, for our purposes, the more important question of just what it was, after all those decades of studious
avoidance, that suddenly drew Goitein so magnetically to the modest
bunch of twenty-one Geniza fragments that Löwinger and Scheiber
entrusted to him during his long wait in what he called their "ruined
city." In fact only seven of these fragments were, to his mind, of any
value. These included an eleventh-century letter from Jerusalem to Fustat, in which one man consoled another about the loss of a great deal of
money; an emotionally charged business letter concerning the delay of a
wood shipment sent to Spain from Kairouan; an epistolary account "in
very animated language" of a violent pirate attack; and a draft of plans
for a medieval fund-raising drive. (Slave girls and dancers figure prominently in the summary of the potential donors' valuable property.) The
rest of the fragments were, Goitein would later write—need we say
it?—just "scraps and tattered remains."

The ghostly presence in Budapest of the late Ignaz Goldziher, the
haunting psychological effects of the recent war, or wars—whatever the
cause, it is hardly an exaggeration to say that this little handful of nine-
hundred-year-old documents that had traveled the long distance from
the Nile basin to behind the Iron Curtain would turn out to be for
Goitein what the Archaic Torso of Apollo was for Rilke, an inanimate yet
somehow living presence insisting: *You must change your life.*

And he did. Although he would later tell the story as if it happened in
a flash, it seems to have taken several years for the implications of his
close encounter with the Kaufmann-Goldziher fragments to fully sink in.
(As late as 1952, he was still wondering aloud in his diary: "What should
I do now? Geniza & Yemen—both extremely difficult subjects though
also compelling.") But something had shifted, and, as a result of his
Hungarian trip, Goitein really did become in time a man with a special
mission: the unprecedented and obsessive collection of all the Geniza's
"daily" documents and their arrangement into a mosaic pattern as vast
and ornate as Goldziher's. So much so, in fact, that the name Goitein

would one day become practically synonymous with "Geniza." "Just now I feel I've entered into the period of creativity in my life," he would confide in his diary, a few years later, "which is to say, the period of long-term plans that will last till the grave, and beyond it." Already more than half a century old, S. D. Goitein had found his calling.

B orn in the first year of that century, Goitein had also—by the time he reckoned with the chill of cold war Budapest and the heat of war-torn Jerusalem, 1948—witnessed enough bloody history, Jewish and general, to make him seriously doubt the whole human race. This did not distinguish him from other members of his generation, though he was, by nature and according to those who knew him well, a pessimist, albeit a forward-looking and phenomenally enterprising pessimist. Having lived through all he'd lived through—what he would describe much later as "the heartbreak, horror and wrath . . . of so much human misery and degradation"—he might easily have seen in that diminished heap of Hungarian fragments nothing but a sign of woes past and still to come: further proof, if any were needed, that the Jews were congenitally condemned to cycle through an endless Möbius strip of "pain and piety," and this legacy destined to be ground into dust. Twenty years before Goitein reached Budapest, this "lachrymose" approach to Jewish history had been recognized, named—and challenged—by the eminent social historian Salo Baron, who saw in the works of earlier Jewish chroniclers a distorting tendency to overemphasize the place of suffering in accounts of their people's past. "Surely," Baron wrote in one of his most famous essays, published in 1928, "it is time to . . . adopt a view more in accord with historic truth."

For Baron, historic truth meant the record of what was, seen as grand demographic, economic, and communal themes that emerged slowly, almost geologically, over centuries. For Goitein, it meant descent into thousands and thousands of discrete particulars, grounded in the grittiest minutiae of daily life and language, and their eventual deployment in a larger frame. (Goitein invented a term to describe his work, calling himself an "interpretive sociographer," one who describes a culture by means of its texts.) The two visions were distinct yet connected in spirit, and, Goitein's pessimism notwithstanding, he would in time turn that "lachrymose conception of Jewish history" on its mournful head—not through polemic, but with his steady and even compulsive emphasis on a brimming history of *life.*

As he set out to begin writing that history, his excitement at the vividness of these weathered texts only grew. In one of his first published articles about the India trade—which Goitein called the "backbone" of medieval international commerce and which was the first subject he took up when he began his Geniza research—he described the thrill of holding in his hands these globe-trotting, thousand-year-old documents. Sailing with the merchants from India to Arabia to East Africa, then traveling across the desert and back on a boat down the Nile, they had finally made their way to Fustat, where they landed in the Geniza—and then crossed other seas to libraries in Europe and America, where Goitein sat and peered at them through his sensible mid-twentieth-century horn-rimmed glasses.

But what would he do with this literal and figurative sea of script? How could he begin to make sense of it? As he evolved a system for working with these letters and lists—whether elegantly calligraphed scrolls copied by trained scribes, or hastily scrawled scraps that the merchants themselves had dashed off on deck as their ships pulled out of harbor—Goitein proved himself a master pointillist with a keen ability to grasp, perhaps even more fully than Goldziher could, the allure of the micro *and* the macro, and the cosmos each implied. He knew that in order to prepare the work he had conceived as his "India Book"—a collection of documents concerning these North African Jewish traders, whose business drew them east—it would not be enough to pluck out and carefully read a handful of texts; rather, he would need to comb through enormous tracts of Geniza documents to find all the letters, court records, and business accounts relevant to the theme, and only then proceed with parsing. By 1954 and the publication of his "preliminary report" on the subject, he had already surveyed all the known documentary contents of eleven Geniza collections on four continents; he'd copied the contents of hundreds of fragments by hand and begun the laborious process of deciphering, translating, and annotating them. Tools, dyes, drugs, perfumes, utensils, articles of clothing—the names of these medieval things were often obscure to even a highly knowledgeable and philologically savvy modern reader like Goitein. So it was that he also went about fashioning a "card index of technical terms," as if he were compiling a dictionary— unpacking the roots and lexical implications of the merchants' words themselves for clues to the nature of these garments, vessels, and potions.

Meanwhile, like those traders, he too had set sail from a Mediterranean port as, in 1957, he accepted a regular position at the University of Pennsylvania, and, with a certain heaviness of heart but an extremely clear sense of purpose, left Israel and its multiple distractions (and minuscule research budgets) behind, turning himself over—when he wasn't teaching—almost exclusively to work on the Geniza. As he was beginning to consider the prospect of widening the lens of his research both methodologically and geographically and starting to reckon with the contents of those unsorted crates in the Cambridge library attic, chance once again played a part: an offer to write a more general book for an American publisher arrived, and "this decided the matter," as he wrote later. "I was off India and on the Mediterranean."

From his first contact with the Fustat documents, Goitein had understood that all the Geniza's bits and shards would be next to useless unless placed into meaningful relation and somehow glued back together. This refusal to simply settle for one part of a larger whole, this need for connection—between the tiny detail and the big picture, Judaism and Islam, East and West, past and present—would be the force that propelled and inspired him to labor doggedly for the next three decades. His typed research reports from this time refer to "The Cairo Geniza Documents Project," as though he were the head of a large, lab-coated team building the bomb or mapping the genome. Setting out to create a mammoth collection of thousands of index cards, photostats, and transcriptions that he came to call his "Geniza Lab(oratorium)," he apportioned different parts of the work to a small group of graduate students; at this early stage he envisioned an eight-volume collection of texts to be brought out in twelve years, under the names of these various "workers." (This was his word.) Yet during this period he labored mostly alone, and the devotion he displayed was as ecclesiastical as it was scientific. And as the project evolved in shape and emphasis, his collaborators faded out of the picture—though he would still insist, as Schecter had, that "a whole generation of scholars will be needed to do this job, each working in a specialized field." Rather comically, he considered his own nearly superhuman undertaking just a preliminary "inventory" of the documentary Geniza. Making gradual pilgrimages to every Geniza collection throughout the world—he referred to Cambridge as "Mecca"—and attempting to reckon in the most exacting manner with all the nonliterary material contained there, he became a kind of Geniza-divine, dedicated with monastic fervor to his vocation.

"I've completely stopped living and become the 'Genizer,'" he scribbled in his diary at around the time he made the switch from "India" to "the rest," as he put it. And what was "the rest"? He called it *A Mediterranean Society.*

The Geniza was, in Goitein's view, a massive and "erratic" repository of texts that offered "a true mirror of life, often cracked and blotchy, but very wide in scope and reflecting each and every aspect of the society that originated it. Practically everything for which writing was used," he enthused, "has come down to us." Fording through this sprawl

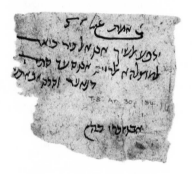

of disparate documents, Goitein was able to reconstruct in vital fashion and often astonishing detail everything from the nature of the medieval Mediterranean postal service to the Tuesday and Friday distribution of free bread to Fustat's Jewish poor to the practice of issuing letters of payment, remarkably similar to modern checks. (As Goitein discovered, one twelfth-century Fustat dweller wrote twenty such checks in a single month alone, each inscribed with the Hebrew word for truth, *emet*—also an abbreviation for Psalms 85:12, "Truth springs out of the earth," a rough medieval precursor to "for deposit only.") He surveyed with the same unflagging rigor nine-hundred-year-old attitudes toward messianism, remarriage, homosexuality, foreign travel, and pigeon-racing, and plumbed ancient correspondence and business accounts for clues about excommunication, social drinking, the price of flax, the Judeo-Arabic terminology for so-called sweating sickness, the total absence in this older Middle Eastern world of the Bar Mitzva ritual, and the prevalence in the same context of good, hot take-out food.

The bracelets and pendants, wimples and robes, silver spoons and sofas of the time were conjured by Goitein in all their subtle texture.

Colors in particular are enumerated with fanatical precision in the documents, and he was zealous about getting each tint right, describing partridge-eye-hued and chickpea-patterned silks alongside linens the shades of honey, lead, cream of tartar, gazelle's blood, asparagus, pomegranate, and pistachio. And this "color intoxication" was, he reported, shared by the sexes: the veils that covered the women when they went outdoors were shed at home to reveal a "gorgeous variety of colorful robes," while "medieval males . . . must have looked like tropical singing birds." And such vibrancy wasn't just a matter of clothing: as he closely read wills, estate inventories, and especially trousseau lists (handwritten accounts of all the pretty and practical things that Jewish brides brought with them into marriage, and which served as a tactile kind of insurance in case of divorce, widowhood, or desertion), he was also able to see—and unfurl for readers—the spectacular tapestry of medieval Mediterranean culture at large.

In this relatively open "religious democracy" Jews were free to practice nearly all the professions, from dyer to stucco worker to banker to phlebotomist to cheese maker to clerk to specialist in carp pickles. They could and did enter into close business partnerships with Muslims and Christians, and lived in any part of town they pleased. "The Geniza reveals a situation very similar to that prevailing today in the United States," he wrote in the mid-1960s, linking, as he often did, his own present to the past of Fustat. "There were many neighborhoods predominantly Jewish, but hardly any that were exclusively so." No ghetto existed in that setting, and members of different communities and religions often owned or rented apartments in the very same building. In Goitein's estimation, even in the more heavily Jewish areas of Fustat, at least half the Jews had gentile neighbors.

The "loosely organized and competitive" society reflected in the Geniza documents reminded Goitein of the "vigorous, free-enterprise society" of the United States, while the American obsession with "endless fund-raising campaigns and all that goes with them, . . . [the] general involvement in public affairs and deep concern (or lip service, as the case may be) for the underdog" also had their medieval Egyptian antecedents.

"We do not," he wrote, "wear turbans here; but, while reading many a Geniza document one feels quite at home."

The "classical Geniza period," Goitein announced on the opening pages of the very first volume of *A Mediterranean Society*, was characterized by "relative tolerance and liberalism," and he closed the circle, five volumes, some three thousand pages, and several decades later by praising this "civilized world, of people who knew how to behave, who were considerate, paying proper attention to their fellowmen." That said, he was careful not to blur too casually the boundaries between medieval and modern sensibilities: "Before characterizing the Jewish community in Geniza times as a 'religious democracy,' I hesitated very much," he wrote, years after first coining the term. "I use the word 'religious' in its Latin sense of 'binding.' It was a democracy bound by divine law. This means that there were certain tenets, injunctions, and practices that could not be questioned because they were laid down in the Torah or Talmud. That democracy had no 'law makers,' only authorized interpreters of a law that was freely recognized by everyone."

Neither did he paint an overly idealized picture of that time and place. As *dhimmi*, or "protected" citizens, the Jews and Christians of the Fatimid (and later Ayyubid) empires were—from the age of nine and without exception—each expected to pay a yearly poll tax. For all but the most well-off, the charge was onerous. Goitein described the "season of the tax," when payment was due, as a time of "horror, dread, and misery." And there were occasional periods—under the rule of the psychotic caliph al-Hakim, for instance—when the *dhimmi* were harshly persecuted. (Like the Church of the Holy Sepulcher in Jerusalem, the Ben Ezra synagogue was demolished during al-Hakim's reign, around 1012, and rebuilt afterward: the Geniza chamber dates, it would seem, from the time after its reconstruction.) It is clear from Goitein's rendering, however, that such bald oppression was the exception, not the rule; likewise, the regular payment of the poll tax was, all things considered, a small price to pay for the power it granted these prosperous, Arabic-speaking Jews to more or less govern their own communities and practice their religion as they saw fit. A certain deference to Islam and to Muslims was expected among those the Prophet Muhammad had dubbed the "People of the Book" (non-Muslims to whom scripture had been divinely revealed)—but for the most part, the Jews of this Mediterranean society fared much better than they did under Christian rule; they were left to pray, work, study, eat, marry, divorce, dress (in most circumstances), and even hand down legal judgment as they themselves determined.

Apart from the broader social synthesis he coaxed from the heaps of raw material he'd gathered over decades, Goitein was able to limn striking portraits of some of the individuals who made up that Mediterranean society. His fascination with a huge array of the "characters" who formed this cast of actual thousands was periscopic, swiveling to take in people like the previously overlooked—though thoroughly unforgettable—"Wuhsha the Broker," about whom, Goitein's family recalls, he would often gossip, as though he had just bumped into her that morning.

Known in the documents by her nickname—which Goitein translates as "Désirée" or "Object of Yearning," though the three-letter Arabic root also implies "Wild One"—Wuhsha (whose real name was Karima, the daughter of Ammar) turns up more often than any other woman in the papers once held in the Ben Ezra synagogue. A rich, eleventh-century divorcée with a flourishing business as a sort of private pawnbroker, she also had a (Jewish) lover named Hassun, and bore him a son out of wedlock.

Despite the patriarchal nature of Geniza society, and the fact that the economic lives of its women were, as a general rule, constricted, Wuhsha seems to have been perfectly able to take care of herself. Various weathered legal documents give us a strong sense of Wuhsha the shrewd businesswoman, Wuhsha the hard-nosed wheeler-dealer. But in many respects the most interesting fragments related to Wuhsha are those that concern her private life—or the place where her private life became very public indeed.

A single page remains of a remarkable court deposition, written after Wuhsha's death. Her son, Abu Sa'd, was now grown and apparently eager to marry; in order to do so, he had to prove that he was not the product of an incestuous relationship, and so witnesses were summoned to attest to his paternity. The first man described how he had been sitting one day, years before, with Hillel ben Eli—a well-known scribe of the time, who had written Wuhsha's trousseau list, and whom Goitein describes as her confidant. Wuhsha turned to Hillel, in urgent need of advice. "I had an affair with Hassun and conceived from him," she explained. (The words for "I had an affair," *waqat ma'*, mean literally "I fell with," though as Goitein explains, they might be translated as "I got into a quagmire with" or, with a slightly altered preposition and more bluntly, "I slept with.") She was afraid that Hassun—who was a Palestinian refugee, so to speak, from Ascalon, which was under threat of Crusader invasion, and who Goitein suspects already had a wife there—would deny being the father of her child.

Her friend Hillel seems to have been unfazed by this news of Wuhsha's dalliance. Without batting a scribal eyelid, he advised her to set up a trap in which several witnesses would surprise Hassun in Wuhsha's apartment. (For a man to relax alone like that in the home of an unmarried woman could—to modesty-minded medievals—mean only one shameful thing.) By doing so she would be able to confirm a sexual relationship with Hassun and, at least by circumstantial evidence, prove him the would-be deadbeat dad.

The story of Wuhsha's little sting operation is repeated in the document by a ritual slaughterer who lived downstairs from her and who described how she had invited a couple of other neighbors to come up to her place "for something." He explains: "The two went up with her and found Hassun sitting in her apartment and . . ." the badly damaged manuscript gives out here, but picks up with the telling " . . . wine and perfumes . . ." and breaks off again, suggestively.

Others were less understanding than Hillel and the neighbors. According to testimony provided in the same document, Wuhsha—whose unorthodox sexual situation was apparently no secret around town—had put in an appearance at the Babylonian synagogue on Yom Kippur, and the head of the community had noticed her . . . and promptly kicked her out.

However mortifying it must have been for Wuhsha to be expelled from synagogue on the holiest day of the year, she had her pride—and she also had the last laugh. In her will, written by the same Hillel ben Eli, she made a point of leaving an equal amount of money to each of the synagogues of Fustat, including the Babylonians who had given her the boot. The funds were earmarked "for oil so that people may study at night." And while she piously promised a respectable 10 percent of her estate to charity, she also stipulated that "not one penny" should go to Hassun, and she provided lavishly for her own funeral: At a time when two dinars could support a lower-middle-class family for a month, she set aside a full fifty dinars for this posthumous extravaganza since "the socially ostracized Wuhsha wanted," according to Goitein, "to show off and prove to everyone what a great woman she was."

Finally, though, it was Wuhsha's son, Abu Sa'd, then still a child, who was her main concern: she left him a good deal of money, as well as "all I possess in cash and kind, in rugs and carpets," and she made provisions for his education. She named a teacher who should instruct him about the Bible and prayer book "to the degree it is appropriate that he should know them," and she set aside funds for the teacher's salary, ordering that he be given "a blanket and a sleeping carpet so that he can stay with" the boy. Wuhsha may have been unusual for her time, but she was still a Jewish mother.

.   .   .

At the very opposite end of the Egyptian social scale was the tortured figure of Abraham Maimonides (1186–1237), with whom Goitein chose to bring *A Mediterranean Society* to its melancholy close. Although time has not been especially kind to Abraham and though he faced serious controversy in his day, this "perfect man with a tragic fate" was much more than the only son of the renowned Moses Maimonides. Abraham, in Goitein's words, "stood for everything regarded as praiseworthy in the society described in this book." He was also, as several other commentators have noted, a figure with whom Goitein himself seems to have identified deeply.

The two had a long history together. In 1936, as a hyper-engaged Hebrew University scholar of Islam, Goitein had been asked to translate a book of Abraham's responsa—or rabbinic answers to petitioners' questions—from Judeo-Arabic to Hebrew. "I developed quite a personal affection for him," Goitein wrote of that early encounter with the scholar, physician, and communal leader known for his blend of humility and firmness, as well as for what his doting father called his "subtle intelligence and kind nature." Over the course of Goitein's decades spent in the company of the Geniza materials, he had made the assessment of Abraham's legacy a kind of pet project, and collected numerous letters and records that pertained to him, as well as more than seventy-five Geniza documents in *Abraham's own hand*—a prototypically hard-to-read doctor's hand, as it happens, whose Hebrew letters run together in an almost uninterrupted flow that looks much like Arabic.

Up to Goitein's final months, in 1985, he had been laboring late into his nights to complete *A Mediterranean Society*—the comprehensive, several-thousand-page work that he continued to refer to as "only a sketch." He and Theresa had moved to Princeton in 1971, when he retired from teaching and became a long-term member of the Institute for Advanced Study there; he converted the living room of their modest, green clapboard house into his study and the headquarters of his Geniza

Lab, and wrote most of the last three volumes in this quiet suburban setting. While he had proceeded according to a typically punctilious schedule through the first four install-ments (and continued to pub-lish other books and numerous articles, even as he dashed off

or dictated letters by the score, admitting to one correspondent in 1977 that "sometimes I write up to twenty . . . a day"), the fifth and final volume was, as one of his Princeton colleagues remembered after his death, "the most difficult to conceptualize and write." No precedent existed in either Islamic or Jewish studies for offering, as Goitein did, a summation of this sort: an extended meditation on the *inner* life of the medieval Mediterranean individual as it was revealed in the Geniza documents. Now, at the twilight of a long, fertile, and intensely varied career, he had chosen to return to the place he'd set out from as a young scholar—to Abraham Maimonides, who represented, in Goitein's words, "all the best found in medieval Judaism, as it developed within Islamic civilization."

Like his father before him, the charismatic Abraham had served as Rayyis al-Yahud, the head of the Jews—representative of Egyptian Jewry before the Muslim authorities and the supreme spiritual and secu-lar authority within the community. His political career, though, was not what distinguished him for Goitein. Rather, it was how he "united in a single person three spiritual trends that were usually at odds with each other": a total mastery of traditional Jewish sources; a "fervor bordering on faith" in the Greek sciences; and greatness as a teacher of religious ethics.

Beyond that, he was a visionary religious reformer, a rationally

minded mystic who was outspoken in his condemnation of the superficial and luxury-loving behavior of so many of his fellow Fustat Jews. As
an alternative, Abraham reiterated in detail the laws that bound the Jewish community and proposed various synagogue reforms: the washing of
feet before prayer, numerous prostrations, and the lifting of hands heav-
enward in supplication—as at the mosque. He had also gathered around
him a small band of pietistic disciples. Drawing directly from the Sufi
teachings that swirled through the Middle Eastern air at the time, he
described the virtues of the "special way" or "high paths" to be followed
by this elect group and went so far as to praise the rag-wool-wearing,
night-vigil-keeping bands of Sufi—that is, Muslim—novices as being
truer descendants of the biblical Prophets than the Jews of the age. He
longed, it seems, to bring his select band of "Jewish Sufis" together as a
community of initiates, dedicated to the ascetic life, the contemplation
of secret knowledge, and the striving toward "the arrival at the end of
the way, the attainment of the goals of the mystic."

Yet for all Abraham's prophetic pronouncements about "high paths,"
it was his entanglement in far *lower* matters—in the mundane business of
serving as his community's all-in-one administrator—that emerged
from the pile of Abraham-related documents that Goitein unearthed in
the Geniza. While Moses Maimonides had been the official head of
Egypt's Jews on and off for just a few years and was known to have
"groaned under" the load of this work, his son served in this distracting
capacity for his entire adult life, from the age of nineteen until his death
at fifty-one.

Goitein found it "appalling" that Abraham was forced to play so many
roles at once: he presided as judge at sessions of the Fustat court and
penned numerous written responsa to legal questions, many drafts of
which turned up in the Geniza. (These Dear Rabbi queries concerned
everything from sexual relations with female slaves to the milking of
sheep on the Sabbath.) He was, at the same time, chief of welfare ser-

vices, responsible for the poor and sick, the widows and orphans of his city: Goitein counted more than fifty orders of payment (salaries, subventions, donations) in Abraham's own hand from a single year alone. As Geniza letters attest, he managed the hiring and firing of communal personnel and was frequently required to smooth the ruffled feathers of various miffed provincial dignitaries. Besides having to snuff out the rash of political wildfires that flared around his own tenure as Rayyis, he often served as peacemaker, intervening, for instance, in a nasty power struggle between the warring members of a prominent Alexandria family. He also performed weddings and acted as registrar of all Jewish marriages and divorces, and he worked, too, as his own legal proofreader; scribal standards had fallen off by his time, and Goitein discovered court documents that Abraham himself had corrected.

And then there was his day job in Cairo, where he served as personal physician to the caliph and overworked doctor at the government hospital. All this *before* struggling to find the time to sit still and write his works of religious scholarship. As teacher and leader of his band of disciples, he also had yet another nagging task to attend to—since even wool-wearing, solitude-seeking ascetics required letters of recommendation.

In short, the workload was "staggering," and Abraham was, declared Goitein, "destroyed by it." The constant preoccupation with all this bureaucratic busyness brought about as well the eventual failure of his reforms and the disappearance of much of his writing, a process connected to the gradual decimation—by "persecutions, epidemic, and apostasy"—of the Egyptian Jewish community in the late Middle Ages. Besides the Geniza documents, only a small fraction of what Abraham wrote has come down to us—a collection of responsa and but a single volume of the ten-volume, or twenty-five-hundred-page, composition the younger Maimonides called "my book."

And here it is worth stopping to consider how it is that S. D. Goitein both did and did not resemble this "perfect man with a tragic fate." Like Abraham, Goitein was utterly fluent in the language of both Jewish and

Muslim texts. Like Abraham he combined a keen (if complex) religious faith with a no-less-fervent belief in the power of "science." He, too, had devoted himself to public service and teaching, alongside his own scholarship. Goitein's protégés and students—and the protégés and students of his protégés and students—stand at the forefront of historical Geniza studies today. Many of them express an almost filial affection for the fastidious man with the gentle smile, drill sergeant's attitude toward punctuality, and drily self-deprecating wit.

Like Abraham, Goitein was a traditionalist who had been known to offer up fairly radical ideas about that tradition and its possible transformation. According to his oldest daughter, Ayala, Goitein dreamed—somewhat vaguely—of founding "a new religion," and in the late 1950s he had published several articles about his vision for a political union called EurAfrAsia, which would stretch "between France and Persia on the one hand and between Sweden and Abyssinia on the other." This new world power would emerge from "the cradle of many of humanity's most essential achievements," Greek thinking and art, the three monotheistic religions, constitutional government, and so on. As a "more or less integrated political body" and common market, EurAfrAsia would be "a blessing for the world not only as a safeguard for peace, but also as a fountain for moral and spiritual values." This was just one of the surprising political proposals Goitein put forward over the years.

While he remained a committed and involved Zionist throughout his life, Goitein's precise political attitudes were notoriously difficult to pin down. One person close to him remembers him as being "very left wing," while another has called him a "hard liner [about] Israeli politics, an extreme conservative"; other characterizations have run the gamut between these poles. Perhaps it would be truest to say that his ideas evolved over time and depending on the historical circumstances. During the war in 1948, he wrote to one of his friends who belonged (as he himself did not) to Brit Shalom, a group of Hebrew University professors who advocated the establishment of a binational state in Palestine, and who in 1942 had formed a political party called Ihud (Union): "You know that I never joined 'Ihud'—not because I don't love the Arabs, [and] am not ready to give my life for a pact of friendship with them, but because I know that there's no chance of peace with them, as long as they believe they can just annihilate us." That said, shortly after the Six-Day War he concluded a Hebrew letter to his cousin David Baneth, back in Jerusalem, by asking: "Is there still talk in Israel about the possibility of a binational state? . . . Never before has the possibility existed as it does now—despite the tremendous difficulties."

In their very different contexts, both Abraham Maimonides and S. D. Goitein strove to realize the promise of what Goitein called the historical "symbiosis" between Arabs and Jews. "Biology defines symbiosis as the coexistence of two organisms so that both benefit from their being linked, and neither suffers loss," wrote Goitein, in 1949. "Just a thin line separates this desirable symbiosis from subordination or parasitism, which is to say, a situation in which two bodies are connected to one another and one drains the marrow of the other without giving anything in return. And there is a third kind of living-in-proximity: conflict and competition, which ends in the subjugation or destruction of one partner and the impoverishment of the other." The fact that the Jewish people are building their new life in close proximity to the Arabs, he wrote in Hebrew in that first year of Israel's existence, provides "the possibilities for dangers without measure and blessing without bounds."

He would return repeatedly to this notion of symbiosis throughout his intellectual life—most famously in his popular 1955 survey *Jews and*

Arabs, which was written as a series of lectures, in the context of the political and military tensions that plagued the Middle East at the time, and which offers a slightly gloomier view. By the late 1960s, when he began to publish *A Mediterranean Society*, his attitude was more upbeat. Drawing as it does on all the Geniza realia, the book offers Goitein's most subtle examination of actual (rather than theoretical) coexistence between Arabs and Jews.

His vision of the profound and inextricable bonds that joined the two peoples was, it should be said, not always understood or fully appreciated, even by those closest to him. The Nobel Prize–winning novelist S. Y. Agnon was one of Goitein's oldest and dearest Jerusalem friends (in 1919, when they all still lived in Germany, Agnon's then wife-to-be, Esther Marx—none other than the sister of JTS librarian Alexander Marx—had studied Arabic with Goitein and Hebrew with Agnon), and throughout the years that Goitein spent in America, the two men corresponded frequently. In a letter written during Goitein's total immersion in his research for *A Mediterranean Society*, Agnon urged him to return to Jerusalem ("the main thing is that I miss you") and challenged him—in typically lofty language—to "put aside the study of the Arabs and return heart and soul to the study of the Hebrews. Many of the great and good have given their best to the gentiles, and in the meantime the goyim have come into our legacy and grasped the art of Jacob with the weapons of Esau." Goitein, for his part, wrote eloquently and often about Agnon's fiction, which he held in the very highest esteem— though in a memorial lecture, delivered shortly after his friend's 1970 death, he admitted, "For my taste, both Yehuda HaLevi and Agnon are a little bit too Jewish. I mean, in both the mere human element is too often subordinated to the specifically Jewish aspect."

Although Goitein must certainly have been frustrated, as Abraham Maimonides was, by the failure of many of his ideas to take wider hold, he was careful not to make the same professional mistakes as his absurdly overextended medieval counterpart: Goitein's decision to leave Israel and all its public demands and focus so tightly on his Geniza scholarship may have saved him—and his work—from Abraham's sad fate. In 1948, there were reports that Goitein was being considered by David Ben-Gurion for the position of minister of education in the first Israeli government; one can only wonder what would have happened to the Geniza and its documentary treasures had that appointment come to pass.

Perhaps most important, the difference between Goitein and Abraham is manifest in the relationships both men developed to the mass of daily details that crowded the universe of the medieval Mediterranean—and spilled forth from the Geniza. Engagement with the "trivia" of his culture brought Abraham low—nearly to ruin—and it prompted in him, paradoxically, a kind of hermit's contempt for material existence. (The saints and the Prophets, he believed, were nobler for having shunned the "love of this world" and contented themselves with "reflections of the heart," as they wore wool, fasted, and "gave up women . . . and repaired to mountain caves and secluded deserts.") S. D. Goitein, on the other hand, managed, through his patient attention and almost boundless curiosity, to be *lifted up* by that same detritus, and while far from a sybarite, he made the celebration and disciplined scrutiny of just this quotidian jetsam his all-consuming lifework.

It was also how he absorbed the world: Goitein had been dubbed "a born schoolmaster" by his old friend and shipmate Gershom Scholem (it was a barbed characterization that reportedly hurt Goitein, accurate though it may have been), but he was also, as one admiring former student, Eric Ormsby, now an accomplished Arabist, essayist, and poet, put it in a posthumous tribute to his teacher, "a perpetual student himself," and someone who existed in "a state of concentrated delight at every new fact or hint of a fact." Ormsby recalls once accompanying Goitein to the Polish Catholic funeral of the murdered father of another graduate student, which took place in Philadelphia on the Jewish Sabbath, no less:

"I drove him there and we sat together during the mass. Throughout the service he peppered me with questions. Why is the priest doing that? What does this gesture signify? Can you explain those vestments?" Ormsby then relates how he "listened in horror as [Goitein] interrogated the funeral director about the precise mode of embalming that he used. Were the intestines removed beforehand? How was this done?"

While there was, as Ormsby describes it, something "a bit frightening about his inquisitiveness, something implacable, and relentless," he understands Goitein's passion for all this maniacal minutiae in terms of the "fierce tenacity" at the root of his scholarship and, perhaps more profoundly, as the embodiment of a long Jewish tradition of respect for the smallest things, placed in the service of the largest ones. As the mishnaic tractate *Pirkei Avot* (*Sayings of the Fathers*) counsels, "Despise not any man, and dismiss not any thing, for there is not a man who has not his hour and not a thing which has not its place." Goitein observed this teaching until the very end—mailing off to his publisher the final, chock-full, and meticulous volume of his magnum opus at age eighty-four, and the very next day getting back to work on the "India Book," the project he'd long put off. Six weeks later he was dead.

"Dismiss not any thing . . ." The words of the Mishna's rabbis echo down through the history of the Geniza and its dramatic, incremental retrieval, as they also call to mind lines by the great Polish-born, Yiddish-and-Arabic-speaking modern Hebrew scavenger-poet Avot Yeshurun—whose name means "the fathers are watching," and who, in 1971, wrote in Tel Aviv: "I bring back all I find. / Not all that glitters is gold. / But I pick up / all that glitters."

Which takes us around to that May day in 1896, when Margaret Gibson first handed Solomon Schechter the grimy scrap of Ben Sira and noticed the glint in his eyes. From Schechter and Taylor to Davidson and Mann; from Zulay to Schirmann, Fleischer, and Goitein; and from them to the delta of their successors—the scholars who have devoted their lives to the exalted and often exhausting work of recovering the Geniza have been guided, each in his hour, by a similar fascination with a "hidden light." For some it has been a matter of life and death for Jewish culture. Others have been driven by philological passions and the challenge of bringing order to history's detritus. For others still, an almost mystical sense of resurrection has been involved. For most it was, and is, much of the above—and then some. As it happens, very little in the Geniza glittered; but almost all, in its way, was gold.

AFTERWORD

Once the very hub of a thriving empire, Fustat seems barely to register on the otherwise-occupied residents of crumbling, sprawling, diesel-choked modern Cairo, and taxi drivers find their way to it only after repeated stops to ask for directions. But it remains—marked Misr el-Qadima (Old Cairo) on the maps—hugging the Nile south of downtown and divided in half by the train tracks and the Mari Girgis, or Saint George, Metro station.

The haphazardly parked cars and tinny Koranic recitations pouring forth from storefront radios notwithstanding, it's tempting to say that Old Cairo looks and sounds more or less as it might have when Wuhsha and Hillel ben Eli, Halfon ben Netanel and Abraham Maimonides lived there. A gargantuan man in a turban and galabia stands stern guard over a donkey-drawn cart piled high with swollen cabbages and cauliflowers. A small boy balances on his head a straw basket twice his size, filled with fresh, grainy pita, still puffed with heat. Women in headscarves pick through heaps of oranges, onions, and greens, much as they might have in Fatimid or Ayyubid Fustat. Sludgy-looking Nile fish flap in basins plunked in the dirt. And at the corner, men in long robes sit on stools and silently eye the passersby. The flies and filth are everywhere.

Easing away from this color and squalor, up onto the walkway that leads over the train tracks and toward Qasr ash-Sham' (the ancient Roman Fortress of the Lamp, which holds the Ben Ezra synagogue), one is struck by the made-over feel of the place: English signage, Pharaonic tchotchkes, elaborately epauletted Egyptian soldiers at every turn, and tourist groups with their leaders' flags held high. And then one arrives at the front gate of the Ben Ezra synagogue, where sunglass-wearing security guards man an airport-style metal detector.

Though there are today fewer than a hundred (mostly elderly) Jews left in Egypt, and none at all who live in Fustat, Ben Ezra probably looks better now than it has for centuries. A Canadian team carried out a major renovation project in the late 1980s and the then-derelict synagogue was restored, inch by ornamented inch. Outside, the moldering brick was resurfaced with a pale lemon gypsum facade and cast stucco crenellation affixed to the roof. With its inlaid cabinetwork, richly painted ceilings, hanging lamps, and cool gray marble pillars and floors, there is a modest splendor to the place. And into this echo of authenticity come the guides and their charges, who are regaled with explanations of the synagogue's importance that call to mind the characterization of Ben Ezra by one early-twentieth-century British visitor, Herbert Loewe, as "a perfect storehouse of fable and fancy." Moses was a baby in the rushes right on this spot (a large, engraved slab near the front of the hall is indicated and duly gawked at by groups from France and India, Australia, America, and Indonesia); the Prophet Jeremiah built the synagogue with Alexander the Great's permission; after the destruction of the Temple in Jerusalem, Ezra the Scribe came here with his very own Torah scroll; in the ninth century a wealthy rabbi bought the structure (then, in this version, a Coptic church) for a great deal of cash from the caliph. . . . And so on and fantastically on, with nary a fact in earshot: "It is," marveled Loewe in 1906, "quite wonderful how many miracles they have managed to cram into that small building."

Meanwhile, the true miracles go mostly overlooked. Perhaps in keeping with the modern history of the Geniza—and the frequent dismissal of its contents as "worthless"—the hole in the wall at the upper left corner of the women's gallery barely gets mentioned on these potted tours. Empty and, like the entire women's gallery, off-limits to visitors, the "room" itself draws little interest and, if it merits comment at all, the conversation quickly returns to the far more cinematic subject of the suckling Moses and Pharaoh's daughter.

To reach the Geniza today—the actual Geniza—one has to travel to Cambridge, England, where Schechter's Cairene haul is preserved in neat black binders on rows and rows of shelves a few aisles down from the Charles Darwin papers in the closed stacks of the University Library. Constituting nearly 70 percent of the worldwide Geniza stash, the Taylor-Schechter collection and the library's other Geniza holdings (those received from Wertheimer, Chester, Henriques, and others) were winnowed by scholars throughout the century; yet during that time the bulk of the fragments remained, remarkably, unsorted and dangerously exposed. Systematic examination began only in 1973, when the library hired the energetic young Scottish Jewish scholar and bibliographer Stefan Reif, who laid out an ambitious ten-year plan to bring order to the jumbled mess, by conserving, cataloging, microfilming, and creating a bibliography for the collection in its entirety. (Among Reif's many other, unspoken duties was the gentle weaning of various visiting scholars from their staunch belief that certain Geniza manuscripts were their own private property.)

With this the Taylor-Schechter Genizah Research Unit was born, and over the course of the next eight years, all the previously unconserved materials were cleaned, ironed, provided with shelf marks, and placed in protective Melinex (Mylar), the same flexible polyester film used in the radiation monitoring devices carried by the *Apollo 11* astronauts during their moon walk. At this time, the so-called Additional Series was also

created: these were fragments that earlier scholars hadn't regarded as worthy of sorting, either because of their content or due to their degraded state. (Even Goitein, in his great excitement over the discovery of the boxes in the library attic, failed to recognize the value of these particular pieces.) At final count, the Additional Series would amount to

105,090 folios—more than the Old Series (40,308) and New Series (45,128) combined! Despite the often mutilated or minuscule nature of the fragments, the Additional Series has yielded, and continues to yield, significant finds.

Over the nearly four decades since the founding of the Genizah Unit, scholars working there have prepared an invaluable and ever-expanding array of catalogs and bibliographies. Meanwhile, in the basement of the library, the eight thousand fragments of the Jack Mosseri collection are currently being treated to the most state-of-the-art conservation conceivable. Gone are the dread steam irons; now fragments are examined under an electron microscope and the chemical stability of the iron-gall ink is tested before a scrap may be treated. In a humidification chamber, a sheet clenched in a thousand-year-old fist is gradually coaxed into unfolding. Fragile pages are strengthened with Japanese paper and a mixture of methylcellulose and wheat starch paste. And the process is by no means rote. Creative solutions must be found for every sort of decay and damage. "Inspecting each folder," observed the collection's conservators, "has been like opening a parcel: sometimes a pleasure, sometimes a portent, depending on the prize within."

Beyond Cambridge, Geniza fragments on paper and parchment are held physically in many other library and private storerooms, from the Jewish Theological Seminary in New York to the Bodleian at Oxford. All told, seventy-five collections—from vast to tiny (just a single frag-ment)—have been counted. And copies—on microfilm and photostat, in typescript and in books—are kept elsewhere, making detailed organiza-tion and study possible. They're in Jerusalem, where at the newly renamed Ezra Fleischer Geniza Research Institute for Hebrew Poetry, located in a maze-like back hallway of the National Library, scholars work in a windowless room roughly the size of the Geniza itself. Sur-rounded by tin shelves crowded with files, under framed, black-and-white portraits of Schirmann, Zulay, Fleischer, Goitein, Leopold Zunz, Shalom Spiegel, and others (well aware of his brother's passion for the Geniza, the Hollywood mogul Sam Spiegel left money in his will, which keeps the Institute running), they bear down like detectives on a very cold case: it is sometimes a thousand years old. Using two vintage micro-film machines, a few new computers, and a bank of metallic gray, circa 1970 card catalogs, they are gradually sleuthing their way through the Geniza's poetic holdings, identifying every fragment they can. And those typescripts and microfilms are also in New Jersey, where, under the auspices of the Princeton Geniza Project, one of Goitein's leading disciples, the historian Mark Cohen, has since the mid-1980s given new life to his late mentor's Geniza Lab by supervising groups of knowledge-able students to transcribe and create a large, searchable database of the Geniza's historical documents in Judeo-Arabic and Hebrew. Known by the modern yet somehow medieval name of TextGarden, the database currently includes some four thousand fragments, or nearly a quarter of the Geniza's documentary (nonliterary) materials.

At the same time, and beyond these individual efforts, the nature of Geniza research is in the process of being wholly reimagined—in virtual form—by the Friedberg Genizah Project. Established in 1999 by the Toronto currency trader and avid bibliophile Albert Friedberg, the multimillion-dollar plan is to inventory and digitize in full color and high resolution every Geniza scrap in existence, compiling for each frag-ment identifications, formerly far-flung catalog entries, and comprehensive bibliographies. No such centralized clearinghouse (or nerve center) has ever existed for the Geniza, and in fact "Friedberg," as it is commonly known, represents the largest, most ambitious manuscript computerization project of any kind, anywhere. In his conjoined devotion to business and to Jewish texts, Albert Friedberg himself might best be seen as a kind of latter-day Salman Schocken—a man willing to put his money where his people's manuscripts are. But this sweeping vision of the Geniza as a reconstituted whole—and the highly complex application of that vision (carried out in a day-to-day way by a staff of young ultra-Orthodox women on the fourteenth floor of an unprepossessing office building, surrounded by shwarma stands, banquet halls, and government offices in one of the uglier industrial neighborhoods of Jerusalem)—is, like so much about the study of the Geniza, a product of the combined talents and efforts of dozens of individuals, scattered in all corners of the earth.

Working together with international teams of scholars, expert in various Geniza fields, the cyberwizard behind the Friedberg site, Yaacov Choueka, has—without fanfare though in a distinctly inspired fashion—already begun to revolutionize the study of the Geniza. (It seems not so much ironic as it is fitting that this phase of the Geniza's redemption has become the mission and passion of this veteran, pioneering computer scientist, a Hebrew-and-Arabic-speaking Jew born and raised in—of all places—Cairo.) If everything goes according to plan, when this stage of the project is complete, vividly photographed images of hundreds of thousands of the Fustat manuscripts—the recto and verso of the estimated 331,351 folios from the Ben Ezra cache—will be available at the mere click of a mouse on the Friedberg website, along with nearly half a million items of data about these manuscripts, compiled over the course of the last century. Adapting state-of-the-art face-recognition technology to the medieval context, the Friedberg programmers have also made possible the mechanical identification of candidates for "joins," the reunion of long-separated parts of a torn manuscript, as well as different fragments written in the same scribal hand. The Friedberg project is, one might say, the high-tech, democratic realization of Solomon Schechter's hundred-year-old dream of creating the modern era's "Greatest Historical Work on Jewish Lore"—a corpus of the Geniza.

W e've tried, with *Sacred Trash*, to make our way into that corpus. Rummaging in the attic of an overlooked aspect of communal history, we've known all along we'd find things that some would consider rubbish and others treasure. This, though, is what literature does— what writers do—and, when it comes to it, what faith is. And as this book makes clear, it is also what the scholars of the Geniza have done, in a quietly heroic way, for more than a century now. If, with Cynthia Ozick, we think of history as "what we make from memory," then these scholars have quite literally been *making* history by re-membering it, by putting it back together syllable by syllable under the intense pressure of powerfully informed and at times visionary imaginations. The yield of that labor of remembrance is staggering, and we've drawn on only a small fraction of it, a handful of examples, hoping that they might stand for the marvelous if messy whole. In doing so, we've been led not only by this microcosmic principle, but by the great historian Yosef Hayim Yerushalmi, who understood as well as anyone the complex role that memory plays in history (how memory both is and isn't the finest index) and who spoke often of the importance of the historical "olfactory sense"—one that allows scholars, and also writers, "to sniff out connections."

In short, we've been guided in our choice of subjects by our noses, and another entire Geniza book, or three, could be written around what we've left out. Front and center among our neglected topics is the Bible, which is represented in the Taylor-Schechter collection alone by some twenty-five thousand fragments. Just as the Geniza scrambles "early and late" in its scrap heap, so, too, it sometimes and literally turns things upside down, or downside up—revealing, for example, that the Morse Code–like array of dots and dashes that indicate proper vocalization of the text didn't descend from Sinai—that is, vowels weren't always placed *under* the Hebrew letters, where we are used to finding them today. Once upon a time, the Geniza makes clear, the vowels were placed *above* the Hebrew letters. While the Geniza's two alternative systems of vocalization—Palestinian and Babylonian—were eventually phased out with the adoption of the Tiberian or Masoretic system, and the introduction of "codified" (printed) biblical texts, they remained in limited use in nonbiblical texts through the sixteenth century.

Among the other important subjects that have, alas, been given short shrift in our book are many standard rabbinic modes. Key Geniza fragments expose, for instance, previously unknown (and sometimes mystical) midrashim, as well as a cacophony of legal responsa, dispatched by the heads of the academies in Babylonia and Palestine and by later halakhic authorities to correspondents scattered throughout the Jewish world—from Lucena to Aleppo to Kairouan. These scribbled replies to queries posed from far away offer a fascinating and previously obscured angle onto the medieval rabbis' unedited, unabridged opinions about a sprawling range of topics pertaining to Jewish law as it was actually—not theoretically—practiced. Moving back still further in time, the Geniza also provides us with a Talmud that is—at least visually—not at all talmudic. These early Talmud fragments predate the now-familiar arrangement of a central text surrounded by a constellation of commentaries, and present what *looks* like a more straightforward, if still charged and not-always-easy-to-follow argument. The older versions of the text bring scholars closer than ever before to the origins of this classic expression of Jewish thought—especially as we find it in the Palestinian Talmud, which Schechter described as "in some respects more important for the knowledge of Jewish history and the intelligent conception of the minds of the Rabbis than the 'twin-Talmud of the East,' " the Babylonian version. The Palestinian Talmud had been, however, seriously neglected over the centuries and therefore "little copied by the scribes." The Geniza, as Schechter saw right away while leaning over the Egyptian tea chests, would "open a new mine in this direction."

Sexy subjects such as grammar, lexicography, and paleography have likewise been treated only in passing here, as have various historical topics—including Jewish life in Crusader Palestine and the legendary Jewish kingdom of the Khazars. As with so many other Geniza matters, documentary evidence about the Khazars sends us back to some of the most basic questions about Judaism, including perhaps *the* most basic one: Who is a Jew and how did he or she become one? From an early discovery by Schechter of what appears to be a tenth-century letter that details Khazar history to an important 1962 find of an epistle concerning the medieval Khazar community of Kiev (the earliest known mention of that city in any language), the Geniza has furnished us with convincing evidence of the existence of this legendary and isolated Jewish kingdom of Turkic converts between the Black and the Caspian seas.

And neither last nor least of the major topics untouched upon in this book, the Geniza holds a store of detailed and often intimate information relating to one of the greatest figures of the medieval Jewish day—the philosopher and communal leader Moses (Musa) ben Maimon, or Maimonides, whose somewhat tortured son appears in our final chapter. The Geniza has yielded more than sixty fragments in the philosopher's own handwriting, including marked-up "draft copies" of his famous *Mishneh*

Torah (which was, controversially, intended to replace the Talmud as a core text for study). These drafts are full of crossed-out words and second thoughts—revealing what we might think of as either a perfectionist, conscientious, neurotic, or simply human side of the Rambam. The Geniza has also preserved moving examples of his personal correspondence (to, among others, his beloved traveling-businessman brother, David—who eventually drowned in the Indian Ocean) and numerous specimens of his dashed-off responses to petitioners' questions about Jewish law. At the same time, we see Maimonides the Jewish physician at work, as the Geniza has left us a letter of application to apprentice with Dr. Maimonides, and some of his handwritten prescriptions, including aids to digestion and what appears to be a kind of medieval Viagra, an iron-water-based concoction designed to boost male potency. The Geniza also lets us know that, despite his generally party-squashing, stoic philosophical tendencies, the Rambam seems if nothing else to have been liberal with prescriptions of wine, the curative powers of which he apparently held in high esteem. In fact, the Geniza provides the equivalent of an entire medieval *Physicians' Desk Reference*, describing in precise detail the cause, diagnosis, and treatment of diseases; the preparation of a Mediterranean medicine chest of potions, pills, pastes, ointments, lotions, and gargles; and even the social and ethical aspects of the medical profession.

Alongside this largely unexplored mountain range of fragments relating to the principal modes of medieval Jewish life in the East, the Geniza has turned up a number of curious though by no means trifling items among its foothills. The earliest known piece of Jewish musical notation surfaces there, for example—in manuscripts left by one Obadiah, a messianically minded early-twelfth-century ex–Norman monk of southern Italian origin who converted to Judaism and eventually settled in Fustat. And further testament to the Geniza's ability to blindside us are two of the world's oldest Yiddish documents, which were probably left behind by Ashkenazic visitors to Egypt: a fourteenth-century 420-line anonymous poem in rhymed quatrains about Abraham's destruction of his father's idols, the story of which is told in considerable (midrashic) detail and with what at times seems almost a kind of slapstick humor— and, from the Middle High German epic tradition, a Yiddish narrative poem that has no German analogue and is therefore invaluable for the study of early German literature.

In a much lower Yiddish register, Geniza scholars have found a group of letters from a sixteenth-century Jerusalemite named Rachel Zussman to her grown businessman son Moshe in Cairo. Among the earliest examples of Yiddish letter-writing, and clearly part of a much more extensive correspondence, they tell of the once well-off but now struggling Prague-born woman's complicated relationship with her only child. Apart from warning him to watch over his money carefully and (above all) to keep up his studies, and also not to be proud when he does something good and of course to write her more often—she wastes little time before pressing the inevitable buttons: "God knows what will become of me," she moans, adding that she has already spent such and such amount this month and has had to borrow money from her own grandson, but

God will help me, and all [the people of] Israel in the future. . . . Don't worry, my son. I always ask God that you not be sick and that I suffer in your stead. And I also ask that He not let me die before I see your face again and you lay your hands over my eyes. . . . Don't worry, my son . . . but don't come now. [The situation, she explains, isn't good.] Don't worry, my son, . . . if I died I would not have a sheet to be brought down from my bed in . . . and I don't have a cover for my head. If you can, buy me one, cheaply. . . . Come back to the holy city.

While one would think that our Fustat closet contained a finite amount of material, the end of which will soon be reached, the history of scholars' finds does make one wonder. Within the last decade or two a striking array of discoveries have proven that the Geniza stock is far from spent.

Just a few months back (we write in the first weeks of 2010), a fragment was found by a T-S Genizah Unit researcher that completes one of those previously extant Yiddish epistolary fragments and helps us understand the thrust of an otherwise hard-to-decipher letter from Rachel Zussman—which turns out, once again, to be her complaint that her son hasn't written, that his silence is making her suffer, and that she thinks he's wasting his time in Cairo and would do better for himself (learn more and make a better living) if he moved back home, to Jerusalem. One is tempted to declare "Jewish mothers and their sons" a new Geniza field altogether—between the apple of Wuhsha's eye and a letter from an aristocratic elderly mother who, writing in Judeo-Arabic from Syria in 1067, offers up the familiar and almost conventional complaint that her son hasn't been in touch for months: "I get letters from your brother, may God preserve him, but don't find any from you among them. . . . Nothing less than a letter from you will cheer my spirits. Do not kill me before my time! . . . I fast and pray for you night and day."

And then, in classic medieval and also inimitable Jewish maternal fashion she animates the convention with a marvelous leap to the particular, pleading with him: "By God, . . . send me your worn and dirty shirts to revive my spirit."

Also forced to stand brooding off to the side not only of our book, but of the entire field of Geniza studies for much of the previous century, is the long-scorned subject of magic and mysticism—with its incantations, fumigations, talismans, angels, curses, and cures. Such texts were widespread in medieval Jewish society, and thousands of "magical" pages exist in the Geniza, though they have been examined in serious scholarly fashion only since the 1980s. A particularly spicy specimen of this sort was encountered not long ago—a multilingual curse that begins in Judeo-Arabic, "Take a plate of lead and write on it in the first hour of the day; bury it in a new grave which is three days old," then moves into Hebrew and Aramaic, in which it addresses by name specific angels (Anger, Wrath, Rage, Fury, and the Destroyer), adjuring them to "blot out the life of N. son of N. from this world" (the victim's name is to be filled in by the one who utters the curse). A short sentence in Arabic (and Arabic characters), in a different and later hand, follows as a kind of postoperative report, observing that "it's effective for killing." Other magic fragments outfit us with recipes for sleep, fishing, ease in childbirth, expelling mice from a home, making people shudder in a bathhouse, and causing a would-be beloved's heart to burn with desire.

Quietly spectacular finds have emerged of late beyond the main collections as well. In 2002, a tin box containing 350 Geniza pages was found almost by chance in the Geneva Public and University Library. Archivists came across it while going through the papers of a noted Swiss scholar who had purchased the fragments together with Greek papyri in Cairo at the end of the nineteenth century. The top of the box bears a faint ink inscription that begins "Textes hébraïques . . . Provenant de la Synagogue du Vieux Caire" and goes on to tell us that the manuscripts were purchased by Jules Nicole in 1896–97 and identified in part by his son Albert Nicole.

Having just completed his graduate studies in theology, Albert was passing through Oxford on his way to a fellowship in Edinburgh when he heard from a colleague about the "sensational" recent discovery of parts of the Hebrew Ecclesiasticus from Cairo and began to wonder if the Nicole family tin box might not contain additional passages from this missing scriptural link. In 1898, newly ordained as a minister, the younger Nicole brought his fragments back to Oxford, where—with Adolf Neubauer and A. E. Cowley—he examined the collection; but— *plus ça change*—apparently Neubauer wasn't impressed (though several palimpsests drew his attention) and the material was returned to Geneva, where it lay untouched in a vault for the next 104 years. When the box was rediscovered at the start of the twenty-first century, a local Dominican scholar-priest was called in to examine the documents, which he sorted in rudimentary fashion—and back they went into the collection, until, three years later, the director of the Institute for Microfilmed Manuscripts at the National Library in Jerusalem (the goal of which is to gather copies of every Hebrew manuscript on the planet) just happened to write to the Geneva library about an administrative matter concerning a particular collection. He also asked in passing if the library had acquired any other Judaica over the course of the previous fifteen years.

"*Oui et non,*" responded the Geneva librarian, who then told the story of the newly discovered old tin box, which turned out (after examination by various specialists from Jerusalem) to contain an extremely well preserved and characteristic range of Geniza goods. There was everything from Mishna, Talmud, and Gaonic fragments to liturgical texts, historical documents, Hebrew and Judeo-Arabic correspondence, and of course poetry—including previously unknown work by major and minor writers alike and, amazingly, a copy of that same foundational "wine poem" by Dunash ben Labrat that Hayyim Schirmann had identified from the caption he'd discovered as a young man in a Cambridge manuscript in the 1930s. The Geneva Dunash fragment was just the second copy of this key Spanish Hebrew poem ever seen by modern eyes; more important, this version was considerably longer than the earlier find and so raised a cloud of fresh questions, namely: Which was the "real" version of the poem? Was the shorter poem detached from its end at some point? Or was the new ending tacked on later? The different scenarios can lead to wholly disparate readings of the poem, reflecting divergent understandings of the period's origins. Such are the ways of the Geniza that a development as dramatic as this one leaves us with more riddles than resolutions.

Quieter still is another recent discovery that involves an even more essential sort of poetic justice than does the Geneva find. In the spring of 2007, a British dealer in Judaica put up for sale several unidentified Geniza fragments that had initially been purchased at auction by a German collector in 1898 and held privately ever since. In preparation for the sale, the fragments were submitted to specialists, who identified them tentatively as liturgical hymns, and they were sold to an American collector. A short while later, digitized images of three of the manuscripts came into the skilled hands of Shulamit Elizur, a leading expert in liturgical and medieval poetry, and one of Ezra Fleischer's most distinguished students, as well as his successor at the Geniza Research Institute named for him. Elizur easily confirmed the identification of two of the fragments as medieval poems from Spain and Palestine (one of them by Yehuda HaLevi), but the third gave her pause. This was something different. It contained none of the trademark signs of medieval verse, and its language instantly marked it as a kind of wisdom literature. But which? Though further probing left her with a strong hunch, the clock was ticking and she was late for an important meeting. She put the printout of the photographed manuscript down—and only in the taxicab heading home from her meeting did she confide in her husband, also a seasoned Geniza scholar, what she suspected.

Her excitement mounting, if not her haste, and the ghost of Schechter perhaps lurking, she continued, late into the night and with her husband's help, to inch through the four partly torn pages of blocky letters, as she checked them against different published texts and cross-referenced translations. Preparations for the Sabbath and the Sabbath itself brought the work to a halt. (The Elizurs are strictly observant.) But after nightfall on Saturday, she resumed her investigations, and by Monday she was certain: glowing before her on the computer screen were long-lost passages from the same second-century B.C.E. book, the original Hebrew Ben Sira, which had triggered the initial chase for the Geniza. Missing since the tenth century, here they were well into the first decade of the new millennium being slipped into the puzzle Schechter had begun assembling in the late 1890s—a still gap-filled textual tapestry to which Neubauer, Cowley, Adler, Schirmann, and others had already contributed pieces.

And so it is that month after month Geniza miracles continue to occur, as vigilant scholars sift through the Cairene debris, sometimes on microfilm or in digitized versions, sometimes leaning over, or on, the paper and parchment in person—pliant, resilient, immaculate pages with the ink still vivid, and thumbnail-sized remnants of brittle pages concealing faded words in their grain. If the record of the past decade, or even the past year, is any indication, other treasures, large and small, will no doubt surface as well—in Cambridge and in Oxford, in Princeton, New York, and Budapest, perhaps in another Geneva tin, at the bottom of a forgotten old-world briefcase, or maybe in Fustat itself. "Turn it and turn it," urges the sage Ben Bag-Bag—in that same mishnaic tractate, the *Sayings of the Fathers*, that begins by elaborating the chain of tradition's transmission and enjoins us to take no object for granted—"everything is in it." And there are, it would seem, as many ways to write a history of the Geniza as there are scholars or readers who have stepped, or might step, through the looking glass of its scattered leaves.

ILLUSTRATIONS

the photo include S. Y. Agnon, Hugo Bergmann, and Levi Billig. Courtesy of the Goitein family.

206 Index card from Goitein's Geniza Lab. Courtesy of the NLI.

208 Twelfth-century check. CUL T-S Ar. 30.184(3r).

215 S. D. Goitein with his lab, Princeton. Courtesy of the Goitein family.

218 Goitein in the classroom, University of Pennsylvania, 1970, with Zvi Gabay, Moshe Gil, Gary Leiser, Ellen Seidman, and Yedida Kalfon Stillman. Marion Scheuer Sofer photographer, courtesy of the Goitein family.

227 Additional Series sorting: Stefan Reif, Yisrael Yeivin, Ezra Fleischer. CUL T-S Genizah Research Unit.

228 Ironing manuscripts. CUL T-S Genizah Research Unit.

233 Palestinian Talmud, Berakhot 2:4–3:1. CUL T-S F 17.20r.

234 Rambam draft, with revisions, *Mishneh Torah* (*Malveh veloveh*). JTS MS 8254.4a.

235 Obadiah, musical score. CUL T-S K 5.41.

237 Magical manuscripts, amulet. CUL T-S K 1.94.

239 Geneva box. Courtesy of David Rosenthal.

NOTES

Hebrew book and article titles appear here in English translation and are marked [Heb]. When English translations of the titles are provided by the publishers themselves, we have maintained the spelling used there. Publication information is given the first time a work is cited. Throughout the book, Hebrew transliteration has been simplified in order to aid pronunciation by the general reader.

Archival abbreviations are as follows: CUL (Cambridge University Library); WGL (West-minster College, Cambridge, Gibson-Lewis papers); JTSA (Jewish Theological Seminary Archive); BLR (Bodleian Library Records, Oxford); NLI (National Library of Israel). Other abbreviations are detailed in full the initial time a reference appears. Our thanks to the Syndics of Cambridge University Library and to these other institutions and archives for permission to quote from their holdings.

1. Hidden Wisdom

Information about Agnes Lewis and Margaret Gibson comes from Janet Soskice, *Sisters of Sinai: How Two Lady Adventurers Found the Hidden Gospels* (London, 2009); A. Wigham Price, *The Ladies of Castlebrae: A Story of Nineteenth-Century Travel and Research* (Gloucester, 1985); Stefan C. Reif, *A Jewish Archive from Old Cairo: The History of Cambridge University's Genizah Collection* (Richmond, 2000); Stefan C. Reif, "Giblews, Jews and Genizah Views," *Journal of Jewish Studies [JJS]* 55/2, 2004; Rebecca J. W. Jefferson, "Sisters in Semitics: A Fresh Appreciation of the Scholarship of Agnes Smith Lewis and Margaret Dunlop Gibson," *Medieval Feminist Forum* 45/1, 2009; Editha Klipstein, "The Learned Twin Sisters from Scotland," WGL 8/4; Christa Müller-Kessler, "Agnes Smith Lewis" and "Margaret Smith Gibson," *The Oxford Dictionary of National Biography* (Oxford, 2004); and the twins' own writing, especially Margaret Dunlop Gibson, *How the Codex Was Found: A Narrative of Two Visits to Sinai* (Cambridge, 1893); Agnes Smith Lewis, *In the Shadow of Sinai: A Story of Travel and Research from 1895 to 1897* (Cambridge, 1898); Agnes Smith Lewis, "Two Unpublished Letters," WGL 6/10.

Descriptions of Schechter (whose initial position as "Reader in Talmudic" seems to have been short for "Reader in Talmudic Literature") come from Norman Bentwich, *Solomon Schechter* (Philadelphia, 1938); Mathilde Schechter's unpublished memoir

(JTSA Schechter archive, box 28/1-11); Adolph S. Oko, *Solomon Schechter: A Bibliography* (Cambridge, 1938); Cyrus Adler, *Solomon Schechter: A Biographical Sketch* (*American Jewish Yearbook*, 1916); Norman Bentwich, *Solomon Schechter*, with a foreword by F. C. Burkitt (pamphlet, London, 1931); Alexander Marx, *Essays in Jewish Biography* (Philadelphia, 1947); George Foot Moore, "Schechter, Scholar and Humanist" and Cyrus Adler, "A Tribute to Schechter," both from *Menorah Journal* 2/1, Feb. 1916; Louis Marshall, Joseph Jacobs, et al., "Solomon Schechter," *JTS Students' Annual*, 1916; Louis Ginzberg, *Students, Scholars and Saints* (Philadelphia, 1928/1945); Margaret D. Gibson, "Dr. Solomon Schechter," *The Week-Day*, Jan. 15, 1916; "Schechter Anecdotes Gathered by F. I. Schechter in England," JTSA Schechter 29/17; F. I. Schechter, "Schechteriana," *Menorah Journal* 8/2, April 1922; *A Tradition Renewed: A History of the Jewish Theological Seminary*, Jack Wertheimer, ed. (New York, 1997); Robert Ackerman, *J. G. Frazer: His Life and Work* (Cambridge, 1987). In particular, the authors would like to acknowledge David Starr's dissertation, *Catholic Israel: Solomon Schechter, A Study of Unity and Fragmentation in Modern Jewish History* (Columbia University, 2003), which is an excellent guide to Schechter's thought, and Stefan Reif's *A Jewish Archive from Old Cairo*, a groundbreaking history of the Geniza collection at Cambridge, based on years of Reif's work as the head of the Taylor-Schechter Genizah Research Unit.

For the origins of the term "geniza," see Avihai Shivtiel, "The Genizah and Its Roots," in *The Written Word Remains*, Shulie Reif, ed. (Cambridge, 2004). For more on the notion of geniza in general, see Solomon Schechter, "A Hoard of Hebrew Manuscripts," *Studies in Judaism* II (Philadelphia, 1908); A. M. Habermann, *The Geniza and Other Genizoth: Their Character, Contents and Development* [Heb] (Jerusalem, 1971); S. D. Goitein, *A Mediterranean Society: The Jewish Communities of the Arab World as Portrayed in the Documents of the Cairo Geniza* 1, 5 (Berkeley, 1967–85/1999); Simon Hopkins, "The Discovery of the Cairo Geniza," *Bibliophilia Africana* 4, 1981; E. N. Adler, "Genizah," *The Jewish Encyclopedia* 5, 1903; Mark Cohen and Yedida Stillman, "The Cairo Geniza and the Custom of Geniza among Oriental Jewry: An Historical and Ethnographic Survey" [Heb], *Pe'amim* 24, 1985; Reif, *A Jewish Archive;* Nehemia Allony, "The Practice of Geniza among the Jews" [Heb], *Sinai* 79, 1976; Malachi Beit-Arié, "*Genizot:* Depositories of Consumed Books as Disposing Procedure in Jewish Society," *Scriptorium* 50, 1996; "Geniza," *Talmudic Encyclopedia: A Digest of Halachic Literature and Jewish Law from the Tannaitic Period to the Present Time* 6 [Heb], Shlomo Yosef Zevin, ed. (Jerusalem, 1954).

Biblical references relating to the idea of "geniza" may be found, for instance, in Esther 3:9 and 4:7; Ezra 5:17, 6:1, and 7:20; 1 Chronicles 28:11. Talmudic allusions to the practice appear, among other places, in Shabbat 115a, 116a; Megilla 26b; Gittin 45b; Sotah 20a; and Baba Batra 20b.

For more on the practice of Muslim geniza, see Joseph Sadan, "Genizah and Genizah-like Practices in Islamic and Jewish Traditions," *Bibliotheca Orientalis* 42/1–2,

Jan.–March 1986; Sadan, "New Materials Regarding Purity and Impurity of Books in Islam in Comparison with Judaism," *Jerusalem Studies in Arabic and Islam* 33, 2007; Sadan, "Storage and Treatment of Used Books (Genizah) in the Moslem Tradition, and Jewish Parallels" [Heb], *Kiryat Sefer* 55/1, 1980; Mark Cohen, "Geniza for Islamicists, Islamic Geniza, and the 'New Cairo Geniza,' " *Harvard Middle Eastern and Islamic Review* 7, 2006.

The explanations cited here for the particular geniza practices of the Ben Ezra community come, respectively, from Malachi Beit-Arié, *"Genizot"*; Mark Cohen (correspondence with the authors, Jan. 27, 2010); Marina Rustow, "From the Palace in Cairo to the Synagogue in Fustat: In Search of the Lost Arabic Archive" (unpublished paper, June 2009, courtesy of the author).

For more on the role that the Ben Ezra synagogue played in the life of the Fustat community, see Goitein, *MS* 2; Mark Cohen, *Poverty and Charity in the Jewish Community of Medieval Egypt* (Princeton, 2005); Elinoar Bareket, *Fustat on the Nile: The Jewish Elite in Medieval Egypt* (Leiden, 1999). Measurements of the Geniza's dimensions come from Cohen and Stillman, "The Cairo Geniza and the Custom of Geniza" [Heb] and Malachi Beit-Arié (*"Genizot"*), who calculates the capacity of the chamber as being between 25 and 30 cubic meters. The descriptions of the Geniza quoted here are: "For centuries," Agnes Smith Lewis, introduction to *Palestinian Syriac Texts from Palimpsest Fragments in the Taylor-Schechter Collection* (London, 1900); "that pestiferous wrack," H. F. Stewart, *Francis Jenkinson, Fellow of Trinity College, Cambridge and Cambridge University Librarian, a Memoir* (Cambridge, 1926).

The Geniza–Dead Sea Scrolls comparison is discussed in Stefan Reif, "Cairo Geniza," *Encyclopedia of the Dead Sea Scrolls*, Lawrence Schiffman and James VanderKam, eds. (Oxford, 2000); Paul Kahle, *The Cairo Geniza* (Oxford, 1959); Habermann, *The Geniza* [Heb]; Norman Golb, "Geniza Studies in Jerusalem," *Studies and Reports* II, Yad Ben Zvi, Jan. 1956; Joel Kraemer, *Maimonides: The Life and World of One of Civilization's Greatest Minds* (New York, 2008). See also T. Gaster, *The Dead Sea Scriptures* (New York, 1976). Goitein's comments about the "Living Sea Scrolls" come from an unpublished lecture, Goitein Geniza Lab 2K.1.1, NLI.

The most recent and accurate count of fragments at the Cambridge Library is 193,654 items. For a detailed reading of this number, see Rebecca J. W. Jefferson, "The Historical Significance of the Cambridge Genizah Inventory Project," in *Language, Culture, Computation: Studies in Honour of Yaacov Choueka*, Nachum Dershowitz and Ephraim Nissan, eds. (Berlin, forthcoming). Grateful acknowledgment is due to Rebecca Jefferson for showing us her article and for providing further helpful information about the inventory, which was carried out on behalf of the Friedberg Genizah Project.

2. Serpents and Secrets

All quotes from Heine come from *Memoirs of Heinrich Heine*, Thomas W. Evans, ed. (London, 1884). Further information about Von Geldern is drawn from Jeffrey L. Sammons, *Heinrich Heine: A Modern Biography* (Princeton, 1979); Hopkins, "The Discovery"; Habermann, *The Geniza* [Heb]; Elkan Adler, "An Eleventh Century Introduction to the Hebrew Bible," *Jewish Quarterly Review* [*JQR*] 9/4, 1897. The account of both of Safir's trips appears in Yaakov Safir, *Even Safir* (Lyck, 1866).

For more on Europe's fascination with ancient Egypt, see Joyce Tyldesley, *Egypt: How a Lost Civilization Was Rediscovered* (Berkeley, 2005); Elliott Colla, *Conflicted Antiquities: Egyptology, Egyptomania, Egyptian Modernity* (Durham, 2007); and especially Leo Deuel, *Testaments of Time: The Search for Lost Manuscripts and Records* (New York, 1966). James Baikie's words appear in *A Century of Exploration in the Land of the Pharaohs* (London, 1924).

Details about Firkovitch (and quotations from his correspondence) are gathered from Zeev Elkin and Menahem Ben-Sasson, "Avraham Firkovich and the Cairo Genizas in the Light of His Personal Archive" [Heb], *Pe'amim* 90, winter 2002; Tapani Harviainen, "Abraham Firkovich," in *Karaite Judaism: A Guide to Its History and Literary Sources*, Meira Polliack, ed. (Leiden, 2003); Tapani Harviainen, "The Cairo Genizot and Other Sources of the Second Firkovich Collection in St. Petersburg," in *Proceedings of the Twelfth International Congress of the International Organization for Masoretic Studies*, E. J. Revell, ed. (Atlanta, 1996); Marina Rustow, *Heresy and the Politics of Community: The Jews of the Fatimid Caliphate*, introduction (Ithaca, 2008); Dan Shapira, *Avraham Firkowicz in Istanbul (1830–1832): Paving the Way for Turkic Nationalism* (Ankara, 2003); Mikhail Kizilov, *Karaites through the Travelers' Eyes: Ethnic History, Traditional Culture and Everyday Life of the Crimean Karaites according to the Descriptions of the Travelers* (Simferopol, Warsaw, 2002). The more skeptical view of Firkovitch's methods is put forth, for example, in Kahle, *The Cairo Geniza*.

The differences between the Fustat genizot are discussed in Rustow, *Heresy*, chapter 1; Haggai Ben-Shammai, "Is 'The Cairo Genizah' a Proper Name or a Generic Noun? On the Relationship between the Genizot of the Ben Ezra and Dar Simha Synagogues," in *From a Sacred Source: Genizah Studies in Honour of Professor Stefan C. Reif*, Ben Outhwaite and Siam Bhayro, eds. (Leiden, 2010). On the Basatin, see Jack Mosseri, "A New Hoard of Jewish MSS. in Cairo," *Jewish Review* 4/21, 1913.

Elkan Adler's account of his first visit to Ben Ezra comes from "Notes of a Journey to the East," *Jewish Chronicle* [*JC*], Dec. 14, 1888. Descriptions of the once-derelict state of Ben Ezra come from Jack Mosseri, "The Synagogues of Egypt: Past and Present," *Jewish Review* 5/25, 1914; Charles Le Quesne, "The Modern Period," in *Fortifications and the Synagogue: The Fortress of Babylon and the Ben Ezra Synagogue, Cairo*, Phyllis Lambert, ed. (Montreal, 1994).

Information about Chester is drawn from E. A. Wallis Budge, *By Nile and Tigris: A Narrative of Journeys in Egypt and Mesopotamia on Behalf of the British Museum between the Years 1886 and 1913* (London, 1926); Rebecca J. W. Jefferson, "The Cairo Genizah Unearthed: The Excavations Conducted by Count d'Hulst on Behalf of the Bodleian Library and Their Significance for Genizah History," in *From a Sacred Source*, Outhwaite and Bahyro, eds.; Stefan C. Reif, *Hebrew Manuscripts at Cambridge University Library: A Description and Introduction* (Cambridge, 1997); Gertrud Seidmann, "Greville John Chester," *Wolfson College Records*, 2005–6; Gertrud Seidmann, "Thunder, Lightning and a Ray of Sunshine," *Romulus Voices*, Wolfson College, 2006; Margaret S. Drower, *Flinders Petrie: A Life in Archaeology* (Madison, 1985); Charles Q. Choi, "World's First Prosthetic: Egyptian Mummy's Fake Toe," www.LiveScience.com, July 27, 2007. Quotations from Chester come from Greville J. Chester, "Notes on the Ancient Christian Churches of Musr el Ateekah, or Old Cairo and Its Neighborhood," *Archaeological Journal* 29, 1872; "The Jew Earl," *JC*, Sept. 8, 1876; "Archaeological News," *The American Journal of Archaeology and of the History of the Fine Arts* 8/1, 1893; letters from Chester to Nicholson, the Bodleian librarian, dated Dec. 20, 1889, Jan. 18, 1890, Dec. 14, 1890, BLR, e. 479. (All sterling equivalents have been calculated using the U.K. National Archives currency converter.)

The two otherwise forthright scholars were Richard Gottheil and William H. Worrell in *Fragments from the Cairo Genizah in the Freer Collection* (New York, 1927). For more on Cyrus Adler and the Egyptian role at the Columbian Exposition, see his *I Have Considered the Days* (Philadelphia, 1941); Egypt-Chicago Exposition Co., *Street in Cairo: World's Columbian Exposition*, 1893; Erik Larson, *The Devil in the White City: Murder, Magic and Madness at the Fair That Changed America* (New York, 2004).

Information about Wertheimer comes from *Manuscript and Book* [Heb] (Jerusalem, 1893/1990); Shelomo Aharon Wertheimer, *Batei midrashot* (Jerusalem, 1980); Wertheimer, *Ginzei Yerushalayim* (Jerusalem, 1901/1992); Reif, *A Jewish Archive*; and interviews with Shelomo Leshem and Shelomo Aharon Wertheimer (the elder Wertheimer's descendants), Aug. 5, 2008, Jerusalem. The postcards and letters from Wertheimer to the Cambridge librarian quoted here are as follows: June 8, 1893, CUL Or. 1080.13viii; April 1893, CUL Add. 8398/12; Oct. 12, 1893, CUL Or. 1080.2viii. The list in Jenkinson's hand is CUL Or. 1080.13iii, v, vi. Wertheimer's reference to the "poor man" is to Ecclesiastes 9:14–15.

Neubauer's biography is drawn from Stefan Reif, "A Fresh Look at Adolf Neubauer as Scholar, Librarian, and Jewish Personality," unpublished paper (our thanks to Stefan Reif for showing us this paper); Rebecca J. W. Jefferson, "A Genizah Secret: The Count d'Hulst and Letters Revealing the Race to Recover the Lost Leaves of the Original Ecclesiasticus," *Journal of the History of Collections* 21/1, 2009; H. Loewe, "Adolf Neubauer, 1831–1931" (pamphlet, no date); S. R. Driver, Sinéad Agnew, "Adolf Neubauer," *Oxford Dictionary of National Biography*; Alexander Marx, "The Importance of the Geniza for Jewish History," *Proceedings of the American Academy for Jewish Research*

16, 1946–47. Quotations from Neubauer come from "The Mail," *University Intelligence*, Oxford, Nov. 24, 1876; "Miscellanea Liturgica," *JQR* 6/2, 1894; "Grammatical and Lexicographical Literature," *JQR* 6/3, 1894.

Accounts of the synagogue "repairs" may be found in Mosseri, "The Synagogues"; Cohen and Stillman, "The Cairo Geniza and the Custom of Geniza" [Heb]; Lambert, *Fortifications*. According to one version of events, a certain German had in 1888 "been sinking a well in the neighbourhood of the Fostat Synagogue [when he] excavated a number of Hebrew MSS." Documents had, in other words, been interred in the area before the synagogue was razed. See "The Cairo Geniza: How It Was Found," *JC*, May 5, 1933. For further discussion of the "repairs," see Elazar Hurvitz, *Catalogue of the Cairo Geniza Fragments in the Westminster College Library, Cambridge* 1, introduction [Heb] (New York, 2006).

Rebecca J. W. Jefferson is single-handedly responsible for uncovering the remarkable story of d'Hulst and his role in the Geniza's retrieval. We are enormously grateful to her for sharing her research with us. For more about d'Hulst, see Jefferson, "A Genizah Secret" and Jefferson, "The Cairo Genizah Unearthed." Quotations from d'Hulst and Sayce are all drawn from BLR, d. 1084.

Elkan Adler's second trip to the Geniza and its aftermath are described in his "An Eleventh Century Introduction"; "The Hebrew Treasures of England," *Transactions of the Jewish Historical Society of England*, 1918; "Ecclesiasticus," *JC*, March 11, 1904.

3. All Sirach Now

Background information relating to Solomon Schechter's interest in Ben Sira is drawn from David Starr, *Catholic Israel*; Y. Zussman, "Schechter the Scholar" [Heb], *Madda'ei haYahadut* 38, 1998; Francis Jenkinson's 1891, 1894, and 1896 diaries (CUL Add. 7414, Add. 7417, Add. 7419); Stefan Reif, "The Discovery of the Cambridge Ben Sira MSS," in *Proceedings of the First International Ben Sira Conference, 28–31 July 1996, Soesterberg, Netherlands*, Pancratius C. Beentjes, ed. (Berlin, 1997); Mathilde Schechter's memoir; Schechter, "A Hoard of Hebrew Manuscripts," "The Study of the Bible," and "Jewish Life in the Time of Ben Sira," all in *Studies* II. The last Jewish scholar to quote from the Hebrew Ben Sira was Saadia Gaon (about whom, see chapter 5, chapter 6, and especially chapter 8). "Badly mutilated" is Leo Deuel's description in *Testaments of Time*.

For general information about the Book of Ben Sira, see *The New Oxford Annotated Bible* (Apocrypha, Ecclesiasticus, or The Wisdom of Jesus the Son of Sirach), Revised Standard Version (New York, 1973); *The Wisdom of Ben Sira* (the Anchor Bible), A. A. Di Lella, ed., P. W. Skehan, trans. (New York, 1987); "Ecclesiasticus," *The Catholic Encyclopedia*; Bernard Mack, *Wisdom and the Hebrew Epic: Ben Sira's Hymn in Praise of the Fathers* (Chicago, 1985); James Kugel, *The Bible As It Was* (Cambridge, 1997) and *How to*

Read the Bible (New York, 2007); John J. Collins, "Ecclesiasticus," in *Oxford Bible Commentary*, J. Barton and J. Muddiman, eds. (Oxford, 2001); Daniel J. Harrington, *Jesus Ben Sira of Jerusalem: A Biblical Guide to Wise Living* (Collegeville, 2005). The best introduction to the book is still the Hebrew critical edition, *The Complete Book of Ben Sira* [Heb], M. Segal, ed. (Jerusalem, 1958).

The lectures Schechter was "feverishly preparing" became *Some Aspects of Rabbinic Theology* (London, 1909); their initial publication was in the *JQR* in three installments between 1894 and 1895. On Schechter and the Higher Criticism, see "The Law and Recent Criticism" and "The Study of the Bible," in *Studies* I and II; Schechter, "Higher Criticism, Higher Anti-Semitism," in *Seminary Addresses and Other Papers* (Cincinnati, 1915); D. Fine, "Solomon Schechter and the Ambivalence of Jewish Wissenschaft," *Judaism* 46/1, 1997; Julius Wellhausen, *Prolegomena to the History of Israel*, J. Sutherland Black and Allan Menzies, trans. (Edinburgh, 1885). The first German edition was published (under a different title) in 1878.

Much of the so-called source critical approach would prove to be sound, and Jewish scholars would adopt it. For more on this, see Marc Zvi Brettler, *How to Read the Bible* (Philadelphia, 2005); Starr, *Catholic Israel*; Paul Mendes-Flohr, "Jewish Scholarship as a Vocation," in *Proceedings of the International Conference Held by the Institute of Jewish Studies, University College, London, 1994*, A. L. Ivry, E. Wolfson, and A. Arkush, eds. (London, 1998). See also L. H. Silberman, "Wellhausen and Judaism," *Semeia* 25, 1983; and Kugel, *How to Read the Bible*.

Schechter's comments about the "German dogs" and Wellhausen are quoted in Starr, *Catholic Israel*. See also Robert Irwin, *For Lust of Knowing: The Orientalists and Their Enemies* (London, 2006). Schechter's first article was "Antisemitische Ethnografie," *Die Neuzeit* 21, 1881; an English translation appears in Starr. Schechter's comments on Wissenschaft in England are from a letter to Gottheil, July 10, 1883, JTSA Schechter 101/7.

For more on Schechter's relation to Zunz, see Schechter, "Leopold Zunz," *Studies* III (Philadelphia, 1924), and Starr, *Catholic Israel*. On Ben Sira's importance for Jewish literary tradition, see Reif, "The Discovery of Ben Sira," and R. Jefferson, "A Genizah Secret."

The descriptions of the Book of Ben Sira and its author are as follows: "A kind of rabbinic self-help manual," *The Bible*, D. Norton, ed. (London, 2006); "the first of the Paitanim," Schechter and C. Taylor, *The Wisdom of Ben Sira: Portions of the Book of Ecclesiasticus* (Cambridge, 1899); "a tissue of old classical phrases," Taylor, *The Wisdom of Ben Sira*; "to adapt the older Scriptures," Di Lella, *The Wisdom of Ben Sira* (Anchor Bible); "Polonius without Shakespeare," *The Bible*, Norton, ed.; "tedious," E. Fleischer, "Hebrew Poetry in a Biblical Mode in the Middle Ages" [Heb], *Te'uda* 7, 1991; "an idiom which is . . . hideous," H. L. Ginsberg, "The Original Hebrew of Ben Sira 12:10–14," *JBL* 74/2, 1955; "the most attractive book," *The Apocrypha: An American Translation*, Edgar J. Goodspeed, trans., Moses Hadas, introduction (New York, 1938/1989); "a self-conscious . . . artist," Menahem Kister, "A Contribution to the Interpretation of Ben

Sira" [Heb], *Tarbiz* 59/3–4, 1990; "The chapters containing the praise of wisdom," Schechter, *Expositor* 5/4, July 1896. On Ben Sira and the Jewish liturgy, see Cecil Roth, "Ecclesiasticus in the Synagogue Service," *Journal of Biblical Literature* 71/3, 1952.

Quotations from Ben Sira are given in the RSV (with changes), and are from (in order): 1:1–3, 24:2–6, 24:7–8, and 24:30–33. "Let us now praise famous men" is Ecclesiasticus 44:1–2. For more on this "teachable, practical sort of knowledge," see especially chapter 38 of Ben Sira, and *The Wisdom of Ben Sira* (Anchor Bible); also Segal, and James Kugel, *Great Poems of the Bible: A Reader's Companion with New Translations* (New York, 1999). Schechter's comment about Judaism's not knowing itself is from "Saints and Saintliness," *Studies* II.

Quotations from, and information about, D. S. Margoliouth's writing on Ecclesiasticus come from his *An Essay on the Place of Ecclesiasticus in Semitic Literature* (Oxford, 1890); D. S. Margoliouth, *The Expository Times* 16, 1904; A. Di Lella, *The Hebrew Text of Sirach* (The Hague, 1966); Gilbert Murray, "David Samuel Margoliouth, 1858–1940," in *Proceedings of the British Academy* 26, 1940; "the kind of beautiful mind," Irwin, *For Lust of Knowing*.

Schechter's article was "The Quotations from Ecclesiasticus in Rabbinic Literature," *JQR* 3/4, 1891. "I do not pretend to understand [them]" refers to Margoliouth's reconstructed Hebrew passages; see Schechter, *Expository Times*, Jan.–Feb. 1900. For more on all this see Mathilde Schechter's memoir.

In 1964, Yigal Yadin discovered at Masada badly damaged leather fragments of a scroll containing the Book of Ben Sira; the text was "invisible to the naked eye," but infrared photographs showed that the Hebrew of these first-century B.C.E. fragments was almost identical to that of the Geniza's Hebrew text and confirm its authenticity. This is the earliest extant copy of the Hebrew Ben Sira. For more on the Ben Sira manuscripts from Masada and Qumran, see Di Lella, *The Wisdom of Ben Sira* (Anchor Bible); Reif, "The Discovery of Ben Sira"; and Y. Yadin, *The Ben Sira Scroll from Masada* (Jerusalem, 1965) and *Eretz Israel* 8, 1967, Hebrew section. Also, Reif, "Reviewing the Links between the Dead Sea Scrolls and the Cairo Genizah," in *The Oxford Handbook of the Dead Sea Scrolls*, T. Lim and J. Collins, eds. (Oxford, 2009).

The only text we have for the passage mentioning Ben Sira's "house of learning" is a translation from the Syriac, so the authenticity of the term is questionable. See M. Kister, "A Contribution to the Interpretation of Ben Sira" [Heb]. Also Shaye J. D. Cohen, *From the Maccabees to the Mishnah* (Louisville, 1987); James Aitken, "Hebrew Study in Ben Sira's Beth Midrash," in *Hebrew Study from Ezra to Ben-Yehuda*, W. Horbury, ed. (London, 1999); and Elias Bickerman, *The Jews in the Greek Age* (Cambridge, 1988).

Ben Sira's first name is sometimes given in English as Jeshua, Joshua, or Jesus. Segal believes his name was Shimon (Simon). There is also uncertainty with regard to the various other parts of his name. Some sources have Yeshua (Jesus) bar Shimon Asira, others Yeshua ben Elazar ben Sira, and others still Shimon ben Yeshua ben Elazar ben Sira.

Schechter describes Ben Sira's world as "a world very much like ours" in "Jewish Life in the Time of Ben Sira," *Studies* II. For background on the way in which Ben Sira absorbed "elements of the surrounding Hellenistic society," see Bickerman, *The Jews*; James Aitken, "Biblical Interpretation as Political Manifesto: Ben Sira in His Seleucid Setting," *JJS* 51/2, 2000; Di Lella, *The Wisdom of Ben Sira* (Anchor Bible); D. Stern, introduction to *Poetics Today* 19/1, 1998; and B. Mack, *Wisdom*. Quotations from Ben Sira about "the full range of life's pleasures, subtleties, and trials" are from 31:27, 22:17, 43:13–14, and 43:18.

Di Lella in the Anchor Bible writes of the "gnawing, unexpressed fear" felt by Jews of Ben Sira's day. See James Aitken, "Biblical Interpretation as Political Manifesto," for a somewhat different perspective. Also Schechter, "Jewish Life in the Time of Ben Sira," *Studies* II. It seems clear from the grandson's preface that the Greek translation was prepared two generations later in Egypt for Jews who had lost direct contact with the wisdom tradition of Hebrew.

D. S. Margoliouth describes the "miserable trap" in *The Origin of the "Original" Hebrew of Ecclesiasticus* (London, 1899). In other words, Margoliouth thought it was not a medieval copy of an ancient book, but a contemporary high-medieval Hebrew version of a much earlier Greek or Syriac translation. Margoliouth, it should be noted, was joined in his skepticism about the authenticity of Schechter's Ben Sira fragment by several Jewish scholars of the day.

The phrase "I am all Sirach now" appears in Meir Ben-Horin, "Solomon Schechter to Judge Mayer Sulzberger: Part I," *Jewish Social Studies* [*JSS*] 25/4, 1963. That letter was from April 1898; Schechter had already written to Sulzberger in January of that year about the need to "save our literature from the goyim," adding that he wanted to oversee the preparation of "a scientific edition of the Apocrypha from a Jewish point of view." (All quotations of Schechter and Mathilde's letters to Sulzberger in what follows come from Ben-Horin's article.) "Sirach" derives from the Greek Sirachides, or son (or grandson) of Sira. See John J. Collins, "Ecclesiasticus," in *Oxford Bible Commentary*, J. Barton and J. Muddiman, eds. (Oxford, 2001).

4. Into Egypt

Mathilde and Schechter's letters to Sulzberger are dated Jan. 3, 1897, and Dec. 22, 1896, respectively. For more on Mathilde, see JTSA Schechter archive: her memoir (box 28/1-11); her novel (box 28/12); her correspondence (box 27). See also Bentwich, *Solomon Schechter*, and Mel Scult, "The Baale Boste Reconsidered: The Life of Mathilde Roth Schechter (M. R. S.)," *Modern Judaism* 7/1, 1987.

Much of the detail in this chapter is drawn from Schechter's letters to Mathilde, from the period of his Egyptian adventure. These letters are all contained in JTSA Schechter archive, box 26. Our thanks to Itta Shedletzky for help with translation of the German parts of Schechter's letters. For further explanation of what led Schechter to Cairo, see his "A Hoard of Hebrew Manuscripts"; Gibson, "Dr. Solomon Schechter"; Marx, "The Importance of the Geniza"; Adler, "Ecclesiasticus"; Jefferson, "A Genizah Secret." Additional descriptions of his time in the Geniza come from his letter to Francis Jenkinson, Jan. 12, 1897, CUL Add. 6463 (E) 3416.

Information about Taylor comes from J. E. Sandys and John D. Pickles, "Charles Taylor," *Oxford Dictionary of National Biography*; Reif, *A Jewish Archive*; Mathilde's memoir; *Charles Taylor and the Genizah Collection: A Centenary Seminar and Exhibition*, Stefan Reif, ed. (Cambridge, 2009). Schechter's obituary for Taylor from *Jewish Comment* is quoted in Bentwich, *Solomon Schechter.*

Details of Schechter's preparations for his trip come from Mathilde's Jan. 3, 1897, letter to Sulzberger; Agnes Lewis to Mathilde Schechter, Feb. 7, 1897, JTSA Schechter 27/33; Schechter, "A Hoard"; an undated letter from Schechter to Elkan Adler, which says "many thanks for your kind letter to the rav in Cairo" (he quotes "*lamdan* and *tzaddik*" here), JTSA Schechter 1/15.

Information about the Cattaui family comes from Samir Raafat, "Dynasty: The House of Yacoub Cattaui," *Egyptian Mail*, April 2, 1994; Gudrun Krämer, *The Jews in Modern Egypt, 1914–1952* (London, 1989); Elkan N. Adler, "Notes on a Journey to the East," *JC*, Dec. 7, 1888. In his "Hoard of Hebrew Manuscripts," Schechter mistakenly refers to Moise Cattaui as Mr. Youssef M. Cattaui. For more on the relationship of Cairo's Jewish aristocracy to the Geniza, see Reif, *A Jewish Archive*; Amitav Ghosh, *In an Antique Land* (London, 1992).

For more on the question of what Schechter took from the "other genizot," see Schechter to Mathilde, Jan. 20, 1897; Schechter to Sulzberger, Jan. 19, 1897. The scholar Nehemia Allony claimed that Schechter got many of the fragments from the graveyard of al-Basatin. Habermann (*The Geniza* [Heb]) quotes Allony as saying "he took little from the Ben Ezra synagogue and most of it he took from the cemetery at al-Basatin." This claim is unsubstantiated by Schechter's letters.

Information about Henriques derives from Henriques to Schechter, April 5, 1898, JTSA Schechter 4/11; Bentwich, *Solomon Schechter*; Jefferson, "The Historical Significance." For more on Raffalovich, see Reif, *A Jewish Archive*; Jefferson, "Historical Significance"; Jenkinson diary, Dec. 4, 1898, CUL Add. 7421.

Agnes and Margaret's account of their Cairo trip are as follows: "the microbe," Lewis, *In the Shadow*; "your dear Husband," Agnes Lewis to Mathilde Schechter, Jan. 21, 1897, JTSA Schechter 27/33; "We have no doubt," Margaret Gibson, "On Two Hebrew Documents of the 11th and 12th Centuries," from the *Cambridge Antiquarian Society's Communications* 10, WGL/6/10; "tea to meet the rabbi," Agnes Lewis to Mathilde Schechter, Feb. 7, 1897, JTSA Schechter 27/33.

5. Sorting

Francis Jenkinson's biography is culled from Stewart, *Francis Jenkinson*; Stephen Gase-lee, "Francis Jenkinson," *The Library* 4/3, Dec. 1, 1923; "Francis Jenkinson," *The Library Association Record*, Dec. 1923; Stephen Gaselee, "Francis Jenkinson," *Oxford Dictionary of National Biography* (1922–30); David McKitterick, "Francis Jenkinson," *Oxford Diction-ary of National Biography* (2004); Reif, "Jenkinson and Schechter at Cambridge: An Expanded and Updated Assessment," *Transactions of the Jewish Historical Society of England* 33, 1993; and especially Jenkinson's diaries (from which all the quotes here come). These are from 1897–1900. (See CUL Add. 7420, 7421, 7422, 7423.)

Information about Oxyrynchus and Flinders Petrie comes from Deuel, *Testaments of Time*; Peter Parsons, *City of the Sharp-Nosed Fish: Greek Papyri beneath the Egyptian Sand Reveal a Long-Lost World* (London, 2007); Flinders Petrie, *Seventy Years in Archaeology* (New York, 1932); Drower, *Flinders Petrie*; Mathilde's memoir; Ann Rosalie David, *The Pyramid Builders of Ancient Egypt: A Modern Investigation of Pharaoh's Workforce* (London, 1986).

Details of Taylor's presentation of the manuscripts to the library are drawn from the CUL Syndicate Minutes, June 9, 1897; May 11, 1898; Reif, *A Jewish Archive*. The des-ignated £500 is worth some $40,000 today.

The description of Schechter at work with the fragments is Mathilde's, from her memoir; Bentwich recycles it almost verbatim in *Solomon Schechter*. The nose-bag quote is H. F. Stewart's, in *Francis Jenkinson*.

Suum Cuique's letter appeared in the London *Times*, Aug. 4, 1897; Schechter's response was published there on Aug. 7, 1897. Schechter wrote to Elkan Adler, Aug. 5, 1897, JTSA Schechter 1/15. His letters to Sulzberger are Aug. 5, 1897, and undated, Bentwich, *Solomon Schechter*.

On the "now-iconic photograph" (which appears on p. 89 and on the cover of this book) and more on the process of sorting, see Reif, "One Hundred Years of Genizah Research at Cambridge," *Jewish Book Annual* 53, 1995–96; "Facts and Fictions about Aquila," *JC*, Oct. 15, 1897; Schechter, "A Hoard" and "A Hoard . . . II," *Studies* II; let-ters to Sulzberger, e.g., Aug. 5, 1897, Aug. 30, 1897, Jan. 14, 1898.

For more on Schechter's decision to leave England for the United States, see, for instance, his letters to Sulzberger, April 16, 1897, May 9, 1897, June 26, 1898; Schechter to Cyrus Adler, Aug. 6, 1899, JTSA Schechter 1/11. Montefiore's critique appears in J. B. Stein, *Lieber Freund: The Letters of Claude Goldsmid Montefiore to Solomon Schechter, 1885–1902* (Lanham, 1988).

Details of Schechter's departure from Cambridge come from Schechter to Jenkin-son, Dec. 29, 1901, CUL Add. 6463 (E) 4963; letter to Schechter from the members of the Cambridge Hebrew Congregation, March 18, 1902 (JTSA Schechter 2/37); Agnes Lewis to Jenkinson, Jan. 24, 1903 (CUL Add. 6463 [E] 5309); Bentwich, *Solomon Schech-*

ter; David Starr, "The Importance of Being Frank: Solomon Schechter's Departure from Cambridge," *JQR* 94/1, 2004. For more on the manuscripts he took to JTS, see Stefan Reif, "The Cambridge Geniza Story: Some Unfamiliar Aspects" [Heb], *Te'uda* 15, 1999; Schechter to Jenkinson, Aug. 28, 1902 (CUL Add. 8809/1902/2).

6. Palimpsests

I

Information on Francis Burkitt is drawn from J. F. Bethune-Baker, *Oxford Dictionary of National Biography*, and Soskice, *Sisters of Sinai*. For details about palimpsests of the sort Burkitt worked with, see M. Sokoloff and J. Yahalom, "Christian Palimpsests from the Cairo Geniza," *Revue d'histoire des Textes* VIII, 1978. On Burkitt's bicycle crash, see "Schechter Anecdotes Gathered by F. I. Schechter in England," JTSA Schechter 29/17.

Quotations by Margaret and Agnes are as follows: "There is nothing that does not leave its mark," Gibson, *How the Codex*; "'ill-scented' ammonium," Gibson, *How the Codex*; "the action of common air," Lewis, *In the Shadow*; "like mending broken chain," Margaret Gibson to Rendel Harris, Feb. 17, 1895 (WGL 5/5). See also Lewis and Gibson, *Palestinian Syriac Texts from Palimpsest Fragments*.

Burkitt's comments on the palimpsests are drawn from his *Fragments of the Books of Kings, According to the Translation of Aquila* (Cambridge, 1897) and from Burkitt, "Aquila," *JQR* 10/2, 1898. See also Schechter's letters to Sulzberger of April 16, May 9, Aug. 5, 1897.

On Aquila's translation see, "Bible, Translations, Ancient Versions," *Encyclopedia Judaica* [*EJ*] 4. In addition to being published in book form by Cambridge University Press, the palimpsests were written about on several occasions in the London *Times* (e.g., Aug. 3, 1897, Dec. 30, 1897, and April 12, 1898), and in the *New York Times* on May 7, 1898. Mention is repeatedly made in both of the Greek and Hebrew texts.

Information about Davidson is drawn from a variety of sources, especially C. Davidson, *Out of Endless Yearnings* (New York, 1946). Davidson's other key work is his monumental *Thesaurus of Medieval Hebrew Poetry*, which appeared in four volumes between 1924 and 1938 and cataloged every published (printed) medieval Hebrew poem known at the time. See Davidson, *Thesaurus of Medieval Hebrew Poetry*, introduction by J. Schirmann (New York, 1970).

For more in English on the history of the term *piyyut*, see Laura S. Lieber, *Yannai on Genesis* (Cincinnati, 2010), and "Piyyut," *Encyclopedia of Judaism* 3. Yannai's only known extant poem was part seven of the *piyyut* beginning *"Onei pitrei rahamatayim,"* in Z. M. Rabinovitz, *The Liturgical Poems of Rabbi Yannai according to the Triennial Cycle of the Pentateuch and the Holidays* 1 [Heb] (Jerusalem, 1985). The section was preserved by recitation in Ashkenazic communities on the Sabbath preceding Passover. This is the hymn mentioned by Ephraim of Bonn. For more on Yannai, and his relation to Kallir, see Davidson, *Mahzor Yannai* (New York, 1919). Wertheimer's Yannai finds were published in *Ginzei Yerushalayim* 2.

The evidence relating to Davidson's discovery is circumstantial and secondhand. See his wife's memoir, and Shuly Rubin Schwartz, "The Schechter Faculty" in *Tradition Renewed*, Wertheimer, ed. "Grotesque" is Menahem Zulay's description in "The Master Hymnist," in *Eretz Israel and Its Poetry* [Heb]. See also Solomon B. Freehof, "Synagogue Poetry: Mahzor Yannai, a Work of the Seventh Century," *American Journal of Semitic Languages and Literature* 37/2, 1921.

For Davidson's own thoughts on his discovery of Yannai, see his preface to *Mahzor Yannai*; also his letter to Schechter, Nov. 14, 1910, JTSA Schechter 2/57.

Descriptions of Palestinian synagogue practice and scriptural recitation are from Davidson, *Mahzor Yannai*; Hayyim Schirmann, *Studies in the History of Hebrew Poetry and Drama* 1 [Heb] (Jerusalem, 1979). Schirmann makes the comparison to the cantatas. Early Palestinian midrashim, such as Genesis Rabba and Leviticus Rabba, are also based on the triennial system. See Stefan Reif, "The Meaning of the Cairo Genizah for Students of Early Jewish and Christian Liturgy," in *Jewish and Christian Liturgy and Worship*, A. Gerhards and C. Leonhard, eds. (Leiden, 2007); M. Freidman, "Opposition to Prayer and Its Palestinian Practice" [Heb], in *Knesset Ezra: Literature and Life in the Synagogue, Studies Presented to Ezra Fleischer* [Heb], S. Elizur, M. D. Herr, et al., eds. (Jerusalem, 1994); Zulay, "Yannai Studies" [Heb], *Yediot hamakhon* 2, 1936; *Mahzor Eretz Israel* [Heb], J. Yahalom, ed. (Jerusalem, 1987).

On the core liturgy, see Ismar Elbogen, *Jewish Liturgy*, Raymond Scheindlin, trans. (Philadelphia, 1993); "Liturgy," *EJ* 11; Ezra Fleischer, "Studies in the Problems Relating to the Liturgical Function of Types of Early Piyyut" [Heb], *Tarbiz* 40, 1971. See also Reif, *Judaism and Hebrew Prayer: New Perspectives on Jewish Liturgical History* (Cambridge, 1993); and Lee I. Levine, *The Ancient Synagogue: The First Thousand Years* (New Haven, 2000). This core liturgy—consisting of the twice-daily recitation of the *shema*, some form of the standing prayer, or *amida*, and public readings from the Torah—developed very early and certainly during the mishnaic period, which is to say, between the destruction of the Temple in 70 C.E. and 200 C.E., when the Mishna was redacted.

The history of attempts to date Yannai's work is discussed in Rabinovitz, *Yannai* [Heb]. Some place him as early as the third century and others as late as the eighth. Information about Romanos is drawn from *Sacred Song: From the Byzantine Pulpit, Romanos the Melodist*, R. J. Schrok, trans. and ed. (Gainesville, 1995). The Greek origin of the term itself—*piyyut*—highlights the Hellenistic context in which it emerged. See Lieber, *Yannai on Genesis*.

The original of "As who . . . on high" comes from Davidson, *Mahzor Yannai*; Burkitt, *Fragments*, Facsimile II, T-S 12.184r. The restored text is based on other manuscripts that have been found since and differ distinctly from Davidson's reading. It appears in the Rabinovitz edition and might be translated (without the acrostic) as follows:

Happy is he whom you hound like a father,	*lest he be left to suffer forever—*
Imprisoned in his life. You'll make him falter	*blood in its issue if [it occurs]*
You made him pure who now is sullied	*Desires divert him toward what is muddied*
His pus is from him, his sentence and majesty	*.............................. [y]*
Impurity comes with devotion's end	*his tormentor gaining the upper hand*
For his sins have swelled since he was young	*and so the issue flows from skin*

The mishnaic quote citation is from Berakhot 4:4. See also Hagiga 14a: "Every day, ministering angels are created from the fiery stream, and utter song, and cease to be, for it is said: 'They are new every morning: great is Thy faithfulness' (Lam 3:23)." See, too, Palestinian Talmud, Berakhot 84:4 and *Midrash Tehillim* (Buber, end of chapter 87). For more on prayer and *piyyut*, see also Zulay, "Between the Walls of the Institute," in *Eretz Israel and Its Poetry* [Heb]; Langer, *To Worship God Properly* (Cincinnati, 1990); Zulay, unpublished lecture, "Hebrew Poetry in the Cairo Geniza" [Heb] (Schocken Institute, Zulay archive, exhibition box); Fleischer, "The Cultural Profile of Eastern Jewry in the Early Middle Ages as Reflected by the Payyetanic Texts of the Geniza" [Heb], *Te'uda* 15, 1999.

For the Hebrew of "You, Lord, who are faithful," see Davidson, *Mahzor Yannai*, Fragment 4; Rabinovitz, *Yannai* [Heb], poem 88, part 3. See also T-S 12.184r.

The educational function of poetry in this context is discussed by Zulay in "The Master Hymnist" [Heb]. On the notion of poetry as a kind of prayer that substitutes for sacrifice, see Michael D. Swartz and Joseph Yahalom, *Avodah: An Anthology of Ancient Poetry for Yom Kippur* (University Park, 2005); J. Yahalom, *Poetry and Society* [Heb] (Tel Aviv, 1999); Yahalom, "The Sepphoris Synagogue Mosaic and Its Story," in *From Dura to Sepphoris: Studies in Jewish Art and Society in Late Antiquity*, L. I. Levine and Z. Weiss, eds. (Portsmouth, 2000); and M. Swartz, "Sage, Priest, and Poet," in *Jews, Christians, and Polytheists in the Ancient Synagogue*, Steven Fine, ed. (London, 1999); and S. Fine, "Between Liturgy and Social History: Priestly Power in Late Antique Palestinian Synagogues?," *JJS* 56/1, 2005. For helpful English descriptions of the "elaborate structure" and "elliptical . . . development" of the *kerova*, see Lieber, "Piyyut," and, for considerably more detail, *Yannai on Genesis*. The description of a "fresh, living, and instructive word" is from Zulay's Motza lecture.

For more on the connection between *piyyutim* and the standard liturgy, see S. Elizur's commentary in Zulay, *From the Lips of Poets and Precentors* [Heb] (Jerusalem, 2004). Elizur makes clear that the origins of the form remain murky. See also S. Elizur, "Poetry Is in the Details: Words in Memory of Prof. Ezra Fleischer" [Heb], *Madda'ei haYahadut* 43, 2006; and E. Fleischer, "Studies in the Problems Relating to the Liturgical Function of Types of Early Piyyut" [Heb].

II

Information on Salman Schocken is drawn primarily from Anthony David, *The Patron* (New York, 2004); Stephen M. Poppel, "Salman Schocken and the Schocken Verlag," *Leo Baeck Institute Yearbook* 17, 1972; Racheli Edelman, "Rediscovering Grandpa Schocken," *Haaretz*, Nov. 9, 2007; and from interviews with Shmuel Glick and Baruch Yunin at the Schocken Institute, Jerusalem (March 26, 2009).

For more on the discovery of Schocken 37, see Hayyim Schirmann, *The History of Hebrew Poetry in Muslim Spain* [Heb], ed., supplemented, and annotated by Ezra Fleischer (Jerusalem, 1995); and in English, Peter Cole, *Selected Poems of Solomon Ibn Gabirol* (Princeton, 2001). Another important manuscript of poems by Schocken 37's copyist has since been found among the Geniza documents (T-S K 25.2 and Or. 1080 4.1). For a detailed description of the mss., see Hayyim Brody, *The Poems of Moshe ibn Ezra, Secular Poetry* 2 [Heb] (Jerusalem, 1942).

Information about Zulay comes mainly from a short memoir by his daughter, Ada Yardeni, "In Memory of Menahem Zulay" [Heb], *Mehkerei Yerushalayim besifrut Ivrit* 21, 2007, and from the authors' interview with Yardeni, Sept. 24, 2009, Jerusalem.

For more about Paul Kahle, see Matthew Black, "Paul Ernest Kahle, 1875–1965," *Proceedings of the British Academy* 51, 1965; Marie Kahle, "What Would You Have Done? The Story of the Escape of the Kahle Family from Nazi Germany" (London, 1945); Norman Bentwich, "German Scholar in London," *Palestine Post*, May 15, 1942. Kahle's *The Cairo Geniza* (Oxford, 1947) was the first general book on the subject.

Zulay's comment on Davidson's publication of Yannai's poetry comes from "The Master Hymnist" [Heb]. On the importance of this literature, see also Zulay, "Yannai Studies" [Heb], and S. Lieberman, "Yannai's Cantorial Poetry" [Heb], *Sinai* 4, 1938. For more on Osiris see James Frazer, *The Golden Bough*, Theodor H. Gaster, ed., abridged edition (New York, 1959). See under "Osiris," sections 242–43.

Quotations by Zulay are as follows: "an entire literature . . . 'In my dream' " is from "From Geniza to Geniza"; "Memory . . . is the finest index" is from "Between the Walls of the Institute"; "a sacred task" is from "Between the Walls"; "Each photostat is a prayer" is from "The Master Hymnist" (all from *Eretz Israel and Its Poetry* [Heb]).

Zulay's description of his own work is taken from an unpublished prose fragment with which he originally intended to open his (Hebrew) essay "Between the Walls of the Institute." The essay appeared in a Festschrift for Schocken in 1952. His draft contains a note in his hand saying, "I took this out and drafted a new version" (Schocken Institute, Zulay archive, exhibition box).

On the last Hebrew volume published in Nazi Germany, see M. Schmelzer, "The Contribution of the Geniza to the Study of Liturgy and Poetry," *Proceedings of the American Academy for Jewish Research* 63, 1997–2001; E. Fleischer, "Perspectives on Our Early Poetry after One Hundred Years of Studying the Cairo Geniza" [Heb], *Madda'ei haYehadut* 38, 1999.

For a description of the sometimes "obscure or bizarrely exegetical" nature of the *kerova*, see S. Elizur, "The Congregation in the Synagogue and the Ancient Qedushta" [Heb], in *Knesset Ezra*, S. Elizur, M. D. Herr, et al., eds.; Laura S. Lieber, "The Rhetoric of Participation: Experiential Elements of Early Hebrew Liturgical Poetry," *Journal of Religion* 90, 2010. For examples of how Yannai's sequences could open into a more resonant and emblematic mode, see "You, Lord, who are faithful" (pp. 111, 260) and, in the same sequence, poem 7B, "He is human and so will be humbled," Rabinovitz, *Yannai*, p. 428. Also see "Our eyes are weak with longing" (p. 121) and S. Elizur, *From the Lips*, pp. 10–11. The likening of Yannai's poems to "a new midrash" is Ernest Simon's, as quoted by Yehoshua Granat, *Haaretz*, April 29, 2005. The *rahit* is described in Elizur, "The Congregation and the Qedushta" [Heb].

The manuscript of "Angel of Fire" is Bodl. MS Heb. e 73.54. It is based on the weekly reading beginning at Exodus 3:1 and focuses on the second verse of that reading, which serves as a kind of lead-in to the poem (here an epigraph). See Zulay, *The Liturgical Poems of Yannai* [Heb], poem 33, part 7; Rabinovitz, *Yannai* [Heb], poem 46, part 7; see also commentary in Elizur, *A Poem for Every Parasha* [Heb] (Jerusalem, 1999), *Parashat Tzav*, and Nahum M. Bronznik, *The Liturgical Poems of Yannai: A Commentary* 1 [Heb] (Jerusalem, 2000), notes to poem 46. The translation departs in several places from the literal Hebrew in order to preserve the spirit and form of the poem. As Ezra Fleischer has noted with regard to the Hebrew liturgical poetry of late antiquity, "Sometimes what the poet is saying is not important; what's important is how he says it and the intensity of the magic and the wizardry of the words" (*Yediot aharonot*, March 20, 1987). The translation of the poem here is by the authors. A different translation appears in T. Carmi, *The Penguin Book of Hebrew Verse* (New York, 1981).

The *kerova* "Our eyes are weak with longing" is based on the reading starting with Genesis 29:31: "And the Lord saw that Leah was hated," *The Liturgical Poems of Yannai* [Heb], M. Zulay, ed., supplementary poems to *kerova* 17, part 4; poem 27, part 4 in Rabinovitz. Schirmann has a fine brief analysis of this poem in his essay on Yannai, in Schirmann, *Hebrew Poetry and Drama* [Heb]. See also T. Carmi, *Penguin Book of Hebrew Verse*.

Quotations by Zulay are as follows: "Mr. Zulay will continue to write the reports," interview with Zulay's daughter, Ada Yardeni; "remnant of a vital faith and naiveté," Zulay, "From Geniza to Geniza," *Eretz Israel and Its Poetry* [Heb]; "mute orphans," Zulay, "Between the Walls," *Eretz Israel and Its Poetry* [Heb]; "the passport of Hebrew literature," Motza lecture. Information about Zulay's health is drawn from the interview with Yardeni and from her article "In Memory of My Father" [Heb]. On Zulay's accomplishment, see S. Elizur, "Fifty Years of Research after Menahem Zulay" [Heb], *Mehkerei Yerushalayim besifrut Ivrit* 21, 2007.

Yannai's *mahzor* has continued to develop. Some half a century after the 1938 Schocken collection a nearly complete edition of the poet's work (by Z. M. Rabinovitz) was published in two volumes with extensive commentary. New fragments of poems by him have continued to surface.

For more on Fleischer as heir to Zulay, see *Yediot aharonot*, July 25, 1975, interview with Penina Meizlisch; Elizur, "From the Depths" [Heb], *Madda'ei HaYahadut* 43, 2006. Fleischer's quotes are as follows: "uniquely Jewish beauty," Fleischer, *Yediot aharonot*, March 20, 1987, interview by Zisi Stavi; "The Geniza didn't change [this] discipline," Fleischer, "The Cultural Profile of Eastern Jewry" [Heb].

Quotations from Ben Sira are: "those who composed musical psalms," 44:5; "who have no memorial," 44:9–10; "maintain the fabric of the world," 38:26–29.

7. That Nothing Be Lost

The "salt-mine" comparison is Gerson Cohen's, in "The Reconstruction of Gaonic History," introduction to the reprint edition of Jacob Mann's *Texts and Studies in Jewish History and Literature* (New York, 1972).

Information about Worman comes from *Ernest James Worman, 1871–1909* (Cambridge, 1910); Reif, *A Jewish Archive;* "Report of the Library Syndicate for the Year Ending December 31, 1909"; and citations below. The account of Abrahams's trip to Cairo is drawn from Phyllis Abrahams, "The Letters of Israel Abrahams from Egypt and Palestine in 1898," *Transactions of the Jewish Historical Society of England* 24, 1975. See Jefferson, "The Historical Significance."

Descriptions of the help Worman gave other scholars are derived from Reif, "A History of the Geniza Collection" [Heb]; Louis Ginzberg, "Preface," *Geonica* (New York, 1909). In "Geonic Jurisprudence from the Cairo Geniza" (*Proceedings of the American Academy for Jewish Research* 63, 1997), Neil Danzig blames Worman for many errors in Ginzberg's texts. Worman's own scholarly articles are "Notes on the Jews," *JQR* 18/1, 1905; "Forms of Address in Genizah Letters," *JQR* 19/4, 1907; "The Exilarch Bustani," *JQR* 20/1, 1908; "Two Book-Lists from the Cairo Genizah," *JQR* 20/3, 1908.

The two documents that Worman accounts for here are T-S 18 J 1.10 and T-S 18 J 1.11. Both are transcribed, translated, and discussed in Norman Golb's "Legal Documents from the Cairo Genizah," *JSS* 20, 1958. Worman's transcription contains several mistakes; we have replicated the notebook entry as it appears, without correcting those errors.

Descriptions of Mann come from A. M. Habermann, "Jacob Mann—The Man and the Scholar" [Heb], in *Men of the Book and Men of Action: Reflections on Writers, Scholars, Bibliographers, Printers and Book-Dealers* [Heb] (Jerusalem, 1974); Gerson Cohen, "The Reconstruction of Gaonic History," in Mann, *Texts and Studies;* Victor Reichert, "Jacob Mann, 1888–1940," *American Jewish Year Book* 5702; Dov Nitzani, "Professor Dr. Jacob Mann," in *Sefer Przemysl* [Heb] (Tel Aviv, 1964); Mark Cohen, *Jewish Self-Government in Medieval Egypt: The Origins of the Office of Head of the Jews, ca. 1065–1126* (Princeton, 1980);

Menahem Schmelzer, "One Hundred Years of Genizah Discovery and Research in the United States," in *Studies in Jewish Bibliography and Medieval Hebrew Poetry* (New York, 2006). Mann's "cautious and laborious . . . method" is outlined in the preface to his *Texts and Studies.* The account of the value of Mann's *The Jews* is based on S. D. Goitein, "Preface and Reader's Guide" to the reprint edition of Jacob Mann, *The Jews in Egypt and in Palestine under the Fatimid Caliphs* (New York, 1970). All quotes from Goitein in this chapter come from this preface.

Mann's description of his working method appears in his letter to Israel Davidson, dated July 5, 1918 (JTSA Davidson 5/32). The gas mask anecdote is J. D. Pearson's, from "Curiosities of Bygone Days," *Genizah Fragments* 28, Oct. 1994. Mann's account of the scope of *The Jews* appears in his introduction to the same.

The description of Schechter's foreign accent and the European bent of the early JTS faculty are derived from Mel Scult, "Schechter's Seminary"; Schwartz, "The Schechter Faculty"; Robert Liberles, "*Wissenschaft des Judentums* Comes to America"; Jonathan Sarna, "Two Traditions of Seminary Scholarship"—all in *Tradition Renewed*, Wertheimer, ed.; Eli Ginzberg, *Louis Ginzberg: Keeper of the Law* (Philadelphia, 1966); Starr, *Catholic Israel.* "Far too highbrow" is Sarna's description.

For more on the language of Jewish scholarship, see Menahem Schmelzer, "One Hundred Years of Genizah Discovery"; Sarna, "Two Traditions." On the move of Wissenschaft to Palestine and into Hebrew, see David N. Myers, *Re-inventing the Jewish Past: European Jewish Intellectuals and the Zionist Return to History* (New York, 1995); Myers, "Between Diaspora and Zion: History, Memory, and the Jerusalem Scholars," in *The Jewish Past Revisited*, Myers and David B. Ruderman, eds. (New Haven, 1998). The German-Jewish commentator was Israel Elbogen, as quoted in Myers, *Re-inventing.* For more on Albert Einstein and the Hebrew University, see "The Hebrew University," *EJ* 8. Schechter and Adler's announcement appears in *JQR* new series, 1/1, 1910.

David Kaufmann's Geniza connection is described in A. Scheiber, "The Kaufmann-Genizah: Its Importance for the World of Scholarship," *Jubilee Volume of the Oriental Collection, 1951–1976*, Éva Apor, ed. (Budapest, 1978). Information about Jack Mosseri comes from Mosseri, "A New Hoard of Jewish MSS"; Israel Adler, "Forward," *Catalogue of the Jack Mosseri Collection*, ed. by the Institute of Microfilmed Hebrew Manuscripts with the collaboration of numerous specialists (Jerusalem, 1990); "Treasure Trove," *Genizah Fragments* 53, April 2007. The description of "the raid on our . . . - treasure-house" comes from "In the Land of the Pharaohs," an interview with Mosseri, *JC*, May 5, 1911. For more on the Dropsie collection, see B. Halper, *Descriptive Catalogue of Genizah Fragments in Philadelphia* (Philadelphia, 1924). The Freer's holdings are described in Gottheil and Worrell, *Fragments.*

The fact that Adler bought Geniza manuscripts from the Bodleian was recently discovered and documented by Rebecca Jefferson. See Jefferson, "The Cairo Genizah Unearthed," for the intriguing details. The efforts by JTS to buy Adler's library may be traced through the following letters: Marx to Sulzberger, Nov. 17, 1916, in *The Mayer*

Sulzberger–Alexander Marx Correspondence, 1904–1923, Herman Dicker, ed. (New York, 1990); Cyrus Adler to Jacob Schiff, Sept. 9, 1919, in Cyrus Adler, *Selected Letters*, Ira Robinson, ed. (Philadelphia, 1985); Louis Marshall to Cyrus Adler, Jan. 31, 1923, and the rest of the extensive correspondence in JTSA Cyrus Adler, 17/1. See also Herman Dicker, *Of Learning and Libraries: The Seminary Library at One Hundred* (New York, 1988); Nahum M. Sarna, "The Library of the Jewish Theological Seminary of America," *Jewish Book Annual* 21, 1963–64; Neil Danzig, introduction, *A Catalogue of Fragments of Halakhah and Midrash from the Cairo Genizah in the Elkan Nathan Adler Collection of the Library of the Jewish Theological Seminary of America* [Heb] (New York/Jerusalem, 1997). The embezzlement by Adler's business partner is described in "Elkan Adler," *EJ* 2. The last two letters quoted here are Elkan Adler to Cyrus Adler, March 27, 1923, JTSA Cyrus Adler 17/1; and Cyrus Adler to Elkan Adler, C. Adler, *Selected Letters* 2.

8. A Gallery of Heretics

The manuscript that puzzled Schechter is T-S 10 K 17. It consists of six leaves of paper, 20.7 cm x 15.2 cm. Schechter writes about the find in "Geniza Specimens: The Oldest Collection of Bible Difficulties, by a Jew," *JQR* 13/3, 1901. All of Schechter's descriptions of that text come from the *JQR* article.

The small book Davidson published after his trip to Cambridge is *Saadia's Polemic against Hiwi al-Balkhi* (New York, 1915). Information about Hiwi al-Balkhi comes from that volume as well as from Robert Brody, *The Geonim of Babylonia and the Shaping of Medieval Jewish Culture* (New Haven, 1998); "Hiwi al-Balkhi," *EJ* 8; Judah Rosenthal, *Hiwi al-Balkhi: A Comparative Study* (Philadelphia, 1949); Henry Malter, *Saadia Gaon: His Life and Works* (Philadelphia, 1921/1942); E. Fleischer, "A Fragment from Hivi al-Balkhi's Criticism of the Bible" [Heb], *Tarbiz* 51, 1982; Avraham Naftali Zvi Roth's response to Fleischer in *Tarbiz* 52, 1983; and Haggai Ben-Shammai, *Abu Yusef Yaakub al-Kirkisani's System of Religious Thought* [Heb] (dissertation, The Hebrew University, 1968).

The "quasi-Jewish sect" that sought to change the Sabbath to Wednesday was— according to one source—the Ananites (followers of Anan). See Moshe Gil, "The Origins of the Karaites," in *Karaite Judaism*, Polliack, ed. For more about Saadia Gaon, see R. Brody, *The Geonim and Rav Sa'adya Gaon* [Heb] (Jerusalem, 2006), and H. Malter, *Saadia*. The scrap of Saadia's reply that Davidson had fished out of the Cambridge pile is T-S 8 J 30. Brody sums up Saadia's contribution well, noting that his influence on the development of the Jewish medieval tradition is "more comprehensive and profound" than that of any other individual. The quote that begins "transforming almost beyond recognition" is Brody's, from *The Geonim*.

Davidson's misidentification is explained by Fleischer, "Hivi's Commentary" [Heb]. Davidson also states that Hiwi's questions were most likely composed in Arabic, but later scholars believed, for a variety of reasons, that they had to have been composed in Hebrew. See Jefim Schirmann, *New Hebrew Poems from the Geniza* [Heb] (Jerusalem, 1965).

Saadia's acrostics deployed the letters of the alphabet in a complicated arrangement. See Davidson, *Saadia's Polemic*. On Saadia as a *payyetan*, see Menahem Zulay, *The Liturgical Poetry of Saadia Gaon and His School* [Heb] (Jerusalem, 1964), and *Siddur Rav Saadia Gaon* [Heb], I. Davidson, S. Assaf, and B. I. Joel, eds. (Jerusalem, 1941/1985).

God's placing the other nations in the care of the angels is, as Hiwi sees it, alluded to in Deuteronomy 4:19, which, as a popular medieval reading had it, sets up this contrast between the Jews and non-Jews. See *The Legends of the Jews* 5, Louis Ginzberg, ed. (Philadelphia, 1925/1953).

Hiwi's theological position is outlined by Davidson, and by Fleischer, who uses the image of the "ax." "A whole millennium ahead of his time" is how Stefan Reif summarizes Hiwi's thought in *A Jewish Archive*. The report of an "expurgated version" of the Bible is treated by Davidson, Brody, and Fleischer. The image of the scholars working like ants is Fleischer's, and he is the Jerusalem scholar who, in 1982, discovered a fragment of Hiwi's text (T-S NS 140.45) at the Geniza Research Institute for Hebrew Poetry.

The phrase "dragging and haggling . . . Heretic's Gallery" appears in Ben-Horin, "SS to Judge MS," Nov. 5, 1901. The italics are ours. See also S. Reif, "The Damascus Document from the Cairo Geniza: Its Discovery, Early Study and Historical Significance," in *The Damascus Document: A Centennial of Discovery*, Joseph M. Baumgarten, Esther G. Chazon, and Avital Pinnick, eds. (Leiden, 2000).

Schechter's "heretic's gallery" appeared as *Documents of Jewish Sectaries* (Cambridge, 1910/New York, 1970). For more on the book and its relation to other Jewish heresies, see Kahle, *The Cairo Geniza*, introduction to the 1959 edition; Brody, *The Geonim*; and S. A. Poznanski, *The Karaite Literary Opponents of Saadiah Gaon* (London, 1908).

On the "vital" center and Jewish sectarian movements, see Starr, *Catholic Israel; Great Schisms in Jewish History*, R. Jospe and S. Wagner, eds. (Denver/New York, 1981); Daniel Lasker, "Rabbanism and Karaism: The Contest for Supremacy," in the same volume; and Schechter, *Documents of Jewish Sectaries*, Joseph A. Fitzmyer's Prolegomenon.

Schechter's views of Reform Judaism and the relation between Karaism and Reform are discussed in Bentwich, *Solomon Schechter*; Haggai Ben-Shammai, "The Scholarly Study of Karaism in the Nineteenth and Twentieth Centuries," in *Karaite Judaism*, Polliack, ed.; "Abraham Geiger," *Jewish Encyclopedia*; and M. Ydit, "Karaite and Reform Liturgy," *CCAR Journal* 18/2, 1971.

The Geniza manuscripts of "Fragments of a Zadokite Work" are T-S 10 K 6 and T-S 16.311. Reif notes that Margoliouth had already suggested in 1910 that the Damascus Document was more important than the discovery of Ben Sira. See Reif's "The

Damascus Document from the Cairo Genizah" and Schechter, *Jewish Sectaries*, Fitzmyer's Prolegomenon.

On the central figure in the Qumran literature, see J. Baumgarten, "Damascus Document," in *The Encyclopedia of the Dead Sea Scrolls*, and F. F. Bruce, *The Teacher of Righteousness in the Qumran Texts* (London, 1957). The term "Teacher of Righteousness" is discussed by Schechter. See also T. Gaster, who, in *The Dead Sea Scriptures*, calls him "The Right Teacher . . . not the Teacher of Righteousness." On the nature of the sect's distinction, see Philip Davies, "The Judaism(s) of the Damascus Document," in *The Damascus Document: A Centennial of Discovery*. The phrase "Make a fence around the Torah" is from *The Sayings of the Fathers*, I:1, T. Herford, trans. (New York, 1962). Other views of the Damascus Document also emerged, including that of Louis Ginzberg, who felt it was composed by a Pharisaic community, though one much more extreme in its views than mainstream Pharisees. For more on this, see Reif, "Damascus Document," and Fitzmyer, Prolegomenon.

Schechter's quotations about the Damascus Document and the Zadokite sect are all from *Jewish Sectaries*. Schechter dated one of his two manuscripts of this text to the ninth or tenth century and the other to the twelfth or thirteenth century. The text itself dates from the beginning of the first century B.C.E. See Reif, "Damascus Document."

On Anan's reform and his commandments, see Moshe Gil, *History of Palestine, 634–1099* (New York, 1992); Gil, "The Origins of the Karaites"; D. Lasker, "Rabbanism and Karaism"; Leon Nemoy, *Karaite Anthology: Excerpts from the Early Literature* (New Haven, 1952); and Abraham Harkavy, "Anan ben David," *Jewish Encyclopedia*. Recent scholarship has weighed in convincingly against calling the newly "united" movement a "sect." See Ben-Shammai, "The Scholarly Study of Karaism," and Rustow, *Heresy*, chapter 2.

For more on normative Judaism's resistance to Anan and the Karaites, see Leon Nemoy, "Al-Kirkisani's Account of the Jewish Sects," *Hebrew Union College Annual* [*HUCA*] 7, 1930; Gil, "Origins of Karaism"; Rustow, "Karaites Real and Imagined: Three Cases of Jewish Heresy," *Past & Present*, no. 197, Nov. 2007; and Brody, *The Geonim*. The Geniza's contribution to the study of Karaism is made clear in Gil, "Origins of the Karaites" (and in Meira Polliack's volume generally), and especially the recent groundbreaking work by Marina Rustow, *Heresy*.

A "shortened" version of the Haggada can be found, among other places, in *The Complete Haggada* [Heb], M. Kasher, ed. (Jerusalem, 1961). See also S. Reif, "Variations in the Haggadah Text," in *Genizah Fragments* 55, April 2008. Reif notes differences in the wording of the kiddush (the blessing over the wine) in T-S H 2.124, as well as the alternative formulation of the traditional Four Questions (in T-S H 2.152).

Our account of the contents of this "alternative Haggada" is based in large part on David Stern, *Chosen: Philadelphia's Great Hebraica*, with E. Cohen, J. Guston, and

E. Schrijver (Philadelphia, 2007), and D. Stern, *Breaking New Ground: Scholars and Scholarship at the Center for Advanced Judaic Studies, 1993–2004* (Philadelphia, 2004). See also Ezra Fleischer, "Fragments of Palestinian Prayerbooks from the Geniza" [Heb], *Kovetz al yad* new series, 13, 1996; and D. Goldschmidt, *The Passover Haggada* [Heb] (Jerusalem, 1960). For other Haggadot that differ from standard versions, see also Jay Rovner, "An Early Passover Haggadah according to the Palestinian Rite," *JQR* 40/3–4, 2000, and "A New Version of the Eretz Israel Haggadah," *JQR* 42/3–4, 2002. In Rovner's (Palestinian) version (JTS MS 9560), which may in fact be older than the Dropsie text, the appetizers are extensive and the father—rather than the youngest child—recites the Four Questions, which in this case are only two. The distinguished scholar who describes the hors d'oeuvres is David Stern.

The social and historical context of Karaism's emergence is discussed in Abraham Halkin, "Revolt and Revival in Judeo-Islamic Culture," in *Great Ages and Ideas of the Jewish People*, L. Schwartz, ed. (New York, 1956), and, in thorough detail, in Fred Astren, *Karaite Judaism and Historical Understanding* (Columbia, S.C., 2004).

The discussion of Kumisi, al-Kirkisani, and the evolution of Karaite doctrine is based on Nemoy, *Karaite Anthology*; Nemoy, "Al-Qirqisani's Account of the Jewish Sects"; Gil, *History of Palestine*; "Sadducees," *EJ* 14; and L. Schiffman, "Jewish Sectarianism," in *Great Jewish Schisms*, Jospe and Wagner, eds. Al-Kirkisani lists seventeen different sects. Cf. Palestinian Talmud, Sanhedrin 29c.

The mention of "fourteen 'religions' " is from Goitein, *MS* 5: x, C, 4. See also Nemoy, "Elijah Ben Abraham and His Tract against the Rabbanites," *HUCA* 51, 1980. Marina Rustow's *Heresy and the Politics of Community* has an excellent account of the diversity of Karaite opinion and the movement's conviction that it alone represented the true Judaism.

On the Karaites and the Masoretes, see Rustow, *Heresy*, especially chapter 2; Goitein, *MS* 5: x, C, 4; and G. Khan, "The Contribution of the Karaites to the Study of the Hebrew Language," in *Karaite Judaism*, Polliack, ed. See also Rina Drory, *Models and Contacts: Arabic Literature and Its Impact on Medieval Jewish Culture* (Leiden, 2000), chapters 5 and 6. As Rustow notes, the Karaites may have been influenced by the general trend in the Islamic world, which by the tenth century was experiencing "an explosion of literary production" in fields ranging from the sciences to the arts and humanities and into the world of theology and religious philosophy. She attributes this explosion to both "the exponential growth of speakers of Arabic, and in part . . . the introduction of paper manufacture to the Near East." On the intensified study of grammar and the details of linguistic analysis, see G. Khan's article, above, and Stefan Reif, "A Centennial Assessment of Genizah Studies," in *The Cambridge Genizah Collections: Their Contents and Significance*, Stefan C. Reif, ed. (Cambridge, 2002).

The notion of Karaism as "a leavening agent" or productive irritant is from J. Mann, *Texts and Studies 2*. See also Elinoar Bareket, "Karaite Communities in the Middle East"; Drory, *Models and Contacts*, chapter 6; and Gil, "Origins of the Karaites."

Information on the particulars of Karaite ritual observance comes from the following sources: Judith Olszowy-Schlanger, *Karaite Marriage Documents from the Cairo Geniza* (Leiden, 1998); Rustow, *Heresy*, chapters 1 and 2; Mann, *Texts and Studies* 2; and Poznanski, *The Karaite Literary Opponents*. The coexistence of the two communities is discussed in Goitein, *MS* 5: x, C, 4; Elinoar Bareket, "Karaite Communities"; Gil, "Origins of Karaism"; and, above all, Rustow, *Heresy*, introduction and chapters 9 and 10. The scholar who suggests that the Karaite material remained in circulation long after the movement itself died out is Stefan Reif in "The Damascus Document from the Cairo Genizah."

The relation between the ninth-century discovery of the Qumran scrolls and the Geniza documents in question is described by Kahle in his introduction to the 1959 edition of *The Cairo Geniza*. The Damascus Document, says Kahle, must have been among the manuscripts taken from the cave at the time; it eventually made its way to Jerusalem, where—by the end of the ninth century—it would have interested the nascent Karaite community. See also J. Baumgarten, "Damascus Document," *Encyclopedia of the Dead Sea Scrolls*; S. Reif, "The Damascus Document," citing L. Schiffman's *Reclaiming the Dead Sea Scrolls*.

The fluidity of communal affiliation in Jewish Fustat is discussed by Rustow in *Heresy*, especially in the introduction and chapter 1; Goitein, *MS* 2: v, B, 1; Reif, "The Damascus Document," and Reif, "The Cairo Geniza," in *Encyclopedia of the Dead Sea Scrolls*.

The correspondence between the scribe from Ramla and the judge from Fustat ("Because of you and your son-in-law") is T-S 10 J 29.13. It is analyzed by Rustow in *Heresy*. The judge was none other than Ephraim ben Shemaria, who would go on to head Egypt's Palestinian community for some fifty-five years. See also Bareket, *Fustat on the Nile*, and Goitein, *MS* 2: v, D, 2.

The translation of Yahya and Rayyisa's *ketuba* is adapted from the one that appears in Olszowy-Schlanger, *Karaite Marriage Documents*, as document 56 (Bodl. MS Heb a. 3.42). For the original text, see also Mann, *Texts and Studies* 2, and, on the text in general, see Rustow, *Heresy*, chapter 9.

The translation of Toviyya's letter is (with a few variations) by Rustow, *Heresy*, chapter 9, which also includes an extensive discussion of Rabbanite-Karaite marriages. That Toviyya's letter ended up in the Geniza suggests that the wife and/or daughter at some point returned to Judaism, perhaps to take advantage of the charitable organizations that were so active within the Jewish community of Fustat. See also Gil, *History of Palestine*; Benjamin Outhwaite, "Karaite Epistolary Hebrew: The Letters of Toviyyah ben Moshe," in *Exegesis and Grammar in Medieval Karaite Texts*, Geoffrey Khan, ed. (Oxford, 2001); Goitein, *MS* 5: x, A, 2. Unlike scholars who believe that the mother may have returned to Judaism with her daughter, Gil thinks that she did not convert to Judaism until after the daughter died. Rustow, whose reading we've followed, understands the situation differently.

9. Pieces of the Spanish Puzzle

The descriptions of the Geniza at the start of this chapter are by Agnes Lewis and Laura d'Hulst, respectively. Both appear in Rebecca Jefferson's "The Cairo Genizah Unearthed," which quotes correspondence from Laura d'Hulst (Dec. 11, 1915, BLR, d. 1084) and Agnes Lewis's *In the Shadow*.

On how the Geniza has changed the way we understand the evolution of this poetry, see Fleischer, "Perspectives on Our Early Poetry after One Hundred Years of Studying the Cairo Geniza" [Heb], *Madda'ei haYahadut* 38, 1998; E. Fleischer, "The Culture of the Jews of Spain and Their Poetry according to the Geniza" [Heb], *Pe'amim* 41, 1989–90; E. Fleischer, "Early Hebrew Poetry in the Cairo Geniza" [Heb], *Deot* 25, 2006; and H. Schirmann, "Secular Hebrew Poetry in the Geniza Manuscripts" [Heb], *Te'uda* 1, 1980.

For more information on the major poets of the period, see Peter Cole, *The Dream of the Poem: Hebrew Poetry from Muslim and Christian Spain, 950–1492* (Princeton, 2007); H. Schirmann, *The History of Hebrew Poetry in Muslim Spain* [Heb]; and H. Schirmann, *Hebrew Poetry from Spain and Provence* [Heb] (Jerusalem, 1954).

The history of the scholarship around Dunash's work comes from Leopold Dukes, *Nahal kedumim* (Hanover, 1873), cited in N. Allony, *Dunash ben Labrat, Poems* [Heb] (Jerusalem, 1947). Schirmann's article mentioning the heading is "Poets Contemporary with Moshe Ibn Ezra and Yehuda HaLevi" [Heb], *Yediot hamakhon* 2, 1936. The manuscript is T-S 8 K 15.8. For more about Dunash (and for translations of the poems discussed here), see Cole, *The Dream of the Poem*; R. Scheindlin, *Wine, Women, & Death: Medieval Hebrew Poems on the Good Life* (Philadelphia, 1986); and R. Brann, *The Compunctious Poet: Cultural Ambiguity and Hebrew Poetry in Muslim Spain* (Baltimore, 1991), especially chapter 2.

Biographical information about Schirmann is drawn, for the most part, from a radio transcript that includes excerpts from interviews with Schirmann himself as well as commentary by Ezra Fleischer and program host Shmuel Haupert—*Milim shmenasot legaat*, Y. Levtov, ed. (Tel Aviv, 1991). We have also drawn from 2009 interviews with former students and younger colleagues or acquaintances of Schirmann, including Yosef Yahalom, Malachi Beit-Arié, Dvora Bregman, Ada Yardeni, and Ayala Gordon. The poem "Won't you ask, Zion" appears in Cole, *The Dream of the Poem*.

On Mendelsohn, see Lili Eylon, "Erich Mendelsohn—Oriental from East Prussia," *Architecture Week*, Jan. 24, 2001; Paul Goldberger, *New York Times*, Oct. 30, 1988; A. Cobbers, *Mendelsohn* (Los Angeles, 2007). Mendelsohn's description of Palestine comes from his 1940 essay, "Palestine and the World of Tomorrow," reprinted in *Erich Mendelsohn in Palestine*, a catalog of a 1994 exhibit at the Technion-Israel Institute of Technology. While Mendelsohn was utterly independent and in some respects opposed to the rigidity of the Bauhaus and the International Style, he absorbed elements of each approach into his far more dynamic and flexible design, which comprised a unique synthesis of expression and restraint, function, and what he called "a sensual component."

Schirmann's relationship with Bialik is described by Dan Almagor, "A Young Scholar Is in the Country" [Heb], *Yediot aharonot*, Jan. 25, 1980. The Italian anthology is Schirmann, *Hebrew Poetry from Italy: A Selection* [Heb] (Berlin, 1934).

Schirmann also writes of the heading to the Dunash poem in *The History of Hebrew Poetry in Muslim Spain* [Heb]; see also Raymond Scheindlin, *Wine, Women, & Death*. The ambiguous situation of the poem is discussed in Scheindlin and in Cole, *The Dream of the Poem*.

The poet who introduced this Arabized use of the gazelle figure is Yitzhak ibn Mar Shaul. See Schirmann, *History of Hebrew Poetry in Muslim Spain* [Heb]; Schirmann, *New Poems* [Heb]; E. Fleischer, "New Findings in the Work of R. Yitzhak Bar Levi (bin Mar Shaul)," in *Hebrew Language Studies Presented to Zeev Ben-Haim* [Heb], M. Bar Asher, A. Dotan, et al., eds. (Jerusalem, 1983). The poet who first wrote about fleas is Yosef ibn Sahl. See Cole, *The Dream of the Poem*, and Schirmann, *New Poems* [Heb]; Schirmann, *The History of Hebrew Poetry in Muslim Spain* [Heb]. The poem about the old man caught with the boy is attributed to Yitzhak ibn Ezra. See Cole, *The Dream of the Poem*; Schirmann, *New Poems* [Heb]; and *Yitzhak ibn Ezra, Poems* [Heb], M. Schmelzer, ed. (New York, 1979). Schirmann's landmark anthology is Schirmann, *Hebrew Poetry from Spain and Provence* [Heb], four volumes. The 1965 collection of Geniza poems is Schirmann, *New Poems from the Geniza* [Heb]. His two-volume history is Schirmann, *The History of Hebrew Poetry in Muslim Spain* [Heb] and *The History of Hebrew Poetry in Christian Spain and Provence* [Heb], E. Fleischer, ed. (Jerusalem, 1997). For information on the circumstances of the two-volume manuscript's discovery, see Fleischer's preface to the book.

It was Y. Levtov who described Schirmann as "a riddle to all those around him." See "In a Still Voice," *Davar rishon*, March 29, 1996. The account of Schirmann after the bombing appears in Ayala Gordon, *Between Jerusalem and Neve-Yam, During the War of Independence* [Heb] (Jerusalem, 1995/2008), letters from Feb. 22 and 26, 1948. These and the preceding characterizations of Schirmann are drawn from the sources cited above, as well as from Israel Levin, "A Life's Work" [Heb], *Davar*, June 26, 1981; Ezra Fleischer, "A Triple Jubilee" [Heb], *Maariv*, Jan. 4, 1980; Dan Almagor, "And You Would Hear Your Teacher" [Heb], *Hadoar* 75/15, June 21, 1996. The quotations from Fleischer here are: "he shifted attention," Fleischer, "A Triple Jubilee" [Heb], and "the type of character about which novels might be written," Fleischer, in *Milim*, Levtov, ed.

The story of the discovery of the poem by Dunash's wife is told in full by Fleischer in "On Dunash ben Labrat, His Wife, and His Son: New Light on the Beginnings of the Hebrew-Spanish School" [Heb], *Mehkerei Yerushalayim besifrut Ivrit* 5, 1984, and "Towards an Early History of Secular Hebrew Poetry in Spain," in *Culture and Society in the History of Israel During the Middle Ages: Studies Presented in Memory of Haim Hillel*

Ben-Sasson [Heb], M. Ben-Sasson, R. Bonfil, and J. R. Hacker, eds. (Jerusalem, 1990). See also N. Allony, "Four Poems," *JQR* 35/1, 1944.

The vertically torn fragments are Mosseri VIII.202.2 and Mosseri IV.387. The manuscript of the full poem is T-S NS 143.46. The poem is translated in Cole, *The Dream of the Poem*. The description of it here is based on the analysis by Fleischer in "On Dunash and His Wife" [Heb]. Fleischer discusses the letter from Hasdai ibn Shaprut and the poem in its upper-left corner in "Towards an Early History" [Heb]. This is T-S J 2.71.

Other scholars, including Abraham Geiger, Shmuel David Luzzatto, and David Kaufmann, had written about HaLevi, but their work was based on a very limited number of poems. Schirmann's study was, on the other hand, based on Brody's six-volume edition of the HaLevi Diwan (Berlin, 1894–1930). Schirmann's 1938 *Tarbiz* article appears in Schirmann, *Hebrew Poetry and Drama* 1 [Heb]; see also his supplement to that two-part study. A list of Goitein's relevant articles appears in Schirmann, *The History of Hebrew Poetry in Muslim Spain* [Heb]; E. Fleischer, "The Essence of Our Land and Its Meaning" [Heb], *Pe'amim* 68, 1996. See also Goitein, *MS* 5: x, D; Ezra Fleischer and Moshe Gil, *Yehuda HaLevi and His Circle* [Heb] (Jerusalem, 2001).

The twins' motto, *"lampada tradam,"* echoes Lucretius: *"Quasi cursores vitai lampada tradunt"*—or, "Like runners, they hand on the torch of life."

The letter from the summer of 1129 is found in Goitein, *MS* 5, p. 465; Fleischer-Gil, *HaLevi* [Heb], Doc. 19; Raymond Scheindlin, *The Song of the Distant Dove: Judah Halevi's Pilgrimage* (Oxford, 2008). Scheindlin interprets this differently, dates the letter twelve years later, to 1141, and places it in Alexandria. For yet a third version of the HaLevi chronology, see Joseph Yahalom, *Yehuda Halevi: Poetry and Pilgrimage*, Gabriel Levin, trans., chapter 10 (Jerusalem, 2009).

The line "the dust of the desolate shrine" is from "My Heart Is in the East," which appears in Cole, *The Dream of the Poem* (the final line is translated differently there). Opinions differ as to when HaLevi was born. The date generally given is c. 1075 (or sometime before 1075). Yahalom and Scheindlin believe that it was closer to 1085. See Schirmann and Fleischer in *The History of Hebrew Poetry in Muslim Spain* [Heb]; Scheindlin, *The Dove*; Yahalom, *Yehuda Halevi*. The description of HaLevi as "the quintessence . . . of our country" is found in Goitein, *MS* 5: X, D. The notion of the pilgrimage as "an educational and political model" is discussed in Fleischer-Gil, *HaLevi*. HaLevi's phrase, "all flowers and no fruit," is discussed in R. Brann, "Judah HaLevi," in *The Literature of al-Andalus*, María Rosa Menocal, Raymond P. Scheindlin, and Michael Sells, eds. (Cambridge, 2000), and Brann, *The Compunctious Poet*.

Citations from the letters (followed by analyses) are drawn from the following sources: "The Sultan's new ship," Fleischer-Gil, *HaLevi*, Doc. 40; see also Scheindlin, *The Dove*, pp. 97ff. (Fleischer-Gil, Scheindlin, and Yahalom provide different accounts of when this letter was written.) "Outwardly I participated," Fleischer-Gil, *HaLevi*,

Doc. 41; Scheindlin, *The Dove*, p. 103. "Put an end to this headache," Fleischer-Gil, *HaLevi*, Doc. 42; Scheindlin, *The Dove*, pp. 100–101. *"Burn after reading!"* Fleischer-Gil, *HaLevi*, Doc. 48 (see 49 as well); Scheindlin, *The Dove*, pp. 135–36. "HaLevi is . . . aboard an 'oversized nutshell,' " Fleischer-Gil, *HaLevi*, Doc. 50; Scheindlin, *The Dove*, pp. 141ff; also Yehuda Halevi, *Poems from the Diwan*, Gabriel Levin, trans. (London, 2002). "The ships bound for al-Andalus," Fleischer-Gil, *HaLevi*, Doc. 51. "HaLevi sailed on Wednesday," Scheindlin, *The Dove*, p. 149; Halfon's letter was written five days after the ship sailed—that is, on Monday the nineteenth. "The memory of a saint is a blessing," Fleischer-Gil, *HaLevi*, Doc. 54; Scheindlin, *The Dove*, pp. 150–51. "The gates of Jerusalem," Fleischer-Gil, *HaLevi*, Doc. 53; Scheindlin, *The Dove*, pp. 249–52. "Modest pilgrimages," Yahalom, *Yehuda Halevi*, chapter 24; see also Yahalom's "Yehuda HaLevi and the Western Wind," *Haaretz*, May 20, 1999. "Reasonably convincing evidence," Fleischer-Gil, *HaLevi*, chapter 7. As for where HaLevi was buried, see Scheindlin, *The Dove*, pp. 150, 276. On the condition of the manuscript telling of HaLevi's demise, see Fleischer-Gil, *HaLevi*, Doc. 53; and Scheindlin, *The Dove*, pp. 249–52.

The larger question prompted by HaLevi's activity in Egypt is: Why was the poet writing Andalusian-style poems at all if he was, as Fleischer says, rejecting the Andalusian cultural ethos outright? Was he trying to make a nationalist statement with his decision to settle in the Land of Israel, or, as Scheindlin argues, was the pilgrimage private and spiritual? See Fleischer, "The Essence of Our Land" [Heb], and Fleischer-Gil, *HaLevi*, p. 233; Scheindlin, *The Dove*, pp. 4, 155–56, 170, and 277.

Information about Fleischer is drawn from a variety of sources, including interviews from *Yediot aharonot* (by Zisi Stavi, March 20, 1987, and by Penina Meizlisch, July 25, 1975); obituaries and memorial notices in the *New York Times* (by Ari Goldman, Aug. 1, 2006) and *Haaretz* (by Ariel Hirschfeld, Aug. 2, 2006; by Uri Dromi, Aug. 3, 2006; by Yehoshua Granat, Aug. 4, 2006; and by Michael Handelsatz, Aug. 11, 2006); personal page, the Israeli Academy of Arts and Sciences, http://www.academy.ac.il/data/persons_data/55/EzraFr.pdf; Shulamit Elizur, "From the Depths" [Heb], *Madda'ei haYahadut* 43, 2006; Shulamit Elizur, "The Scholarly Project of Ezra Fleischer: General Observations" [Heb], unpublished article, 2006 (quoted by permission of the author); and Yehoshua Granat, "Diverse Colors, Threads of Delicate Echoes, an Authenticity Deep and Sharp: On Ezra Fleischer's Studies of Medieval Hebrew Secular Poetry" [Heb], *Madda'ei haYahadut* 45, 2009. Fleischer stopped publishing poetry after he immigrated to Israel.

In "Diverse Colors" [Heb] Granat discusses Fleischer's complex relationship to the Hebrew poetry of Spain. See also H. Schirmann, *Yehosef HaNagid: The Tragedy of a Jewish Statesman* [Heb], with a foreword by Ezra Fleischer (Jerusalem, 1982). Fleischer's astonishing response to the Hebron massacre—"A Cry"—appeared in *Haaretz*, March 25, 1994. Our thanks to Yehoshua Granat for alerting us to this article.

Schirmann's avoidance of political and social commentary is apparent in H. Schirmann, "The Study of Hebrew Secular Poetry" [Heb], *Sedarim: me'asef sofrei Eretz Israel.* See also Tova Rosen and Eli Yassif, "The Study of Hebrew Literature of the Middle Ages," in *The Oxford Handbook of Jewish Studies,* M. Goodman, ed. (Oxford, 2002).

For more on Ben Saruk and Ibn Avitor, see Schirmann, *The History of Hebrew Poetry in Muslim Spain* [Heb]; Fleischer, "On the Early History of Our Poetry in Spain: The Secular and Liturgical Poetry of R. Menahem ben Saruk" [Heb], *Asufot* 2, 1988; "On the Poetry of R. Ibn Avitor" [Heb], *Asufot* 4, 1990, as well as Fleischer's doctoral dissertation, *The Works of Yosef ibn Avitor* [Heb] (The Hebrew University, 1967); and "Towards an Early History of Secular Hebrew Poetry in Spain," in *Culture and Society* [Heb], Ben-Sasson, Bonfil, and Hacker, eds. See also Cole, *The Dream of the Poem.*

The phrase "a fourfold miracle" is Fleischer's, from "Early Hebrew Poetry in the Cairo Geniza" [Heb]. "The study of the Geniza" is from the same essay. Shulamit Elizur discusses Fleischer's work as a whole in "The Scholarly Project of Ezra Fleischer" [Heb]. See also Y. Granat, *Haaretz,* Aug. 11, 2006. Fleischer's articles on the subject are collected in *The Hebrew Poetry of Spain and Its Offshoots* [Heb], S. Elizur and T. Be'eri, eds. (Jerusalem, 2010). In "A Triple Jubilee" [Heb], Fleischer mentions "the tens of thousands of hitherto unknown poems" released by the Geniza. The image of their ancient authors all around him is from S. Elizur, "Poetry Is in the Details" [Heb].

10. A Mediterranean Society

We are extremely grateful to Ayala Gordon, Elon Goitein, and Ofra Rosner for permission to quote from their father S. D. Goitein's letters and journals, which are in their private possession. The letter that begins "SECRET" is dated Oct. 8, 1955.

For more on Baneth, see, for example, Goitein, "David Hartwig (Zvi) Baneth, 1893–1973," *Studia Orientalia Memoriae D. H. Baneth,* J. Blau et al., eds. (Jerusalem, 1979); Hava Lazarus-Yafe, "The Transplantation of Islamic Studies from Europe to the Yishuv and Israel," in *The Jewish Discovery of Islam,* Martin Kramer, Menachem Milson, eds. (Tel Aviv, 1999).

Goitein's published account of the discovery of the New Series appears in Goitein, "Involvement in Geniza Research," in *Religion in a Religious Age,* Goitein, ed. (Cambridge, 1974). The description in his diary is dated Oct. 7, 1955. For another vivid description of the work with the New Series' crates and their contents, see Hayyim Schirmann's radio interview (notes to chapter 9), where he tells of his first encounter with the new finds in the summer of 1957: "Immediately after my arrival, Miss Skilliter brought me to the library's storeroom, and before my wonder-struck eyes stretched a long row of thirty tall crates, full of Geniza fragments, mostly to the brim. . . ." A brief examination was enough to convince Schirmann that the discovery was every bit as valuable as the Old Series and that the crates had to be gone through systematically. "Examination of this sort called for qualities normally found in a natural-born archeologist. Call it an ability to take pleasure in drudge work in the fullest sense of the term. A willingness to swallow clouds of dust which rose up after the slightest motion of the hand inside the Geniza crates, [and] a power of endurance, because one had to sit with the crates for weeks on end. I didn't have these traits, but as no one else had come to [sort the literary fragments], I had no choice but to lock myself in with the enormous crates and send up the dust that had settled in them. I washed myself several times a day, and still couldn't completely get rid of the traces of the Geniza." Schirmann's account recalls that of Schechter in Cairo in 1897 and his coining of the unforgettable term—*"Genizahschmutz."*

The comparisons of the Geniza to garbage are as follows: "contents of a huge waste paper basket," D. S. Margoliouth, "The Zadokites," *The Expositor* 8/32, Aug. 1913; "nothing of any interest," Reif, *A Jewish Archive* (he is quoting the library assistant B. C. Nightingale); "I have . . . once or twice rummaged," A. F. Schofield, "Librarian's Report: 4 April 1944," CUL ULIB 6/4/1/104.

For more on Judeo-Arabic, see Joshua Blau, *The Emergence and Linguistic Background of Judaeo-Arabic: A Study of the Origins of Neo-Arabic and Middle Arabic* (Jerusalem, 1999); Goitein, *MS* 1, introduction; Ghosh, *In an Antique Land*; "Judeo-Arabic," *Encyclopedia of Islam.*

For the Carlyle quote, see Thomas Carlyle, *On Heroes, Hero-Worship and the Heroic in History* (New York, 1888). See Starr's chapter on "The History of Great Men," in *Catholic Israel*, for more on Schechter's relationship to Carlyle's notion of history. Simha Assaf's contribution to Geniza research is described in Goitein, "What Would Jewish and General History Benefit by a Systematic Publication of the Documentary Geniza Papers?," *Proceedings of the American Academy for Jewish Research* 23, 1954; Reif, *A Jewish Archive*; Goitein, *MS* 1, introduction. His role in naming Rehavia's streets is described in Amnon Rimon, *Rehavia: A Neighborhood in Jerusalem* [Heb] (Jerusalem, 1998). Goitein calls Baneth the "father of the Geniza project" in "S. D. Goitein: Scientific Projects/Instructions in Case of a Fatal Accident," dated July 25, 1961, which is held in the SDG Geniza Lab, 2J.1.2, NLI.

Biographical information about S. D. Goitein and overviews of his work come from Goitein, "The Life Story of a Scholar," in Robert Attal, *A Bibliography of the Writing of Prof. Shelomo Dov Goitein* (Jerusalem, 1975/2000), and from the bibliography itself; S. D. Goitein, "Involvement in Geniza Research"; Ayala Gordon, *Shelomo Dov Goitein and Shmuel Yosef Agnon: Criticism and Letters, 1919–1970* [Heb] (Jerusalem, 2008); *The History of the Goitein Family* [Heb] (Jerusalem, 2008); Ayala Gordon, *Between Jerusalem and Neve-Yam* [Heb]; Avraham Udovitch, preface to Goitein's *MS* 5; Mark Cohen, "Shelomo Dov Goitein," in *The American Philosophical Year Book*, 1987; Mark Cohen, "Goitein, the Geniza, and Muslim History," *Middle Eastern Lectures*, no. 4, Moshe Dayan Center, Tel Aviv University, 2001; Eric Ormsby, "The 'Born Schulmeister,' " *The New Criterion* 22/1, Sept. 2003; Mordechai Akiva Friedman, "A Note on the Contribution of S. D. Goitein to the Interdisciplinary Study of Judaeo-Arabic Culture" [Heb], *Sefunot* 5/20,

1991; Mordechai Friedman, "Prof. S. D. Goitein, Man and Scholar" [Heb], *Yedion haIgud haOlami leMadda'ei haYahadut* 26, 1986; Joel Kraemer, "Goitein and His Mediterranean Society" [Heb], *Zmanim*, no. 34–35, summer 1990; Gideon Libson, "Hidden Worlds and Open Shutters: S. D. Goitein between Judaism and Islam," in *The Jewish Past Revisited*, Myers and Ruderman, eds.; Franz Rosenthal, "Shlomo Dov Goitein," *Proceedings of the American Academy for Jewish Research* 53, 1986; Avraham Udovitch et al., *Shelomo Dov Goitein, 1900–1985* (Princeton, 1985); Steven M. Wasserstrom, "Apology for S. D. Goitein: An Essay," in *A Faithful Sea: The Religious Cultures of the Mediterranean, 1200–1700*, Adnan A. Husain and K. E. Fleming, eds. (Oxford, 2007); Shaul Shaked, "S. D. Goitein: Scholar of the Historical Cooperation between Judaism and Islam" [Heb], *Pe'amim* 22, 1985; Trude Weiss-Rosmarin, "Shlomo Dov Goitein—Scholar Extraordinary," *Judaism* 33/3, 1984; Moshe Gil, "Shlomo Dov Goitein, 1900–1985: A Mediterranean Scholar," *Mediterranean Historical Review* 1/1, 1986; Noam A. Stillman, "From Oriental Studies and Wissenschaft des Judentums to Interdisciplinarity" [Heb], and Miriam Frankel, "The Historiography of the Jews in the Middle Ages—Landmarks and Prospects" [Heb], both in *Pe'amim* 92, 2002; *Studies in Judaism and Islam: Presented to Shelomo Dov Goitein on the Occasion of His Eightieth Birthday by His Students, Colleagues and Friends*, Shelomo Morag, Issachar Ben-Ami, Norman A. Stillman, eds. (Jerusalem, 1981); and interviews (conducted throughout 2008–9) with Ayala and Amirav Gordon, Elon and Harriet Goitein, Mark Cohen, Joshua Blau, Stefan Reif; e-mail exchanges with Mordechai Friedman, Norman Stillman, Paula Sanders. Goitein's arrival in Palestine with Gershom Scholem is described by the latter in *From Berlin to Jerusalem: Memories of My Youth*, Harry Zohn, trans. (New York, 1980).

For the drama surrounding the publication of *Pulcellina* (Tel Aviv, 1927), see B. Z. Kedar, "S. D. Goitein and Pulcellina on the Banks of the Loire" [Heb], *Haaretz*, April 14, 1995; Shalom Spiegel, "A Play about the Martyrs of Blois" [Heb], *Davar*, Oct. 7, 14, 21, 1927.

Information about Theresa Goitein comes from Ayala Gordon, *Theresa Gottlieb Goitein* [Heb] (Jerusalem, 2008); Ayala Gordon, "Shelomo Dov Goitein and His Wife Theresa (Gottlieb)" [Heb], in *History of the Goitein Family* [Heb], and interviews with Ayala and Amirav Gordon and Elon and Harriet Goitein.

The descriptions of Goitein are as follows: "like a bumblebee," Joshua Blau, conversation with the authors, Oct. 5, 2009; "trains constantly coming and going," SDG diary, Jan. 5, 1955. His letter "I fear that our entire existence" was written to Ernest Simon, Dec. 18, 1947 (NLI Arc 4 1751/426).

The account of Goitein's "special mission" is compiled from "The Life Story of a Scholar"; Mordechai Friedman, preface, Goitein and Friedman, *India Traders of the Middle Ages: Documents from the Cairo Geniza ("India Book")* (Leiden, 2008); Friedman, "A Note" [Heb]; Gordon, *History of the Goitein Family* [Heb]; interviews with Ayala Gordon, Elon Goitein, and Mark Cohen; Friedman, e-mail to the authors, Sept. 15, 2009; Norman Stillman, e-mail to the authors, Oct. 1, 2009.

Goitein reported on his trip to Paris in "The Congress of Orientalists" [Heb], *Haaretz*, Sept. 17, 1948, and wrote of being in Budapest (without specifying why he was there) in "A Visit to Hungary" [Heb], *Haaretz*, Nov. 19, 1948, and again in "On the Jews of Hungary" [Heb], *Haaretz*, Jan. 7, 1949. His description of the plane filled with chickens is from his diary, Sept. 26, 1948, when he was making plans to fly home. He returned to Jerusalem on Oct. 12. (Our thanks to Ayala Goitein Gordon for help with the timeline of his trip.)

For more on the atrocities that Theresa witnessed, see, for instance, Goitein's letter to Ernest Simon, April 19, 1948, in which he describes her disgust at having to provide medical care to the perpetrators of the Deir Yassin massacre (NLI Arc 4 1751/426), and her own letter to Goitein (then in Paris) in *Between Jerusalem and Neve-Yam* [Heb] from Aug. 8, 1948, about their neighbor who died from a bullet to the stomach.

Accounts of the fate of the David Kaufmann collection are contradictory. In "The Life Story of a Scholar," Goitein says that it was thought at the time of his trip that the collection had been destroyed during the war, but in July of 1948, at the International Congress of Orientalists, Samuel Löwinger and Alexander Scheiber presented their *Genizah Publications in Memory of Prof. Dr. David Kaufmann* (Budapest, 1949) and announced that the collection had mostly survived. Goitein was present at the congress and would have known this. It is true that several years earlier it was believed that the whole collection was lost. See Dov Schidorsky, *Burning Scrolls and Flying Letters: A History of Book Collections and Libraries in Mandatory Palestine and of Book Salvaging Efforts in Europe after the Holocaust* [Heb] (Jerusalem, 2008).

Information about Goldziher comes from Raphael Patai, *Ignaz Goldziher and His Oriental Diary* (Detroit, 1987); Goitein, "Goldziher as Seen through His Letters" [Heb], *Ignace Goldziher Memorial Volume*, part I, Samuel Löwinger and Joseph Somogyi, eds. (Budapest, 1948); Goitein, review of Alexander Scheiber, ed., *Ignaz Goldziher Tagebuch*, in *JSS* 41, 1979; Goitein, "Goldziher, the Father of Islamic Studies" [Arabic], *al-Katib al-Masri* 5, 1947; Goitein, "I. Goldziher's Hebrew Writings" [Heb], *Kiryat Sefer* 23, 1946–47. Goldziher's description of the Kaufmann fragments is recounted in A. Scheiber, "The Kaufmann-Genizah: Its Importance for the World of Scholarship," in *Jubilee Volume of the Oriental Collection*. Goitein's comments about Goldziher's work as a mosaic come from "Goldziher as Seen through His Letters" [Heb]. For more on the connection between Goldziher and Goitein, see Gideon Libson, "Hidden Worlds and Open Shutters."

For more about Scheiber, see *Occident and Orient: A Tribute to the Memory of Alexander Scheiber* (Budapest, 1988); Menahem Schmelzer, "Scheiber's Beloved Books," in *Studies in Jewish Bibliography*. Details about the Hungarian fragments appear in S. D. Goitein, "Early Letters and Documents from the Collection of the Late David Kaufmann" [Heb], *Tarbiz* 20, 1950. Goitein's diary entries are as follows: "What should I do now?" Goitein diary, Nov. 15, 1952; "Just now I feel," Sept. 16, 1954.

Goitein's description of "the heartbreak, horror and wrath" comes from Goitein,

"The Life Story of a Scholar." The term "pain and piety" is Leopold Zunz's. See Yosef Hayim Yerushalmi in *Shelomo Dov Goitein*; Ismar Schorsch, "The Lachrymose Conception of Jewish History," in his *Text and Context: The Turn to History in Modern Judaism* (Waltham, 1994). Baron's famous comments about the lachrymose conception are drawn from "Ghetto and Emancipation," reprinted in *The Menorah Treasury*, Leo W. Schwarz, ed. (Philadelphia, 1964). For more on the connection between Goitein and Baron, see Mark Cohen, *Under Crescent & Cross: The Jews in the Middle Ages* (Princeton, 1994); Goitein, "Jewish History—the First 2,000 Years," *Jewish Observer and Middle East Review*, Aug. 14, 1953; Goitein review of *A Social and Religious History of the Jews* in *Speculum* 36/3, July 1961. See also Mark Cohen, "The Neo-Lachrymose Conception of Jewish History" and Norman Stillman, "Myth, Countermyth and Distortion," both in *Tikkun* 6/3, 1991.

Goitein's study of the India trade is described in his "Involvement in Geniza Research"; "The Jewish India-Merchants of the Middle Ages," *India and Israel* 5/12, 1953; "From the Mediterranean to India: Documents on the Trade to India, South Arabia, and East Africa from the Eleventh and Twelfth Centuries," *Speculum* 24/2, part 1, April 1954. For the history of the "India Book," see also Friedman, preface, *India Traders*; Goitein, *Letters of Medieval Jewish Traders* (Princeton, 1973). Goitein repeats the story about the offer to write a more general book almost verbatim in the preface to *MS* 1 and "Involvement in Geniza Research."

Details of the "The Cairo Geniza Documents Project" appear in SDG Geniza Lab 2J.1.2, a report on his work during the summer of 1958. This seems to be an account that Goitein prepared for Fernand Braudel's Ecole pratique des hautes études (VI° section) in Paris, which was partially funding his research. His initial description of an "eight-volume collection" comes from the June 15, 1955, letter to Clemens Heller that he mentions on the first page of *MS* 1. Our thanks to Peter Miller for generously showing us this letter (from the files of l'Ecole des hautes études), and for sharing with us his research about the failed Goitein-Braudel connection. The quotes that involve the "workers" and "a whole generation of scholars" also come from the Heller-Goitein correspondence housed there. For the contents of the lab, see Goitein, "Involvement in Geniza Research." Goitein's diary entries are as follows: "I've completely stopped," Dec. 2, 1957; "the rest," undated.

For all of the references to the material covered in *A Mediterranean Society*, see the five volumes of text and, especially, volume six, the cumulative index, edited by Goitein and Paula Sanders. All Goitein quotes in what follows come from *MS* unless otherwise noted. Readers should note that the single-volume abridgement of *A Mediterranean Society* (made by another scholar, after Goitein's death) lacks most of the daily, economic, linguistic, and human detail that distinguishes the original; it is therefore in no way representative of Goitein's work.

The description of the "gorgeous variety of colorful robes" comes from "The Mediterranean Jewish World in the Light of the Cairo Geniza," SDG Geniza Lab 2J.2.1.

The term "religious democracy" figures prominently in *MS* 2 (see preface). Goitein's use of the term is described in Goitein, "Political Conflict and the Use of Power," in *Kinship & Consent: The Jewish Political Tradition and Its Contemporary Uses*, Daniel I. Elazar, ed. (New Brunswick, 1997). For more on the *dhimmi*, see Mark Cohen, *Under Crescent & Cross*; Cohen, "The Neo-Lachrymose Conception of Jewish History."

Information about Wuhsha comes from Goitein, *MS* 3: viii, D; Goitein, "A Jewish Business Woman of the Eleventh Century," *JQR* 57, seventy-fifth anniversary issue, 1967; Friedman-Goitein, *India Traders*, section 2, chapter 1. For more on the economic life of women in Geniza society, see Goitein *MS* 1: ii, 6; *MS* 3: viii, D; Mark Cohen, *Poverty and Charity*; Cohen, *The Voice of the Poor in the Middle Ages: An Anthology of Documents from the Cairo Geniza* (Princeton, 1985). For more on the sexual context in which Wuhsha lived, see Goitein, "The Sexual Mores of the Common People," in *Society and the Sexes in Medieval Islam*, Afaf Lutfi al-Sayyid Marsot, ed. (Malibu, 1979).

Accounts of Abraham Maimonides' life and work come from Goitein, *MS* 5: x, D; Goitein, "Abraham Maimonides and His Pietist Circle," in *Jewish Medieval and Renaissance Studies*, Alexander Altmann, ed. (Cambridge, 1967); Goitein, "A Treatise in Defense of the Pietists by Abraham Maimonides," *JJS* 16, 1965; Goitein, "The Renewal of the Controversy Surrounding the Prayer for the Head of the Community at Abraham Maimuni's Time" [Heb], *Ignace Goldhizer Memorial Volume*, part 2 (Jerusalem, 1958); A. H. Freimann and S. D. Goitein, *Abraham Maimuni: Responsa* [Heb] (Jerusalem, 1938); Goitein, "Documents on Abraham Maimonides and His Pietist Circle" [Heb], *Tarbiz* 33, 1964; Samuel Rosenblatt, *The High Ways to Perfection of Abraham Maimonides* (New York, 1927/Baltimore, 1938); Goitein, review of *The High Ways to Perfection*, in *Kiryat Sefer* 15, 1938–39; Mordechai A. Friedman, "Responsa of R. Abraham Maimonides from the Cairo Geniza: A Preliminary Review," *Proceedings of the American Academy for Jewish Research* 56, 1990; Friedman, "Responsa of Abraham Maimonides on a Debtor's Travails," in *Genizah Research after Ninety Years: The Case of Judaeo-Arabic*, Joshua Blau and Stefan C. Reif, eds. (Cambridge, 1992); Paul B. Fenton, "Abraham Maimonides (1168–1237): Founding a Mystical Dynasty," in *Jewish Mystical Leaders and Leadership in the 13th Century*, Moshe Idel and Mortimer Ostrow, eds. (Northvale, 1998); Gerson Cohen, "The Soteriology of R. Abraham Maimuni," *Proceedings of the American Academy for Jewish Research* 35/36, 1967–68; Y. Tzvi Langermann, "From Private Devotion to Communal Prayer: New Light on Abraham Maimonides' Synagogue Reforms," *Ginzei Qedem* 1, 2005. All of Goitein's quotes about Abraham come from *MS* 5: x, D. Quotes from Abraham are from Rosenblatt, *High Ways* (1938), translation adjusted slightly by the authors. For more on the comparison between Goitein and Abraham Maimonides, see Udovitch, "Foreword"; Libson, "Hidden Worlds"; Wasserstrom, "Apology."

The notion of *MS* as "only a sketch" is described in Mark Cohen, "Shelemo Dov Goitein." Abraham Udovitch is the colleague who saw the fifth volume as "the most difficult to conceptualize" (see "Foreword," *MS* 5). Goitein's account of the number of letters he wrote every day is drawn from Friedman: "Prof. S. D. Goitein, Man and Scholar" [Heb].

"Goitein's protégés and students" include those scholars who completed their doctoral work with him. Among these were Mordechai Friedman, Norman Stillman, Yedida Stillman, Moshe Gil, and Gershon Weiss. Later, after his retirement, Goitein was an important mentor to others, including Mark Cohen. See Cohen, "Shelomo Dov Goitein."

For more on "EurAfrAsia," see Goitein, "M.E.'s Future in Eurafrasia," *Jerusalem Post*, Feb. 15, 1957; Goitein, "EurAfrAsia," *New Outlook* 1/11, 1958. Goitein's letter about Ihud was written to Ernest Simon, March 25, 1948 (NLI Arc 4 1751/426). His letter to Baneth is dated Nov. 11, 1967.

Goitein wrote often on symbiosis. The quote cited here is drawn from Goitein, "On Jewish-Arab Symbiosis" [Heb], *Molad* 2/11, 1949. For more on the historical context in which *Jews and Arabs* was written, see Mark Cohen, "Introduction to the Dover Edition," in *Jews and Arabs: A Concise History of Their Cultural Relations* (Mineola, 2004). The quote from Agnon is from a 1961 letter (no month or day) in Gordon, *Between Shelemo Dov Goitein and Shmuel Yosef Agnon* [Heb].

Although Goitein worked for many years in the United States without honors or much public attention, at the very end of his life he was awarded one of the first MacArthur fellowships. He was the oldest fellow that year. See Kathleen Teltsch, "20 Get Cash Prizes in 'Genius' Search," *New York Times*, Jan. 19, 1983. The description of Goitein as "a born schoolmaster" is from Scholem, *From Berlin*. All quotes from Eric Ormsby are from "Born Schulmeister."

That Goitein returned immediately to work on the "India Book" is indicated in a letter to Stefan Reif, Dec. 21, 1984 (files of T-S Genizah Research Unit) and another to Mordechai Friedman, Jan. 5, 1985 (Friedman, preface, *India Traders*). After Goitein's death, Friedman completed the work on the "India Book." It was published in 2008 as *India Traders of the Middle Ages*.

Avot Yeshurun's poem is "The Collection" [Heb] in Avot Yeshurun, *Complete Poems* 2 (Tel Aviv, 1995–2001).

Afterword

For a detailed look at the contemporary fate of Egypt's Jews, see Joel Beinin, *The Dispersion of Egyptian Jewry: Culture, Politics, and the Formation of a Modern Diaspora* (Cairo, 2005). A full account of the Ben Ezra renovation appears in Phyllis Lambert, *Fortifications and the Synagogue*, as does Herbert Loewe's description, from "Some Traditions of Old Cairo," *JC*, July 20, 1906. The description of Fustat and the synagogue is also based on the authors' December 2009 visit to Ben Ezra—and up the ladder into the Geniza.

The (inaccurate) description of Ben Ezra as a former church is repeated in nearly every English-language guide book to Cairo. Scholars now agree that the church-turned-synagogue in question was probably the nearby Babylonian synagogue, once the Melkite church of St. Michael. See Goitein, *MS* 2: v, D, 1, a; Charles Le Quesne, "The Synagogue," in Lambert, *Fortifications;* Reif, *A Jewish Archive.*

The history of the Genizah Research Unit is drawn from Rebecca Jefferson, "Thirty Years of the Taylor-Schechter Genizah Research Unit," in *The Written Word Remains,* Shulie Reif, ed.; Stefan Reif, "One Hundred Years of Genizah Research at Cambridge," *Jewish Book Annual,* no. 53, 1995–96; Reif, *A Jewish Archive;* Rebecca Jefferson, "The Historical Significance"; interviews with Stefan and Shulie Reif (August 25, 2008, Beit Shemesh) and Ben Outhwaite (July, 2008, Cambridge). Stefan Reif retired in 2006, at which point the Bible scholar and bibliographer Ben Outhwaite became director of the Unit; he continues to run it today. For more about the Unit's current activities see www.lib.cam.ac.uk/Taylor-Schechter/.

Particulars of the Unit's early conservation methods are detailed in Sue Greene, "Conserving History," *Genizah Fragments* 1, April 1981; "Conservation Nears End," *Genizah Fragments* 2, October 1981; A. E. B. Owen, "Space-Age Technology Helps Unit," *Genizah Fragments* 9, April 1985; "A New Use for Moon Film," *Cambridge Evening News,* Oct. 29, 1969. The description of the Additional Series is Ezra Fleischer's, from his report (dated Sept. 11, 1974), CUL ULIB 6/7/6/51. Details of the conservation of the Mosseri collection come from Rebecca Jefferson and Ngaio Vince-Dewerse, "When Curator and Conservator Meet: Some Issues Arising from the Preservation and Conservation of the Jacques Mosseri Genizah Collection at Cambridge University Library," *Journal of the Society of Archivists* 29/1, April 2008; interview with Ngaio Vince-Dewerse (July 2008, Cambridge). The quote from the conservators comes from Jan Coleby and Ngaio Vince-Dewerse, "Mosseri Collection's Challenge," *Genizah Fragments* 53, April 2007. For more on the Princeton University Geniza Project, see http://www.princeton.edu/~geniza/.

The description of the Friedberg Project is drawn from the following sources: http://www.genizah.org/; Yaacov Choueka, lecture [Heb], Fifteenth World Congress of Jewish Studies, Friedberg Genizah Project panel, Jerusalem, August 2009; Roni Shweka, Yaacov Choueka, Lior Wolf, et al., "Automatically Identifying Join Candidates in the Cairo Genizah," Post ICCV Workshop on eHeritage and Digital Art Preservation, 2009; interview with Yaacov Choueka (Feb. 2, 2010, Jerusalem). The Friedberg Project is a joint venture with the Jewish Manuscript Preservation Society. Schechter's words about the corpus appear in Bentwich, *Solomon Schechter.*

Cynthia Ozick's comments on remembering come from *Quarrel and Quandary* (New York, 2000). For Yosef Hayim Yerushalmi's ideas of history and memory, see Yerushalmi, *Zakhor* (Seattle, 1982), and *Jewish History and Jewish Memory: Essays in Honor of Yosef Hayim Yerushalmi,* Elisheva Carlebach, John M. Efron, David N. Myers, eds. (Waltham, 1998).

For more on the Bible and the Geniza, see Reif, *Jewish Archive*; Reif, "A Centennial Assessment of Genizah Studies," in *The Cambridge Genizah Collections*; Kahle, *The Cairo Geniza*; G. Khan, "Twenty Years of Genizah Research," in *EJ Yearbook, 1983–85*. See also C. Sirat, *Genizah Fragments* 23 and 24, and Ben Outhwaite's entries in *In the Beginning: The Bible Before the Year 1000*, M. Brown et al., eds. (Washington, D.C., 2006).

On midrashim and responsa in the Geniza, see, for instance, Reif, *A Jewish Archive*; Danzig, *A Catalogue of Halakhah and Midrash Fragments* [Heb]. The many responsa found in the Geniza are also described in Robert Brody, *The Geonim*, and in works by Louis Ginzberg, Jacob Mann, Simha Assaf, and M. A. Friedman. See also Shmuel Glick, *Kuntress hateshuvot hehadash: Bibliographic Thesaurus of Responsa Literature Published from ca. 1470–2000* [Heb] (Ramat Gan, 2006–7) and his forthcoming catalog of the responsa contained in the Mosseri collection. The Talmud's role in this context is discussed in Reif, *A Jewish Archive* and "An Assessment"; Yaakov Sussmann, "Talmud Fragments in the Cairo Geniza," *Te'uda* 1, 1980. See also Shelomo Morag, *Vocalised Talmudic Manuscripts in the Cambridge Geniza Collections* (Cambridge, 1988), and Robert Brody and E. J. Wiesenberg, *A Hand-list of Rabbinic Manuscripts in the Cambridge Geniza Collection* (Cambridge 1998). For more particular examples, see, for instance, Abraham Katsch, "Unpublished Cairo Genizah Talmudic Fragments from the Antonin Collection in the Saltykov-Shchederin Library in Leningrad," *JQR* 69/4, 1979; Shamma Friedman, "An Ancient Scroll Fragment (B. Hullin 101a–105a) and the Rediscovery of the Babylonian Branch of Tannaitic Hebrew," *JQR* 86/1–2, 1995; and Binyamin Elizur, "Towards a New Publication of Yerushalmi Fragments," lecture [Heb], Fifteenth World Congress of Jewish Studies, the Academy of Hebrew Language session, Aug. 3, 2009. Schechter's description of the Palestinian Talmud appears in "A Hoard II."

For more on grammar, lexicography, and paleography, see, for instance, Reif, *Jewish Archive*; Kahle, *The Cairo Geniza*; Khan, "Twenty Years of Genizah Research"; Malachi Beit-Arié, "The Contribution of the Fustat Geniza to Hebrew Paleography" [Heb], *Pe'amim* 41, 1989.

The Khazar connection to the Geniza is described in Schechter, "An Unknown Khazar Document," *JQR* 3/2, 1912; N. Golb and O. Pritsak, *Khazarian Hebrew Documents* (Ithaca, 1982). See also *The World of the Khazars: New Perspectives*, Peter B. Golden, Haggai Ben-Shammai, András Róna-Tas, eds. (Leiden, 2007).

Maimonides' role in the Geniza world is detailed in, among other places, Sarah Stroumsa, *Maimonides in His World: Portrait of a Mediterranean Thinker* (Princeton, 2009); Kraemer, *Maimonides*; J. Kraemer, "Six Unpublished Maimonides Letters from the Cairo Genizah," *Maimonidean Studies* 2, 1991; H. Isaacs and C. Baker, *Medical and Para-Medical Manuscripts in the Cambridge Genizah Collection* (Cambridge, 1994); Reif, "An Assessment." See the "Fragment of the Month" for October 2007, by Esther-Miriam Wagner, and April 2007, by Ben Outhwaite, both on the T-S Genizah Research Unit's Web site.

For more on medicine in this context, see Isaacs and Baker, *Medical and Para-Medical*

Manuscripts; Haskell D. Isaacs, "Medical Texts in Judaeo-Arabic from the Genizah," in *Genizah Research after Ninety Years,* Blau and Reif, eds.; Goitein, "The Medical Profession in the Light of the Cairo Geniza Documents," *HUCA* 34, 1963; Ephraim Lev and Zohar Amar, "Practice versus Theory: Medieval Materia Medica according to the Cairo Genizah," *Medical History* 51/4, 2001; E. Lev, "Medieval Egyptian Judaeo-Arabic Prescriptions," *Journal of the Royal Asiatic Society of Great Britain & Ireland* 18, 2008, and other publications by Lev.

Obadiah's life and work are discussed in N. Golb, "The Music of Obadiah the Proselyte and His Conversion," *JJS* 18, 1967; Golb, "Obadiah the Proselyte: Scribe of a Unique Twelfth-Century Hebrew Manuscript Containing Lombardic Neumes," *Journal of Religion* 45/2, 1965; J. Prawer, "The Autobiography of Obadyah the Norman, a Convert to Judaism at the Time of the First Crusade," in *Studies in Medieval Jewish History and Literature,* I. Twersky, ed. (Cambridge, 1979); *Giovanni-Ovadiah da Oppido, proselito, viaggiatore e musicista dell'eta normanna,* A. De Rosa and M. Perani, eds. (Florence, 2005).

For more on the unearthing of Yiddish manuscripts in the Geniza, see Leo Fuks, *The Oldest Known Literary Documents of Yiddish Literature* (Leiden, 1957); J. Frakes, *Early Yiddish Texts 1100–1750* (Oxford, 2004); Dovid Katz, *Words on Fire* (New York, 2004). The poems mentioned here are part of a bound volume and were discovered by Fuks in 1953. In Fuks's opinion, by the fourteenth century an Ashkenazic community—seeking shelter from persecution in the north—may have settled in Egypt and Palestine, among other Eastern places. More recent scholars have argued that the codex may have belonged to travelers passing through. For the letters, see Ch. Turniansky, "A Correspondence in Yiddish from Jerusalem from the 1560s" [Heb], *Shalem* 4, 1984; S. Assaf, "A Yiddish Letter from Jerusalem" [Heb], *Zion* 7, 1941; and A. M. Habermann, "On Ashkenazim in the Geniza" [Heb], *Te'uda* 1, 1980. The letter quoted is T-S Misc 36.152. The more recent Yiddish find is T-S AS 202.383, discovered by T-S Genizah Unit researcher Esther-Miriam Wagner and published as the Unit's Fragment of the Month, Oct. 2009. The fragment it completes is T-S NS 298.18. The exchange also contains Moshe's answer.

Wuhsha and the Syrian mother don't represent new finds, but they do represent a field that began to draw interest relatively late in the Geniza game. See Joel Kraemer, "Women Speak for Themselves," in Reif, *The Cambridge Genizah Collections,* and Goitein, *MS* 3: viii, D. The Judeo-Arabic letter in question is T-S 13 J 23.5.

Magic and the Geniza are discussed further in Mark Cohen, "Goitein, Magic and the Geniza," *Jewish Studies Quarterly* 13, 2006; Steven Wasserstrom, "The Magical Texts in the Cairo Genizah," in *Genizah Research after Ninety Years,* Reif and Blau, eds.; Wasserstrom, "The Unwritten Chapter: Notes towards a Social and Religious History of Geniza Magic," in *Officina Magica: Essays on the Practice of Magic in Antiquity,* Shaul Shaked, ed. (Leiden, 2005); Gideon Bohak, *Ancient Jewish Magic: A History* (Cambridge, 2008); Bohak, "Reconstructing Jewish Magical Recipe Books from the Cairo

Geniza," *Ginzei Qedem* 1, 2005; Bohak and F. Neissen's "Fragment of the Month," Sept. 2007, T-S Unit Web site; L. Schiffman and M. Swartz, *Hebrew and Aramaic Incantation Texts from the Cairo Genizah: Selected Texts from Taylor-Schechter Box K1* (Sheffield, 1992); N. Golb, "Aspects in the Historical Background of Jewish Life in Medieval Egypt," in Altman, *Jewish Medieval and Renaissance Studies;* P. Schafer, "Jewish Magic Literature in Late Antiquity and Early Middle Ages," *JJS* 41, 1990; "Medieval Jewish Magic in Relation to Islam: Theoretical Attitudes and Genres," in *Judaism and Islam. Boundaries, Communications and Interactions. Essays in Honor of W. M. Brinner,* B. H. Hary, J. L. Hayes, F. Astren, eds. (Leiden, 2000).

Details of the Geneva Geniza are drawn from *The Cairo Geniza Collection in Geneva: Catalogue and Studies* [Heb], David Rosenthal, ed. (Jerusalem, 2010). See, especially, David Rosenthal, introduction, Barbara Roth-Lochner, "Fragments from the Cairo Geniza in the Geneva Library"; Shulamit Elizur, "New Findings in the Study of Hebrew Poetry from the Geniza." See also articles by Rosenthal, *Haaretz,* May 26, 2006, and June 9, 2006. Information regarding the correspondence with the Geneva library is courtesy of Benjamin Richler, at the time director of the Institute for Microfilmed Manuscripts, NLI (author interview and e-mail correspondence between Richler and Barbara Roth-Lochner, Oct. 7, 2005). Our thanks to Richler and Roth-Lochner for supplying this and other helpful information.

The riddles that arise in the wake of the new Dunash finding include the following: Was this originally a shorter polemical poem onto which Dunash attached an ending in praise of Hasdai—perhaps in order to camouflage the poet's own disapproval of the looser ways of the Andalusian court and thereby win Hasdai's approval? Or was this originally a poem that celebrated the ways of the court and the court's patron, even as it acknowledged resistance to those ways? In the latter scenario, it would have then been truncated (by the poet or by someone else) so as to make it seem either more ambiguous or in fact to make it a poem that denounced the courtly ways.

Information regarding the new Ben Sira find is from author interviews with Shulamit Elizur and Binyamin Elizur and S. Elizur, "A New Fragment of the Hebrew Ben Sira" [Heb], *Tarbiz* 76/1–2, 2007. (For an English version of this article see S. Elizur, "Two New Leaves of the Hebrew Version of Ben Sira," *Dead Sea Discoveries* 17, 2010.) The manuscript in question was ms. "C," a medley of verses.

In what might be called the Case of Krengel, the "forgotten old-world briefcase" scenario has in fact taken place. At the start of the twentieth century, the German rabbi Johann Krengel came into possession of several hundred Geniza fragments and wrote an article about some of them. According to former JTS librarian Menahem Schmelzer, in "One Hundred Years of Genizah Discovery and Research," the manuscripts "disappeared during World War II and were found in the Seminary Library in the 1970s in an old, worn, leather briefcase, mixed up with Krengel's typewritten sermons in German. The collection is now called the Krengel Genizah."

ACKNOWLEDGMENTS

This is a book about a lost culture and the scholar-heroes who have been retrieving it bit by dusty bit for well over a century. To do justice to the ongoing aspect of that project would have required adding numerous chapters to the volume, detailing the contribution of the scores of men and women hard at work with the Geniza material today. Without their seemingly tireless efforts this book would not have been conceivable; nor would its composition have been as pleasurable as it was without the magnanimity of so many of them. We've been fortunate beyond measure to have had the guidance—on the page and in person—of scholars who have lived with the Geniza day and (often well into the) night for many years now.

First and foremost, our gratitude to members—past and present—of the Cambridge University Library Taylor-Schechter Genizah Research Unit can't properly be put into words. With patience, warmth, precision, and humor, they brought us into their fold and gave us a world. No gift could be greater. Above all, we're grateful to Rebecca Jefferson for her sustained and vital assistance, advice, and encouragement, and for generously sharing the fruits of her research into the early history of the Geniza's recovery; and to Ben Outhwaite, director of the Unit—who first opened the Unit's doors and drawers to us and personally helped us rummage through its various treasures over a period of several years. Both have become partners of a kind in the making of this book. We're also deeply indebted to the Unit's founder and former director, Stefan Reif, for his endless openness and willingness to share his stores of knowledge and experience with us. The late Shulie Reif was a gracious and welcoming presence as well, and we remember her for her valuable work with the Unit and for her kindness. Mark Cohen of Princeton University, and the Princeton Geniza Project, has been a close consultant on this project from the very start, and he has been generous in the extreme with his learning and his wisdom, helping us get our bearings, answering questions huge and minuscule, feeding us valuable material, and putting us in touch with critical contacts. Our debt to him is major. Early readers of parts of this book provided invaluable feedback. We're especially glad to have been advised, prodded, boosted, and improved by the likes of (alphabetically) Yehoshua Granat, Matti Huss, James Kugel, Gabriel Levin, Laura Lieber, Stephen O'Shea, Marina Rustow, Steven Wasserstrom, Larry Yarborough, and again, Mark Cohen, Rebecca Jefferson, and Ben Outhwaite. While they can and should take credit for much that is here, all blunders and howlers are, it goes without saying, ours.

Acknowledgments

The families, friends, and former students of our book's protagonists have also been exceptionally gracious and patient with our repeated inquiries. We hesitate to think what this book might have been without the cooperation and trust of Ayala Goitein Gordon and Amirav Gordon, Elon and Harriet Goitein, Ofra Rosner, Ada Yardeni, Shelomo and Dafna Leshem, Shelomo Aharon Wertheimer, and Shula Bergstein; Shulamit Elizur, Binyamin Elizur, Mordechai Friedman, Norman Stillman, Eric Ormsby, Joshua Blau, Paula Sanders, Dvora Bregman, and Dan Almagor. Malachi Beit-Arié, Janet Soskice, Peter N. Miller, Itta Shedletzky, Mikhail Kizilov, David Rosenthal, Yaacov Choueka, Reuven Rubelow, Shuly Rubin Schwartz, and Samir Raafat were unstintingly helpful as well. Special thanks to Yosef Yahalom for his willingness to entertain every sort of question, and, above all, for his extensive work with the Geniza documents themselves.

Heartfelt thanks are likewise due to the librarians and archivists at the Israel National Library (Avraham David, Benjamin Richler, Ezra Chwat, and the staff in the General Reading Room, the Judaica Reading Room, and the Manuscript Reading Room); the Jewish Theological Seminary, New York (Ellen Kastel, Menahem Schmelzer, Jerry Schwarzbard, David Kraemer, and David Sclar); the Schocken Institute, Jerusalem (Shmuel Glick, Baruch Yunin, Racheli Edelman); Cambridge University Library (Ngaio Vince-Dewerse); the Bodleian Library, Oxford (Piet van Boxel, Linda Needham); Westminster College, Cambridge (Margaret Thompson); St. John's College, Cambridge (Jonathan Harrison); the Bibliothèque de Genève (Barbara Roth-Lochner); the Israel Museum (Amalyah Keshet, Rachel Laufer); the Hebrew University (Annette Freeman); and the Ezra Fleischer Geniza Research Institute for Hebrew Poetry (Sarah Cohen). We left Cairo in grateful debt to Raymond Stock, Carmen Weinstein, Mohamed el-Hawary, Nevette Bowen, Peter Kenyon, and Barbara Surk.

Various other friends and colleagues have provided critical doses of advice, company, and/or assistance of one sort or another along the way to this book, and we're in their debt as well: Jenny Diski, Ian Patterson, María Rosa Menocal, Miriam Altshuler, Ivan Marcus, Jacob Abolafia, Giddon Ticotsky, Dan Laor, Gidi Nevo, David Stern, Paul Mendes-Flohr, Gali Gamliel-Fleischer, Francesco Spagnolo, Emily Levine, Michael Chazan, Yael Cohen, Brian Kitely, Sarah Pessin, and Amiel Vardi.

We're also grateful to the many people who worked on this volume at Schocken Books and Random House. We're especially lucky to have been in the good hands of Altie Karper and Dan Frank, and we thank them for their enthusiastic support.

And last, though he was also first, it's a special pleasure to thank Jonathan Rosen— who believed in this project from the speculative start and saw it through to this inky end.

ABOUT THE AUTHORS

ADINA HOFFMAN is the author of *House of Windows: Portraits from a Jerusalem Neighborhood* and *My Happiness Bears No Relation to Happiness: A Poet's Life in the Palestinian Century*, which was named one of the best twenty books of 2009 by the *Barnes & Noble Review* and one of the top ten biographies of the year by *Booklist*. *My Happiness* also received Britain's 2010 *Jewish Quarterly*–Wingate Prize. Hoffman's essays and criticism have appeared in *The Nation*, the *Washington Post*, the *TLS*, *Raritan*, the *Boston Globe*, *New York Newsday*, *Tin House*, and on the World Service of the BBC. Formerly a film critic for the *American Prospect* and the *Jerusalem Post*, she is—with Peter Cole—one of the founders and editors of Ibis Editions.

PETER COLE's most recent book of poetry is *Things on Which I've Stumbled*—whose title poem revolves around the Cairo Geniza. Cole's translations from Hebrew and Arabic include *War & Love, Love & War: New and Selected Poems* by Aharon Shabtai; *So What: New & Selected Poems* by Taha Muhammad Ali; and *The Dream of the Poem: Hebrew Poetry from Muslim and Christian Spain, 950–1492*, which received the National Jewish Book Award in Poetry and the American Association of Publishers' 2008 Hawkins Award for the outstanding university press book of the year. Cole has received numerous other honors for his work, including an American Academy of Arts and Letters Award in Literature, the PEN Translation Prize for Poetry, and fellowships from the NEA, the NEH, and the Guggenheim Foundation. In 2007 he was named a MacArthur Fellow.

Hoffman and Cole live, together, in Jerusalem and New Haven.